I0292837

Sir William Muir

The Mohammedan controversy;

Biographies of Mohammed; Sprenger on tradition; The Indian liturgy; and the

Psalter

Sir William Muir

The Mohammedan controversy;
Biographies of Mohammed; Sprenger on tradition; The Indian liturgy; and the Psalter

ISBN/EAN: 9783337730208

Printed in Europe, USA, Canada, Australia, Japan

Cover: Foto ©ninafisch / pixelio.de

More available books at **www.hansebooks.com**

THE MOHAMMEDAN CONTROVERSY

BIOGRAPHIES OF MOHAMMED

SPRENGER ON TRADITION

THE INDIAN LITURGY

AND THE

PSALTER

BY

SIR WILLIAM MUIR, K.C.S.I.,

D.C.L., LL.D., Ph.D. (Bologna)

EDINBURGH

T. & T. CLARK, 38 GEORGE STREET

1897

CONTENTS

FIFTH ARTICLE

PREFACE

THESE Essays are taken from the *Calcutta Review*, in which they appeared many years ago.[1] They are now republished as containing matter which, it is hoped, may still, in various quarters, have some special interest.

FIRST ESSAY, 1845 A.D. *The Mohammedan Controversy.*—The immediate object of this paper was a review I was called on to make of Dr. Pfander's famous Apologies for the Christian faith. As leading up to the subject, the Essay opens with an account, chiefly from Dr. Lee's great work, of the controversy in previous times, and of Henry Martyn's discussions with the Moollas of Persia. The three chief writings of Pfander—the *Mízân-ul-Haqq*, *Miftâh-ul-Asrâr*, and *Taríq-ul-Hyât*—are then described. The debates which these give rise to between their Author and his Moslem opponents follow, notably that with the Mujtahid, or royal Apologist of the King of Oudh. In the latter part of the Second Essay the subject is resumed, and an account given of the continued controversy with the champions of the North-West Provinces and Lucknow brought up to date (1852).

SECOND ESSAY, 1852 A.D. *Biographies of Mohammed.*—The Essay opens with a warning against the danger of publishing incorrect biographies of the Prophet. Certain treatises, founded on imperfect sources (as Washington Irving's *Life of Mohammed*), and circulated by the London and Bombay Tract Societies, are

[1] Excepting the last, published in a London journal.

shown to be of this type. Several passages are quoted full of such gross misstatements as could not fail to damage our authority, and bring discredit on the Christian apologist. A description follows of Native biographies abounding in the East, whose authors, in entire neglect of early tradition, build their story on the fanciful fictions of later days. An illustration is given at length of a remarkable biography, *The Ennobled Nativity*, which tells us how the LIGHT of Mohammed, created a thousand years before the world, passed from father to son, down to the Prophet's birth. The whole forms a kind of celestial romance, the playful fantasy of an uncontrolled imagination.

THIRD ESSAY, 1868 A.D. *Sprenger on the Sources and Growth of Moslem Tradition.*—This is Dr. Sprenger's monograph on Mohammedan tradition, being a preface of 180 pages to his great work, *Das Leben und die Lehre des Mohammad*, and by far, as I think, its most valuable part. It has never been given to the public in English, and the present résumé may therefore with the greater confidence be commended to the notice of those interested in the life of Mohammed; for it is only by a thorough acquaintance with the rise and growth of tradition that we can, with any approach to certainty, distinguish between fact and fiction. For this end, the special value of each of the great sources of tradition—the *Sunna*, *Genealogies*, *Biographies*, and *Commentaries*, in addition to the *Coran* itself—has to be carefully weighed; and this the researches of Sprenger have enabled us to do.

The almost incredible mass of matter which has survived must be traced chiefly to the SUNNA, or "practice" of the Prophet; for his life and example, as law to his followers, has been sought out and recorded in every possible shape and detail. Another cause of the prodigious growth of tradition is, that the most distant connection with the Prophet—a word or a glance—conferred honour on him who could claim it; and so a vast body of all kinds of tales was ready to the eager collector's hand. Hence the necessity, in forming an estimate of Mohammed's life and the early rise of Islam, of such a study as will enable us to test the evidence on which such traditions stand; and here Sprenger is our guide.

For I need hardly say that no authority comes near to that of one whose researches in this branch of Moslem history are unexampled in their range and familiarity with the subject.

FOURTH ESSAY, 1850 A.D. *The Indian Liturgy.*—Our Prayer-Book is altogether inadequate to meet the needs of the Indian Church. Among other things for which there is no provision, two stand out pre-eminently. Prayers for the early and the latter Rain are nowhere to be found; and yet on these in India hang life and death, fruitful seasons or fatal dearth. Then there are the surrounding masses of Heathen and Mohammedans, and the dangers to our converts resulting from their influence and example; the necessity also of unceasing supplication for the ingathering of all around them. Hence the importance, as urged in this Essay, of such an enlargement of the Indian Liturgy as will meet these and other objects of time and place. The reasonableness is also urged of permission to use unfixed forms, as borne out by the example of the early Church. The authority of Bingham, Palmer, and others, as to the practice of the apostolical age and the gradual introduction of liturgical services, is referred to as a lesson to ourselves. This historical outline (though, I fear, carried to an unnecessary length) will, it is hoped, be found of interest, and to abound with lessons bearing on the reasonableness of the adoption of such a service as may best suit the wants of churches planted in the midst of heathen nations.

FIFTH ESSAY, 1887 A.D. *The freer and more varied use of the Psalms in our churches.*—Looking to the Eastern and Roman Churches, we find that the serial repetition of the Psalter is modified by the use in its stead of the Proper Psalms appointed for the Ferial and Saints' days constantly recurring in their services. Such being not the case in our own Church (six holy days excepted), the daily and monthly repetition of the Psalms in the same serial form is with us never changed from one year's end to another.

This want of freedom has long been felt in America to be a serious disadvantage. And, to remedy it, two measures have for

b

many years been there observed. First, by substituting a table of Proper Psalms for sixteen holy days. And secondly, another table containing ten series of selected Psalms was long ago introduced into the Prayer-Book, "to be read, instead of the Psalms for the day, at the discretion of the Minister." The American services are thus enriched in no ordinary degree, and made suitable to time and occasion. A further object has been to escape the imperative use of the minatory passages in the Psalms, a subject which has long exercised the American mind. The alternative table entirely avoids these; so that it is in the power of the Minister, when they occur in the Psalms for the day, to read out of the other table instead.

Following the example of their American sister, the Conventions of Canterbury and York, some twenty years ago, approached Her Majesty with a table of Proper Psalms. It is earnestly to be hoped that the endeavour thus already made will not be lost sight of, but be prosecuted till it meet with the desired success.

W. M.

Edinburgh, 1897.

THE MOHAMMEDAN CONTROVERSY

FIRST ARTICLE

From the "Calcutta Review," 1845

1. *Controversial Tracts on Christianity and Mohammedanism, etc.* By the Rev. S. Lee, A.M. Cambridge, 1824.
2. *Mohammedanism Unveiled.* By the Rev. Charles Forster, B.D. 2 vols. London, 1829.
3. *Mîzân-ul-Haqq; or, a Resolution of the Controversy between Christians and Mohammedans.* In Persian. By the Rev. C. G. Pfander. Shûshy, 1835. Ditto translated into Urdoo. Mirzapore, 1843.
4. *Miftâh-ul-Asrâr: A Treatise on the Divinity of Christ and the Doctrine of the Holy Trinity.* In Persian. By the same author. Calcutta, 1839. Ditto in Urdoo. Agra, 1843.
5. *Tarîq-ul-Hyât: A Treatise on Sin and Redemption.* In Persian. By the same author. Calcutta, 1840.
6. *Controversial Epistles between the Rev. C. G. Pfander and Syad Rehmat Ali and Mohammed Kâzim Ali.* Urdoo Manuscript.
7. *Controversy between the Rev. C. G. Pfander and Moulavi Syad Ali Hassan.* In Urdoo. Published in the *Khair Khâh Hind*, newspaper, from January to August, 1845.

8. *Khulâsa-i-Saulat-uz-Zaigham: An Urdoo Tract in Refutation of Christianity.* Lucknow, 1258 Hegiri.
9. Answer to the above. In Urdoo. Allahabad, 1845.
10. *Kashf-ul-Astâr li Kasri Miftâh-ul-Asrâr; or, The Key of Mysteries Shattered.* Lucknow, 1845.

MOHAMMEDANISM is perhaps the only undisguised and formidable antagonist of Christianity. From all the varieties of heathen religions Christianity has nothing to fear, for they are but the passive exhibitions of gross darkness which must vanish before the light of the Gospel. But in Islam we have an active and powerful enemy;—a subtle usurper, who has climbed into the throne under pretence of legitimate succession, and seized upon the forces of the crown to supplant its authority. It is just because Mohammedanism acknowledges the divine original, and has borrowed so many of the weapons of Christianity, that it is so dangerous an adversary. The length, too, of its reign, the rapidity of its early conquests, and the iron grasp with which it has retained and extended them, the wonderful tenacity and permanent character of its creed,—all combine to add strength to its claims and authority to its arguments.

When the first tide of Mohammedan invasion set in towards the West, its irresistible flood seemed about to overwhelm the whole of Europe and extinguish every trace of Christianity, just as its proud waves were repelled by the Pyrenees; but though Europe, as a whole, successfully resisted the attack, yet Mohammedan settlements continued for centuries in various quarters to exist upon it. Again, during the twelfth and thirteenth centuries, when Europe poured forth her millions into the East, the Crusaders established for a length of time in Syria and the Holy Land, a succession of posts which in the end were gradually swept away by Moslem arms. And, finally, in the fifteenth century, the closing conquest of Constantinople and establishment of the Turkish empire with its extended frontier towards Hungary and Italy, confirmed and perpetuated the last and most intimate relations which have taken place between Europe and Islam.

Here, then, we have a long period of twelve centuries, during which Christianity has been in contact with her mortal foe; while upon three marked occasions that foe was the grand object of her hopes and fears. It would have been natural, therefore, to expect that Christian Europe would have entered the lists not merely with the sword and with the shield. We might have anticipated that her learned divines and apologists would have advanced to the combat clad in the celestial armour of the Gospel; and that Rome, besides pouring forth the martial bands of Christendom, would have strenuously and unremittingly applied its hosts of learned monks and ecclesiastics to overcome the adversary with such spiritual weapons as would better have suited the sacred contest. The banners of Islam approached close to the papal See; and the Crescent, almost within sight of Imperial Rome, shone brightly upon Spain, Turkey, and Sicily. Might we not then have hoped that its inauspicious rays would have waned before the transcendent glory of the Sun of Righteousness? How fallacious were such expectations! We learn, indeed, that "in later times, when, in the vicissitudes of military adventure, the arms of the Mohammedan were found to preponderate, some faint attempts were made, or meditated, to convince those whom it proved impossible to subdue"; and again, that, "in 1285, Honorius IV. in order to convert the Saracens strove to establish at Paris schools for Arabic and other Oriental languages. The council of Vienna, in 1312, recommended the same method; and Oxford, Salamanca, Bologna, as well as Paris, were places selected for the establishment of the professorships. But the decree appears to have remained without effect until Francis I. called it into life."[1] And where are the marks and effects of this feeble and tardy resolution? As far as practical controversy is concerned, they are buried in obscurity. Learned works upon the Arabic tongue, translations from its authors, or at best, dissertations and commentaries which too often fight with the air, and sometimes betray gross ignorance of the real views and tenets of Islam, are all that remain. The dominion of the false Prophet needed

[1] Waddington's *History of the Church.*

to fear but little from such contemptible efforts, which, even had they been known to his followers, would most probably have served only to confirm them in their unbelief. In truth, the spirit of the age was adverse to any spiritual success. Clogged and obscured by error, the Church, as well in the East as in the West, had abandoned her vantage ground, and what but defeat and dishonour were to be looked for? We are not prepared, indeed, to say that the entire labours of the Christian world, from the time of Mohammed to the Reformation, were of this futile character. On the contrary, we believe that devoted Christians, during this interval, frequently and with zeal attempted the conversion of the Mussulmans; but it is a melancholy reflection that we have not a single account of their success, or of any beneficial effects resulting from their efforts. We find, it is true, in the twelfth century, the eastern Emperor erasing from his creed the anathema against the god of Mohammed, as likely to offend those Mohammedans who had embraced, or were disposed to embrace, Christianity; but, except for such transient hints, we should hardly be aware that the controversy was going on;—no *fruits* at least give token of vitality.[1]

How, then, are we to account for the want of success which characterised these long ages, in which neither party gained ground in the grand and momentous struggle? There are four causes to which it may be attributed. The first and chiefest was the superstition which had already gained ground in the Church before the rise of Islam, and which afterwards so rapidly increased and sprang up so thickly, crippling its exertions and stifling its efforts. The use of images and pictures, so hateful to the Moslem, and other superstitious practices of the Church, froze the current, which should have flowed unceasingly, diffusing to the nations around the genial and healing streams of Christianity. Again, the want of any communication or interchange of sentiment, the want even of the usual offices of courtesy between the contending parties, occasioned partly by the mutual intolerance which separated them, and partly by political circumstances,—

[1] [I had not then seen, or of course would here have mentioned, the *Apology of Al Kindy*, published by the S.P.C.K.]

not only stopped the mouth of the Christian advocate by affording him no opportunity for discussion, but even debarred him from those scenes and intimacies of social life, which, by rendering him conversant with the ideas and tenets of Mohammedans, would have enabled him to dispute with them to advantage. Thirdly, the bigotry of the Mussulmans, the licence of concubinage and slavery, and their otherwise low standard of morality, acted then, even as they act now, excluding light and rebutting conviction with contempt. Lastly, the hostility of the Mohammedan governments towards Christianity checked inquiry, prohibited any attempt at missionary labours, and suppressed every approach to conversion by sanguinary measures and summary punishment. The last three causes extenuate, though they by no means remove, the charge during those long ages of indifference towards this great controversy.

The fourth grand era of the connection of Christianity with Islam arose with the dominion of Europeans in India. And here every circumstance was in our favour. The presence of Europeans was generally the effect of conquest which, after the first feelings of irritation subside, invests the conqueror's faith and opinions with the prestige of power and authority. Here, too, our opponents are greatly outnumbered by the Hindoos; and the mixed character of the population might be expected to have broken the bond of Mohammedan union, so far at least as to weaken the thraldom of opinion and custom, to diminish the intensity of bigotry, and to exchange the narrow-mindedness of the Turk and the Persian, for somewhat of enlightened liberality in the Mussulman of India. Now, at least, we might have expected that Christian Europe would early have improved her advantages for evangelising the East;—that Britain, the bulwark of religion in the West, would have stepped forth as its champion in the East, and displayed her faith and her zeal where they were most urgently required. How different are the conclusions which the eighteenth century forces us to draw! England was then sadly neglectful of her responsibility; her religion was shown only at home, and she was careless of the spiritual darkness of her benighted subjects abroad; while her sons, who adopted India as their country, so far from endeavouring to impart to its inhabitants the benefits of their religion, too often banished it from their own minds, and exhibited to heathens and Mohammedans the sad spectacle of men without a faith. Were they then neutral and inactive in the contest? Alas, no! for their lives too often presented a practical and powerful, a constant and a living, argument against the truth of our holy faith. The great controversy was thus silently advancing in favour of the Mohammedan, whose views, arguments and faith, were receiving so convincing a corroboration from the conduct and manners of their apparently infidel conquerors.

But the nineteenth century dawned with brighter prospects; and, as it advanced, the dark incubus of idolatry, superstition and bigotry began gradually to receive the light and teaching of the Gospel. Buchanan and Martyn, Brown and Thomason, are among the harbingers of this better era, in which Britain started from her lethargy; and, as if she had been treasuring up strength during her long inaction, came forth as a giant to the encounter. Her missionaries, with the venerable Carey at their head, led the van in a strong array; many of her exiled sons began to perceive their responsibility for India's regeneration, and their number has since steadily increased. England now pours forth her gold in the merciful and blessed work of enlightening the people; while a material portion of her people in India has assumed a new aspect, and acknowledges by its deeds that its highest object is the enlightenment of India. How, then, has the great argument between the Christian and the Moslem fared in this altered position: has it advanced as rapidly in the direction of *truth* as we might have anticipated: what has been effected since the tone of society has thus improved?

In endeavouring to answer this question, we propose to examine several works which have lately appeared and given rise to some important discussions,—indicating remarkable signs of the times, if they do not indeed constitute a new epoch in the controversy. To give, however, as complete a view of the state of the argument as possible, we notice first a previous treatise of great merit and interest, which was published twenty-one years ago by

Dr. Lee, the learned professor of Arabic in the Cambridge University. It is entitled "Controversial Tracts on Christianity and Mohammedanism" (1824), and consists of three portions: a preface, embracing the previous state of the argument; translations of the controversy carried on in Persia between Henry Martyn and the Mohammedan doctors; with Dr. Lee's own continuation and conclusion of the argument. As this excellent work has not obtained that currency and circulation to which, at least in this country, its subject and worth entitle it, we shall now give a brief account of its contents.

It is certainly not very flattering to our national pride that the Portuguese should have so long preceded us in the endeavour to place the arguments for our faith before the Mohammedans. In the beginning of the seventeenth century, Hieronymo Xavier presented an elaborate treatise on the truth of Christianity to the Emperor Jehangir. The preface of Dr. Lee's work opens with an account of this treatise, illustrated by a variety of extracts. Xavier visited Lahore during the reign of the great Akbar, and having finished his book in the year 1609, presented it to his Successor. The table of contents, and the specimens which are produced of his reasoning, appear to justify the author's remark that Xavier was a man of high ability, sparing no pains to recommend his religion to the Mohammedan or Heathen reader, but that he trusted more to his own ingenuity than to the plain declarations of Holy Writ. Indeed, from Lee's brief review of the several chapters and a few of the extracts, we cannot but perceive under what disadvantage a Roman Catholic labours in attempting to argue with the Moslem. He is compelled to leave his strongholds, and descend to the relief of the defenceless outworks; and his skill and subtlety are wasted in arguments for the reasonableness of relics and miracles, of prayers for the dead and worship of images. Such arguments imply not simply a loss of time and trouble; they throw discredit upon the whole reasoning with which they are connected, and weaken the force of the attack. We have space only for two short extracts:—

"The section closes with a panegyric on the advantages arising from observing the days of the Saints and of the Holy Virgin; and stating that

Islamism can boast of no such ordinances. In the sixth section of the last chapter we have a curious account of the elevation of the Pope, which is intended to show that he is the regular descendant of St. Peter, and Vicar of Jesus Christ on earth; and that he is both the spiritual and temporal ruler on earth: that it is in his power to dethrone or set up kings at his pleasure, and to bind or loose both in earth or heaven."—(Preface, p. xl.)

And again: "We have evident intimations that God approves of the worship of these images, and this He has evinced by miracles, which He has wrought in favour of those who have paid particular reverence to them; as it may be seen from past histories, and witnessed even now in Christian countries." Then follows a string of shrines, where the Moslem is invited to go and witness such exhibitions for himself. To all this his opponent quietly replies: "We need not now notice your worshipping wooden images of the Virgin Mary and Jesus, whether such worship be intended as respectful to their persons, or for the purpose of paying them divine honours. And as a word is enough for the wise, believing as we do that you are such, we shall content ourselves with the mere hint."

To this tract an answer was published about twelve years afterwards by a learned Mohammedan, Ahmed Ibn Zain-al-abidin, copious extracts from which, comprising about sixty pages, are given by Lee in his Preface. The author combats Xavier's objections against Mohammedanism, occasionally with skill and sometimes with effect; but his direct arguments against Christianity consist chiefly of the usual components of a Mohammedan attack,—groundless reasonings and perverted interpretations of Scripture. These are, however, more to be excused in this writer, because of his very slender means of acquiring any Christian knowledge. The mode of reasoning does not seem to differ essentially from that adopted in the present day, except that some of the positions taken up by his Romanist opponent afford the Moslem a peculiar and advantageous line of argument. As a specimen of the manifest perversion characterising almost every Mohammedan polemical production, we may quote the passage in which verse 20 of Psalm ix. is turned into a prophecy of Mohammed's advent: "'Oh God, send a lawgiver, that he may come and teach man that he is a man.' Hence it is plain that God informed David of what the Christians would say respecting Christ. After which David is informed that God would send some one who would establish a law, and teach mankind the right way; and that the Messiah would be but a man. Hence to worship him is inexcusable, much more to consider him as a God" (p. xlix.). Mahommed Ruza, in his reply to Henry Martyn, still further alters the passage: "David has also said, Send a lawgiver, oh God, that men may know that Jesus is a man and not a God" (p. 231).

The fact that Christ did not punish the woman taken in adultery, is assumed as conclusive evidence that Christianity abrogated the Mosaical law. The following will serve as a specimen of Ahmed's reasoning:—"Moses was no prophet, because he opposed the law as given by Jacob. In the law of Jacob it was allowable to marry two sisters, for he married both Leah and Rachel; which is contrary to the law of Moses. . . . You Christians are reduced, therefore, to this alternative, either you must deny the mission of Jesus; or must allow that he opposed Moses" (p. lxv.). This is much the same style of reasoning as we have at the present day. The greater part of the remaining arguments consist of attacks upon the credibility of the Scriptures, by showing that they contain discrepancies and unworthy sentiments, and that the apostles and evangelists were men of doubtful character. Ahmed also gives the Catholics a sly hit about the Reformation:—"It appears that you Christians oppose all the prophets. You need not, therefore, reproach and reprobate the English as you do. . . . You say that when some cursed persons came who endeavoured to corrupt the Holy Scriptures, they were unable to succeed; but corrupted only those books, which their own reprobate doctors had written out; and these are the English, some of whom are now at Isfahán" (p. xciv.). What were our English ancestors then about; were the Reformers silent at Isfahán? There is a curious account of the mode in which Gospels are said to have been fabricated, and which is ably replied to at p. cii. Having devoted a few more pages to the refutation of Ahmed's objections, Lee proceeds to describe a Latin work by Philip Guadagnoli, of the College *de Propag. Fide*, in defence of Xavier, and refutation of Ahmed. Lee's silence confirms the opinion one forms of its poverty from the frequent references it contains to the authority of Fathers,

Popes and Councils. We have room for no more extracts from Lee's Preface, which, though a useful introduction to the controversy, is wearisomely long; and turn now to the body of the work.

Henry Martyn's three tracts carry us back to the discussions of that devoted apologist during his residence in Persia. Lee gives us first the treatise of Mirza Ibrahim arising out of Martyn's visit to Shiraz, and his public disputations with the Moslem doctors there. It is evidently the work of an able and learned writer, and is remarkable for its freedom from anything harsh and virulent. His argument chiefly concerns miracles, of which he holds the Coran to be the chiefest. A miracle is an act exceeding human experience, accompanied by a prophetic claim and the challenge to produce the like. It may belong to any art, but must be witnessed by those best skilled in such art to be beyond human experience and power. As such the miracle must belong to the age in which the art in question is in the highest stage of perfection. Thus the miracles of Moses and Jesus belong to the arts of magic and physic, which had each reached perfection in their Prophet's day. The evidence of the magicians is accordingly deemed sufficient proof for the miracles of Moses, and that of the physicians for those of Jesus. But had these miracles occurred in any other age than that in which the respective arts flourished, such evidence would have been imperfect, and the miracles not binding. This strange text,—which Martyn in his reply shows to be founded on an inadequate knowledge of history,—the Mirza applies to the Coran, and proves, entirely to his own satisfaction, that it fulfils all the required conditions. For the miracle here belongs to the art of eloquence, and in it the Arabs of the day were the highest adepts of all ages. The Coran was accompanied by a challenge to produce the like, and when the Arabs confessed inability, then evidence, like that of the magicians and physicians in the case of Moses and Jesus, became equally binding. The Mirza further dilates on the superior and lasting character of the miracle, as an exhibition of supernatural power which will remain when all others have passed away. He touches slightly on the other alleged miracles of his Prophet; and asserts the insufficiency at the present day of all proof, excepting that of the Coran, for the revelations of former prophets.

Martyn's First tract refers chiefly to this subject of miracles. He asserts that to be conclusive, a miracle must exceed *universal* experience; that the testimony and opinion of the Arabs is therefore insufficient, besides being that of a party concerned; that, were the Coran even allowed to be inimitable, that would not prove it a miracle; and its being an *intellectual* prodigy is not a virtue, but rather, by making it inappreciable by the vast body of mankind, a defect. He concludes by denying Mohammed's other miracles, in the proof of which two requisites are wanting, viz., their being recorded at or near the time of their occurrence, and the narrators being under no constraint. The Second tract directly attacks Mohammed's mission; alleges the debasing nature of some of the precepts and contents of the Coran; and holds good works and repentance alone to be insufficient for salvation. He then turns to the atonement, which prefigured in types, was fulfilled in Christ, and made public by the marvellous spread of Christianity. The Third tract commences with an attack upon the strange doctrines of Sufiism, and shows that love and union with the Deity cannot be obtained by contemplation, but only through the manifestation of His goodness towards us, accompanied by an assurance of our safety; and that this is fulfilled in Christianity, not by the amalgamation of the soul with God, but by the pouring out of His Spirit upon us, and by the obedience and atonement of Christ. Vicarious suffering is then defended by analogy, the truth of the Mosaic and Christian miracles upheld, and the argument closes with an appeal to the authenticity of the Christian annals as wholly coincident with profane history.

It will be observed that the most important part of Martyn's reply consists in refuting the assumptions of his opponent; he does not open any new ground, nor does he (except very briefly) touch upon the evidences proper to Christianity. His defence paved the way for a lengthened reply from Mirza Mahommed Ruza; and in the end, to quote from Lee, "However the particular topics discussed by them might be vindicated or refuted, the general question at issue may nevertheless not be advanced by such a method; and the reader, reduced perhaps to the mortifying consideration that time and pains had been thrown away, may at last ask, 'to what purpose has been this waste?' . . . but situated as Martyn was in Persia, with a short tract on the Mohammedan religion before him, and his health precarious, the course which he took was perhaps the only one practicable." In pursuing his argument, Martyn has displayed great wisdom and skill, and his reasoning appears to be in general conclusive; in a few instances, however, he has perhaps not taken up the most advantageous ground.

And first, as to miracles, Martyn does not deny that there might be an *intellectual miracle*, he merely depreciates the Coran as such by saying that it would not be *generally* intelligible. Dr. Lee characterises the Coran as a "miracle of the wrong sort," and declines the subject of miracles altogether, stating that neither the Mohammedan nor Christian definitions are applicable to our argument, and that, so great stress having been laid on magic, it was better to hold by the more certain guidance of prophecy (p. 535). He was probably right, considering the turn the argument had taken; but the weight of miracles is certainly not to be cast off by us in the general discussion. We would, therefore, reject the limitation of Mirza Ibrahim, and demand with Martyn *universal* experience as the test of a miracle, which must be a manifest interference of the Divine power suspending or exceeding the usual laws which He has established, and which have guided the world since the beginning. In accordance with this principle the name of miracle must be denied to any exhibition of *intellectual* power; there can be no such thing as an intellectual miracle, at least so far as man's faculties are capable of judging. A power might, indeed, be conceived of perceiving unseen or future events, but this would constitute really, not an intellectual, but a prophetic miracle. We can ascertain the laws which govern matter, and are therefore able to perceive when those laws succumb to a superior power; but the laws, properly speaking, which govern the intellect, are more obscure, and we have no standard for measuring their limits. Thus we sometimes meet with unexampled, and almost incredible powers of memory and calculation; and those of eloquence and composition are equally irregular,[1] so that a surpassing instance in those arts, though it might be unapproachably excellent, cannot possibly bear any of the marks or requisites of a miracle. Pfander has treated the miracle of the Coran very ably,[2] but he has not exhibited it exactly in this light. He shows that the Mohammedan argument, admitted to its furthest extent, does not prove the Coran to be superior to works in other languages; but to this the Persian Doctors reply, that these were not accompanied, as the Coran, with a challenge and claim to prophecy; and irreverently assert that, when these are brought forward by *any* worker of wonders, it becomes incumbent upon the Deity, if the claim be false, to raise up an equal or superior![3]

Again (p. 117), Martyn says that when Mohammed calls Christ the *Word* and *Spirit* of God, these titles must bear the same relation to the Deity, as the "word and spirit" of man to man. This is combated by his opponent, and Dr. Lee (p. 430) remarks, "It is certainly to be regretted that Martyn did not meet his opponent purely on his own ground. The title, *Spirit of God*, seems here to have been adopted by way of accommodation (it being the language of the Coran), by which, however, nothing could be gained, but much lost in the further prosecution of this question." We have a curious illustration of the truth of this in Pfander's controversy. That writer, in the beginning of his

[1] Had Lord Brougham forgotten the *Coran*, when, speaking of the wonderful composition of Rousseau's *Confessions*, he says, "No triumph so great was ever won by diction; there hardly exists such another example of the miracles which composition can perform."—(*Lives of Men, Letters, etc.*, p. 183.)

[2] *Mîzân-ul-Haqq*, pp. 216-220, and also in the controversy with Kazim Ali.

[3] Compare pp. 192, 204 and 210 of Mahommed Ruza's reply, where it is held, that a miracle does not necessarily exceed human power; but that when *any* wonder or work is brought forward with a challenge by a claimant of prophecy, and is not surpassed, it must be received as a miracle, otherwise the Deity would have interposed.

treatise on the Divinity of Christ, very properly adduces the passage in the Coran alluded to above, not to prove Christ's divinity, but merely to show what illustrious attributes the Mohammedans should ascribe to Jesus from the concessions their Prophet had made to him. Kazim Ali denies the conclusion, and shows that Mohammed has applied the very same expression to Adam: on which Pfander replies that if the Coran makes Adam to share in the Divine nature, his opponent may believe the doctrine if he pleases. Kazim Ali, of course, rebuts the imputation, and holds, with a show of reason, that the application of the expression to Adam proves that it was not meant to imply divinity.[1] So much for the caution and wariness required in this great controversy.

Again, Martyn's references to alchemy (p. 82) and to magic (p. 85) placed his argument upon a false position, which his adversary did not fail to turn to advantage (pp. 203–5). His reply, too (p. 93), is faulty where he says, that to suppose the evidence of miracles to diminish with the lapse of time, would be to imply that a person at sixty has lost part of the conviction as to any fact which he possessed at twenty: the Mirza replies that the cases are not parallel,—one involving personal identity, the other a succession of individuals. He also takes up a weak position (p. 104), when he refutes the miracles of Mohammed by the circumstance that some of them are said to have been performed while he was yet an unbeliever, which at most would prove but little. Mirza Ruza resents the imputation, and devotes fifteen pages (p. 253) to show that the passages produced by his opponent do not refer to belief;—"'Thou wast in error, and I have directed thee,' that is to say, the religion of Jesus was with

[1] The author of the *Saulat uz Zaigham*, or "Lion's onset," has a strange disquisition into the meaning of this phrase "Spirit of God"; in which he endeavours to prove that the possessive case does not imply connection (no more than to say "my meat is cooking" implies that it is yours and not the goat's flesh),—and that from this to argue Christ divine, would be to allow other prophets divine upon whom God's Spirit descended; that Gabriel and other angels are styled "spirits of God," and that Christ was called a spirit *par excellence*, because his laws were pre-eminently spiritual, and he lived like the angels without marriage.

respect to Jesus himself and his followers the true one; but may properly be termed 'error,' with respect to the last Prophet and his followers." Mohammed was, therefore, at first in error because he was a Christian! He also explains the verses where Mohammed's *sins* are mentioned as referring to the sins of his people. Our Indian antagonist Kazim Ali is more candid; for he does apply the words to Mohammed, but alleges that they refer merely to omissions of prayer and other ceremonial observances, which even Prophets are sometimes guilty of, but which imply no *moral* stain. So easy is it by forced reasoning to avoid the point of the clearest expressions!

We must hasten to Mirza Ruza's answer to Martyn, written in 1813, the year after his death. It is very prolix, occupying no less than 289 pages; but not being characterised by any peculiar exhibition of talent, and abounding with perversions of Scripture and unfair conclusions, such as we meet with nowadays in India, the work is not deserving lengthened notice. The Mirza treats many of his opponent's arguments with great injustice, brings forward a grand array of prophecies which he insists upon applying to Mohammed along with the foolish story of the Hebrew child, expatiates upon the wonderful superiority of the Shiea doctrines, and praises with fulsome panegyric the virtues of his Prophet and the Coran. We shall take leave of the Mirza with a few specimens of his style; and first an instance of his proficiency in history:—

"It is told of Plato, that when he heard of Jesus having restored one to life who had been three days dead, he said, I can do the same thing; which we suppose must be understood of a person in the longest possible fit of apoplexy. For it is an established principle with the physicians, that the longest continuance of an apoplectic fit cannot exceed seventy-two hours. . . . And hence it is that when any one dies suddenly, he is not buried for three days; during which time every effort is made for his recovery, because there is still a possibility of his being restored" (p. 217). "And again" (p. 177), "when Plato wrote to Christ to know if anyone could be saved by his intervention, the answer of Jesus was, 'Divine Physician! without my mediation no one can be saved'" (p. 173).

The reason assigned for Mohammed's having nine wives is

amusing, though we do not precisely comprehend its full meaning :—

"Women are in a very dependent state ; to have more than four wives would superinduce oppression, and to observe justice with regard to nine would be next to impossible.

"Therefore, in conformity with the general mercies vouchsafed to the faithful, none but the Prophet were permitted to have more than four. But *as he was the paragon of all justice, he was allowed to have nine.* This might be supposed to forbid a plurality of wives, but every sensible man must see that the reduction of the number of wives to *one* would also reduce men to difficulties. For, it is the desire of most men to take women without any sort of restraint ; and it is well known that the object of Mohammed's law was to diminish difficulties. It has been our object, therefore, to show that Mohammed's taking more wives than he allowed to others was not founded on lust, but with the view of diminishing the difficulties above mentioned ; namely, *to point out the difficulty of other individuals preserving justice among four* ; and that this was not the case (with respect to Mohammed) in a number exceeding five, six, or more."

(A rich specimen of reasoning certainly ; but let us see what he thinks of our law of marriage) :—"The law, however, now in the hands of Christians, is, as every man of sense knows, of a very different description ; and, *therefore*, can never have come from God. . . . Their women, too, being allowed to take any man they may please, and whenever they please, cannot but superinduce great confusion in their tables of pedigrees, and must put an entire end to that chastity which, everyone knows, is both necessary and proper. In such a case no one can possibly know whose son he is" (p. 380).

And then he reads a lecture to Roman Catholics on the evils of monasticism and celibacy, which is recommended to their attention.

We shall quote but one passage more. The Mirza denies that Mohammed ever intended to say that he could not work miracles ;—"To say, therefore, that he pretended to nothing more than merely to be the messenger of a revelation from above : and then to argue that a contrary supposition would involve a manifest contradiction to his own declarations, is evidently unfair ; and particularly so when applied to a period of time not less than three-and-twenty years" (p. 255). This objection should be allowed due weight ; and in order to answer it satisfactorily, it would be useful to find out at what different times the commentators suppose these expressions were used which disclaim the power of working miracles; if they extended over the greater period of the Prophet's ministry, it would render our attack unanswerable.[1]

Dr. Lee now comes forward, and, taking up the question of miracles, adopts a different line of argument. In his first chapter he exposes the insufficiency of the evidence upon which Moslems lean, and shows that the testimony of multitudes, if interested and but partially informed, is worth nothing; he then substitutes instead, the true laws of evidence as enforced by Locke's six considerations. The Second chapter is devoted to the integrity of the Scriptures. The Mirza had asserted that the Old Testament was lost during the Babylonish captivity, and the first section answers the objection in a satisfactory manner. The second section refers to the period between the captivity and the time of Mohammed, during which the purity of the Bible is maintained by convincing arguments. He then takes occasion to show the value of Versions, which the Mirza foolishly imagines to have increased corruption. A third section discusses Kennicott's notion of the Jews having altered their Scriptures, which is shown to be unfounded. The whole chapter is recommended to the particular attention of our missionaries. In his Third chapter, Dr. Lee, foregoing the proof by miracles, shows from Scripture that a true prophet must have the gift of prophecy; and that even then, if he opposes a previous revelation, he is not to be credited: Mohammed is condemned by these premises. The argument concludes with a brief description of our Scriptures, in which, avoiding metaphysical and abstruse arguments, he dwells on their adaptation to man, and refutes the objections of the Moslems.

Where all is excellent it is difficult to select. Two short extracts, however, will give some idea of the Doctor's conclusive mode of treating his subject. The Mirza had discarded the doctrine of the atonement with this contemptuous sneer:—

"The statement" (he says, regarding Martyn's notice of it) "is calculated to provoke the smile even of a child. For all might have been obviated

[1] [The abnegation is absolute throughout.]

by one sentence, which the angel Gabriel could have delivered and explained to any one of the Prophets." Lee replies :—"However this *might have been done* concerns not us to know. Our question is not, as to what *might have been done*, but what has been done. If the Almighty had thought proper, He might have revealed His will in ways totally different from those which He has chosen; but as His will has been revealed, it is our duty to inquire what that is, and not to suggest what might have been" (p. 560).

And, again, as to the miracles ascribed to Mohammed :—

"They are either said to have been performed in private, as his being saluted as a prophet by stocks and stones, when he was a child; or are false, such as his dividing the moon, causing the sun to stand still, etc., which would have been recorded by the Greeks and others had any such thing actually taken place; or they were executed for no adequate purpose whatever, such as the poisoned shoulder of mutton speaking.[1] . . . Again, as to the number of the witnesses to these miracles, they may generally be reduced to one: Ali, for instance, or Ayesha, or Hasan, or Hosein, who delivered the account orally to someone who delivered it to another in the same way:—and so, after many generations, the account is committed to writing by Kuleini, or Bochari, or some other respectable collector of traditions. These, then, are copied by a number of compilers who follow; and then the number calculated to produce assurance is cited as worthy of all credit!" (p. 567).

The subject of such traditions, as evidence competent to prove miracles, is ably treated by Pfander in his *Mîzân-ul-Haqq*, where he shows that the original witnesses were interested, that their testimony never exceeded hearsay, and had already become shadowy before it was committed to paper; and that the traditions refute themselves from the absurdity as well as discrepancy of their contents. This is a topic of extreme importance; what we require, is a sifting analysis of the traditions, according to the probable dates of their being recorded; an account of the individuals who registered them; of the means they possessed for arriving at a true knowledge of the facts; and of the number through whom they successively descended. Such a manual would prove useful to the missionary; and, if written in a proper

[1] [The purpose was sufficient; but according to tradition it was too late, for one of the Prophet's followers died from eating it, and the mouthful Mohammed took himself affected him all his after-life, till on his deathbed.]

spirit, might tend to loosen the hold which such evidence has upon the Mohammedans, of whom the more intelligent are not slow in acknowledging the futility of hearsay, or the insufficiency of interested evidence.[1]

Besides the text of Dr. Lee's work, thus briefly reviewed, there is a great deal of valuable matter in the appendices; especially extracts from Aga Akbar's tract[2] on Mohammed's miracles, to which are added notes on the prophecies of the Coran, and an important disquisition tracing Mohammed's scriptural knowledge to Syria, and many of his stories to Ephrem the Syrian. We should like to see this book in the hands of every missionary; in its present shape, indeed, it is bulky, and in some parts tedious; but if the preface and Mirza Ruza's tract were curtailed, the remainder might be printed in a cheap form fit for general circulation.[3] The portions which regard the *Shiea* doctrines would not, however, be so generally applicable here as in Persia; for, excepting in Oudh, the Indian believers as a rule belong to the Sunni faith.

[1] [Such a work, however, is hardly necessary, as the disavowal of miracles in the Coran itself is sufficiently plain and decided.]

[2] At p. 109, this writer makes a very candid confession. In justifying Mohammed's religious wars, he says that his Prophet "was sent in mercy to mankind; but had he not put some to death, seized upon their property, and carried away the rest captives, the whole world must have remained in infidelity and discord, so that the light which he came to bestow would have fallen upon none. The Arabs, therefore, would have remained idolaters,—the Persians have rested in their doctrines or principles, . . . the Hindoos have continued to worship cows and trees,—the Jews to continue obstinate,—and the Christians to dispute on the genealogies of persons who neither were nor are Father and Son."

From Martyn's memoir, however, as well as from the extracts given by Dr. Lee, it would appear that Aga Akbar was but a poor defender of the faith, and that he was advised by his brethren not to bring forward his discreditable production.

[3] We have heard that an Urdoo translation of Dr. Lee's tract was published by the American missionaries at Ludhiana; but it has not been circulated, nor had the American missionaries at another station (from whom we procured the information) ever seen it. At p. cxxiii. Dr. Lee promises a *Persian* translation of his tract. It is not known whether this ever appeared. It would be highly prized in India.

We pass on to the consideration of Dr. Pfander's writings, which consist of three treatises: first, *Mizân-ul-Haqq*, or "Balance of Truth"; second, *Miftâh-ul-Asrâr*, or "Key of Mysteries"; and third, *Tarîq-ul-Hyât*, or "Way of Salvation." They were originally written in Persian, but have also been published in Urdoo, excepting the last which is in progress of translation. From his residence and travels in Persia, Pfander possesses advantages which fortunately qualify him in an unusual degree for the great controversy with our Moslem population. He was attached for ten or twelve years to the German mission at Fort Shushy on the confines of Georgia, from whence he made frequent and protracted visits to Persia, penetrating as far as Bagdad, and returning by a circuitous tour through Isfahán and Teheran. In 1836, the Russian Government, unable to tolerate the presence of foreign ecclesiastics, put a stop to the mission, and thus proved the means of providing us with labourers who in the field of Persia had acquired so valuable a knowledge of its language and so intimate an acquaintance with the religion and tenets of the Mohammedans. Pfander joined the Indian mission of the C. M. S. in 1838.

Our author has not been backward in improving his peculiar privileges, or in availing himself of the help which the previous controversy and such writings as those of Dr. Lee afforded him. His first and most important work is the *Mîzân-ul-Haqq*, or "Balance of Truth," as between Christians and Moslems; and being of extraordinary value, we shall endeavour to present our readers with a complete account of it. The original Persian edition was published at Shushy in 1835, and the Urdoo translation was lithographed at Mirzapore in 1843. The argument is prefaced by a statement showing that the soul can alone be satisfied with the knowledge and favour of God, to which man in his present state is unable of himself to attain. To secure this end a revelation is necessary which must fulfil the real desires, and satisfy the spiritual wants of man's soul; coincide with the principles of right and wrong implanted in his heart; exhibit the Deity as the just and holy, omniscient and unchangeable Creator; be consistent in all its parts; and not contradict, though it may transcend, human reason.

The choice, it is next proved, lies between the Bible and the Coran, while the Divine origin of the former is admitted by the latter. The notion that each revelation has successively abrogated its predecessor is shown to be unfounded, and unworthy the Divine government; and the hypothesis that each advancing stage of society requires a suitably advanced revelation, refuted. The argument for the integrity of the Scriptures follows and, occupying as it does a considerable space, is sound, able and satisfactory.

About half of the volume is now devoted to the development of the doctrines of the Bible and the scheme of Christianity. In this are treated the attributes of God; man's condition; the nature of the Atonement, its proof from prophecy and practical benefits; the influences of the Holy Spirit; and the character of the true Christian;—the whole system being enforced by a variety of tests. It is difficult to say what is best done where all is good; but the doctrine of the Atonement, and the spread of Christianity, may be specified as remarkably well discussed. The quotations under the head of "Commands" are, perhaps, too long; it is, no doubt, necessary to show that we have a code of morals fully developed in our Scriptures; but when the extracts cover a very large space, and there is nothing to mark their beginning or their end, they become tedious to the native reader, and obstruct the flow of the argument.

The last chapter is reserved for the direct refutation of Islam. The first and second marks given for recognising a true prophet resemble those of Dr. Lee, except that miracles are admitted. They are as follows:—His teaching must not oppose previous revelations; it must be supported by proper evidence, as that of miracles or prophecy; his conduct must befit that of a prophet of God; and his doctrines must not be enforced by violence. Several pages are now allotted to prove that Mohammed was not foretold, and that the prophecies advanced by Mussulmans are shown to have no reference whatever to their Prophet. This portion of the work is very ably executed; indeed the wonder is, that after its perusal any one could ever again have recourse to such arguments. The contents of the Coran are next examined and, while it is acknowledged that it inculcates some excellent precepts and doctrines, it is held that these are mainly taken from the Bible, while the grandest and most important of its truths are denied, omitted, or perverted. The teaching that pardon is attained through Mohammed and God's mercy, is shown to be insufficient; and the sensual rewards, intolerant precepts, and blind predestination set forth in the Coran, opposed to the dictates of reason, as well as to the express teaching of the Gospel. Some canons of correct interpretation are laid down, to obviate the far-fetched and unfounded explanations by means of which our opponents avoid the unfavourable conclusions drawn from the contradictions in the text of the Coran. Mohammed's character is then brought under review; the claim advanced of his miraculous and prophetical powers is refuted; and the grossness with which he indulged his licentious passions held up to deserved reprobation, as well as the measures of violence and other worldly means by which he spread his religion. The whole closes with a statement of the wonderful manner in which the Gospel is now being preached to all the world, preparatory to the glorious advent of Christ; and with a solemn parting admonition to the Moslem reader. As an appendix, are added six narratives of conversion in various nations, by way of exemplifying the practical working of Christianity.[1]

The *Miftâh-ul-Asrâr*, or "Key of Mysteries," is a short treatise devoted to the establishment of the divinity of our Saviour, and the doctrine of the Trinity. It sets out with showing the lofty dignity ascribed in the Coran to Christ, and the reverence with which Moslems ought, therefore, to regard

[1] These are very interesting, but perhaps they might be in parts curtailed without diminishing the effect. *Indian* stories will, in general, be more applicable and better understood than those of distant nations. Would it not be appropriate here to introduce a few instances of Hindoo young men who, in their conversion, have displayed so noble a victory over the world, so complete a subjection to the love of Christ?

him: the weakness of the human intellect is then dwelt on, which can reason only upon the perceptions we receive, and is therefore incompetent for the discovery of subjects regarding which we have no experience; and hence is deduced the necessity of bending to the revelation of God with humble and implicit faith. The First chapter takes up the proof of our Saviour's divinity, and a section is allotted to the evidence derived from His own words. This is a very suitable arrangement, as Mohammedans always ask first for Christ's own assertions, holding that no statements of another party are to be received towards the proof of that which our Saviour did not himself affect to claim. But why are Gabriel and the Angels' evidence admitted into this section? A Maulavi remarked to us, that the Mussulmans would smile at this; "the Padre," they will say, "set out with proving Christ's divinity from his own words, and in the very first page he is obliged to have recourse to other testimony": it is in reality no great blemish, as the object is to usher in the birth of the Saviour whose own words are about to be brought forward: but it may be as well not to give any ground for the eager hyper-criticism of our antagonists. Our only other remark on this section, and on the following which is appropriated to the evidence of the apostles, is that the expression "*only* begotten Son" is not sufficiently insisted upon.[1] This was repeatedly assumed by Christ to himself; and to have more prominently seized upon it would have strengthened our author's position. In other respects this portion of the work is full and satisfactory, as well as the third section, which continues the argument from the Old Testament.

The Second chapter is on the Trinity, and its first section con-

[1] We learn from the author of the *Saulat uz Zaigham* that "White and Williams, Padres," took their stand upon this expression, when pressed by him as to the ambiguous meaning of the word "Son." It is evident that he found it was hard to explain away its meaning, for he has resorted to the convenient argument of *interpolation*;—a subterfuge which the readiness with which he brings interpretations and glosses to suit his purpose seldom renders necessary.

The same author fancies that he has discovered an argument against us in the expression "first begotten Son," because it was applied by Moses to

tains copious selections from the Scriptures to prove that sacred mystery and the personality of the Holy Ghost. There are one or two passages in the concluding paragraph which we doubt the propriety of introducing, especially the threefold blessing which Aaron was directed to pronounce over the people of Israel. We are aware that this is usually applied to the Trinity, and the tradition of the Jews regarding the mode in which the priest disposed his hand as he gave this beautiful benediction, may strengthen the idea. But, at the best, it could hardly be regarded as being more than allusive; and where there is any appearance of forcing an application, we had much rather see it omitted. It is, at the same time, just to mention that in the following page, Pfander clearly explains that the sacred mystery is referred to in the Old Testament by allusion alone, and that it can be interpreted only by the plain teaching of the New Testament on the subject.

The second part of this chapter contains a variety of arguments, which are intended to reconcile the mystery of Trinity in Unity with the conclusions of sound reason. These arguments are not entirely satisfactory. Thus we are told that Nature is the shadowing forth of eternal principles, and to the pure mind is a "ladder" and a "school," whereby we may learn divine mysteries so completely, "that if man had not rebelled against God and thus perverted and darkened his intellect, he would certainly have attained, by reference to creation and the perceptions of his own heart, to a perfect knowledge of God and himself, so fully that no written revelation would have been necessary." But it seems at least doubtful whether man, even in a perfect state, could, without revelation, have discovered the doctrine of the Trinity; whereas the mode of expression here

Israel, by Jeremiah to Ephraim, and in the Gospel to Jesus: he then argues that there can be but *one* "first begotten," therefore the three authors contradict each other; and offers to extricate us from the difficulty by this interpretation, viz. that Israel was termed "first begotten," in opposition to Ishmael, who did not inherit; and that the meaning therefore of Christ's being called God's first begotten Son, is that he was an Israelite; and the word "only" was added as distinguishing and honouring him beyond all other Israelites. To what shifts our interpreter is driven!

adopted implies that there are marks in creation which do plainly indicate the Trinity of the Creator. A number of explanatory instances or analogies are given, after which their force is summed up as follows:—"To conclude, it is clearly proved from these examples, that *nature contains unequivocal marks of the existence of the Divine nature in Trinity*; and, in truth, whoever attentively considers them, will perceive that plurality in unity is possible." There is no serious objection to bringing forward instances of plurality in unity with the object of proving it not to be impossible: nay, if care be taken that they are not used as direct analogies, they may be beneficial in displaying the inability of man to fathom mysteries infinitely short of the sublime doctrine of the Trinity. But the expressions go beyond this, and imply that nature directly *points out* the doctrine; and from this we dissent as unfounded, and as giving the adversary a needless advantage. For example, the *Circle* is stated to be an emblem of the Deity, having neither beginning nor end; and the fact that trigonometry is the key to its measurement and comprehension, is represented as an illustration of the Trinity by which alone the Divine nature can be understood. Such exemplifications only pave the way for our opponents. Thus the author of the *Saulat uz Zaigham*, in a passage which it would be painful to translate, draws the figure of a triangle, and, after some contemptuous remarks upon the inequality of its angles, adds this cutting scoff, "If this be the way of their arguing, why anybody may join the Virgin Mary to the Deity, and drawing a square may assert that here is quaternity in unity"; and to complete the blasphemy he adds the diagram by way of illustration! To shew the species of reply which is given to one of Pfander's less objectionable analogies,—that of the plurality in unity of man,—we give a further quotation from the same work:—

"First, every composite subject is dependent upon parts, and to be dependent is not worthy of the Deity; second, every such subject is liable to change, and cannot therefore be eternal; third, if any one of man's component parts be taken away, the rest is no longer *man*; if God, therefore, be composed of three persons, then when the Son came to this earth the Father and the Holy Spirit were no longer God; and so with the Holy Ghost which descended upon earth after the Son's return: in that case the Almighty were imperfect and liable to change, which God forbid! . . . Illustrations prove nothing, and if they did the Mohammedans might assert a quaternity from the creation consisting of *four* elements, and the Hindoos from their *five* elements a Deity of five in one."

Many similar examples of the disadvantages and ridicule to which such a line of argument exposes us might be adduced,—but we forbear, and close the subject with an extract from Dr. Wardlaw's admirable lectures on the Socinian controversy, the sentiments of which are recommended to Mr. Pfander's consideration :—

"Of the precise import of the term *Personality*, as applied to a distinction in the Divine essence, or of the peculiar nature and mode of that distinction, I shall not presume to attempt conveying to your minds any clear conception : I cannot impart to you what I do not possess myself :—and convinced as I am that such conception cannot be attained by any, it had been well, I think, if such attempts at explanation, by comparisons from nature, and otherwise, had never been made. They have afforded to the enemies of the doctrine, much unnecessary occasion for unhallowed burlesque and blasphemy. The Scriptures simply assure us of *the fact* :—of the *mode* of the fact they offer no explanation. And where the Bible has been silent, it becomes us to be silent also ; for when, in such cases, we venture to speak, we can only "darken counsel by words without knowledge." The fact, and not the manner of it, being that which is revealed, is the proper and only object of our faith. We believe that *it is so* ; but *how* it is so, we are not ashamed to say, we do not presume even to conjecture."

Pfander proceeds to prove that no intelligent actor can exist in *absolute* unity, as that would imply mere existence ;—to which the superadditions of intelligence and will must be given, else the mere *Being* remains passive and inactive ; hence the metaphysical speculations of the Hindoo, Grecian and Moslem philosophers, are shown to have all ended in proving the necessity of the Creator's existing in a species of trinity. As far as this argument and a display of the absurdities of Sufieism are resorted to, merely to shew the conclusion of trinity and unity to which man arrives when he reasons on the nature of his Creator, and even to prove that plurality in unity is not so inconsistent with sound reason as at first appears,—we do not object : but the greatest care must be observed lest this line of reasoning assume the appearance of an obligatory argument,—as if, from the nature of things, the

Deity *must* exist in trinity; and a few of Pfander's expressions seem calculated to give rise to such an impression. For example, he argues thus:—"If you reject the doctrine of trinity, and hold to simple unity, you reduce your Creator to an inanimate existence" (p. 75); to which the Mohammedan retorts—"You confuse the terms of *personal* and *metaphysical* unity; the latter I do not hold: the former, viz., a Creator whose existence is endowed with the attributes of intelligence and will,—such is my God"; and the reply would be just, because, according to the supposed reasoning fully carried out, the Christian Trinity would be not *one* but *three* trinities. It must not, however, be understood that Pfander in any degree intentionally employs the argument as an *à priori* and independent one; on the contrary, his declared object is simply to show that the doctrine of the Trinity as revealed does not oppose reason, and this he repeatedly states. At the same time, we trust that in a future edition the line of reasoning and cast of expression will be so far altered as to leave no possibility of misconception.[1]

The closing section dwells on the truth that our knowledge of God, and hopes of salvation, are bound up in the doctrine of the Trinity; and excepting some expressions of the nature just noticed, its contents are most valuable. The wonderful love of God in effecting man's salvation through His eternal Son, and the blessedness of sanctification through the Spirit, are shown to be so dependent on the Trinity, that he who denies the Son hath not the Father nor the prospect of eternal life.

The *Tarîq-ul-Hyât*, or "Way of Life," takes up a point which was but briefly noticed in the *Mîzân*, namely, the nature of sin;—to all a subject of extreme importance, but especially to the Mohammedan whose loose and imperfect ideas of *inward* sin, lull him to sleep amid the outward ceremonies of a shallow faith, and steel him against the attacks of conscience and the Gospel. The nature of sin to which, in the Introduction, are ascribed all the unhappiness and misery of man, must be sought for in God's word. The first portion of the work is

[1] The quotations from Arabic and Persian metaphysical works are much too long.

accordingly devoted to the Mosaic account of the fall, the effects of which are traced in man's corruption. A searching examination follows into the real evil of sin, and its heinousness is found to consist in the *intention*: hence, and from copious illustrations in Scripture, corrupt desires, even though they do not break out into overt acts, are proved to be offensive and deserving punishment in the sight of God. The erroneous notions of Moslems as to *venial* offences are grounded upon false principles; and it is shewn that *all* sins, though they may differ in enormity, are alike transgressions of the law;—nay, that what appears to us a venial sin may, from the *intention*, be in God's sight one of the most aggravated nature. The dreadful effects of sin are next treated of. The pains of hell will be chiefly mental and spiritual, in opposition to the doctrine of the Coran which depicts, with hideous detail, the various species of bodily torments inflicted upon the damned. The Mohammedan account of the fall of Satan is shewn to be without foundation; the origin of Evil is cautiously touched upon; and the reason of its permission left with Almighty wisdom. The whole of this argument is conducted with great ability.

The next portion of the work is devoted to the doctrine of Pardon, and the means of securing it as held by different religions. Among these the Zoroastrian, Hindoo[1] and Chinese creeds are considered; the opportunity being taken advantage of for describing the compulsory manner in which Islam banished the first of these from Persia. Then the Mohammedan religion is weighed in the balance and, like its predecessors, found wanting; its ceremonies are classed in the same category with heathen rites and practices; while Mohammed acknowledged himself to have been a sinner, and a mere man, incapable of being an atonement for the sins of others. The errors of Islam are shewn to have originated in mistaken notions of the nature of sin; and the doctrine denounced which lays down that the intention to commit any *sinful* act, however rife or fondly cherished, is not

[1] In the forthcoming Urdoo edition, the remarks upon the Hindoo religion might be expanded so as to form a useful episode for the Hindoos who, we may hope, will not be backward in reading the treatise.

counted by God against a Mussulman, while the mere intention to do a *good* action, is reckoned as one and, if it be carried out, as ten good deeds! Inward corruption and impurity are therefore ideas foreign to the Mohammedan creed. The Gospel is now introduced. Faith in Jesus is shewn to be the requisite and only acceptable accompaniment of repentance; and the wonderful splendour thrown upon the Divine attributes by the love of God, in the gift of His Son, is fully dwelt upon. The concluding portion displays by copious extracts from Scripture, and with great power of language, the blessings conferred by participation in this salvation. The springs of the Christian's character and happiness, his restoration to God's favour, his delight in prayer, his love to all mankind, and his glorious prospects for eternity, are described with a fascinating eloquence which cannot fail to captivate the reader. There is no space for details, but attention may be drawn to the vivid parallel between the heaven of the Bible, and the paradise of Mohammed; a species of argument which Pfander frequently adopts with great effect. Thus, after dilating at length on the excellencies and the perfections of some Christian doctrine, he suddenly brings forward the corresponding tenets of the Mohammedan faith, the comparison adding to their native deformity. So again (p. 146), after dwelling upon God's mercy and desire that all should be saved, the teaching of the Coran, that millions were created for damnation, is held up in contrast. Such a course seems more effective, and more likely to produce conviction, than successively to bring up each of the Mohammedan doctrines like culprits to the bar for separate condemnation.[1]

The *Tarîq-ul-Hyât* stands unrivalled as an exposition of Christian doctrine in the Persian language. It is difficult to say

[1] Such a mode is adopted in the *Dîn Haqq ki tahqîq*, "An Inquiry into the True Religion," a prize essay published three years ago in "refutation of Hindooism and Mohammedanism and establishment of Christianity." The most important portion refers to the Hindoo religion,—the subject being elaborately treated, and the arguments in general conclusive. The part which applies to Mohammedanism, though it contains a deal of useful matter, is not so likely to be beneficial; the peremptory tone is likely to excite opposition, and some of the arguments are weak,—such as the impossibility of keeping

whether greater ability is displayed in the argumentative reasoning of the *Mîzân-ul-Haqq*, or in the moral discussions of the *Tarîq-ul-Hyât*; the latter, perhaps, from the abstract nature of the subject, deserve the highest praise. Each, indeed, has its peculiar merit, and with the *Miftâh* form a whole, placing before the Mohammedan almost every point which he is at present prepared for. To be interested or profited by the *Tarîq-ul-Hyât*, requires, no doubt, a state of mind much in advance of that which the ordinary Moslem now possesses, for the subject of inward corruption is one foreign to his ideas; but the day is, we trust, approaching, when this will no longer be the case;—when the leaven of that knowledge which is even now pervading the country will work a mighty change in their feelings and ideas; and then, by the blessing of God, will the heart respond with notes of conviction and repentance to the touches of truth contained in this volume. Pfander has indeed conferred in these books an inestimable boon upon this country; and we are much mistaken if they do not assume the place of standard treatises among such as interest themselves in this great question, and especially among our native Christians; for though primarily adapted to the professors of Islam, their contents must always possess a general interest.

The *Tarîq-ul-Hyât* displays an uncommon exuberance of language and richness of diction,—a perfect facility in the Persian idiom, and a degree of ease in adopting elegant and appropriate illustration, which astonish the Mohammedans of this country, and perplex them to account for the *Padre's* accomplishments.[1] Notwithstanding, therefore, the plainness with which their errors are laid bare, these treatises are viewed with much respect by learned Mohammedans; and that they

the fast of Ramzân and observing the five daily prayers at the poles,—which, though to a certain extent true, is too strongly insisted upon. As this book has been published in English, no more lengthened notice of it is necessary here.

[1] If there is any fault in the style of the *Tarîq*, it is, that some of the words are so difficult and uncommon as scarcely to be known even to the learned of this country; this must be avoided in the Urdoo translation.

have created a great sensation is evident from the discussions which will shortly be mentioned. Some of the learned Maulavis of Tonk having seen a copy of the *Mîzân*, addressed a note to its author, soliciting a further supply of what they term "a wonderful production." [1]

The *Mujtahid* (Shiea Apologist) of Lucknow, in acknowledging the receipt of Pfander's four books, confesses

> that the style of these delightful treatises differs so completely from that hitherto adopted by Christian writers, that he strongly suspected some accomplished Persian of having, from worldly motives, assisted in their composition, for no such charms or merit had heretofore appeared in any writing of the *Padres*.

And his sense of their merit was proved by the threat of a refutation. The surmise of the celebrated critic is sufficiently amusing; in correcting, indeed, and polishing the style of his books, Pfander did avail himself of the services of a converted Mussulman, who, born an Armenian, was, when a boy, carried off by robbers, and, having been sold to a Persian nobleman, was by him educated as his Munshi. Pfander had to tutor both himself and this assistant in the language; and the marked superiority in the style of the *Tarîq*, his latest composition, shows what rapid progress he was attaining in the beauties of the Persian language. The fourth work referred to above by the Apologist of Lucknow, is "The Tree of Life," a small but useful Urdoo tract containing a copious selection from Scripture, illustrative of the Divine perfections and the Christian code of morals. Pfander has also composed a short treatise in English, on the "Nature of Mohammedanism," which is recommended to the perusal of all who are interested in the controversy.

It is difficult to say how the *Mîzân* was regarded in Persia. Its distribution, in which great caution was required, was commenced just as the Mission was called away; but there is reason to suppose that, notwithstanding the bigotry of the Persians, it was liked and perused by them with interest. When on his way to India, Pfander fell in with two respectable Persians, who made inquiries about the book and its author, and stated that the

[1] *Az máâmilât ajîb ast.*

Governor of Casbin had received two copies, the contents of which had excited great attention. It was suspected by them to be the work of some renegade Mohammedan. That the countries about Kabul and Herat are prepared to peruse and receive benefit from it, is clear from the evidence of an Officer who had ample opportunities of forming a correct judgment. Of the *Mîzân* he writes, that, during the period of four years' residence in that country,

he had several opportunities of proving the value of the work in question, having found in it many arguments for the truth of Christianity, which the Mussulmans, with whom he conversed, were unable to refute in a truly Christian spirit, and whenever shewn to the followers of Islam, always excited much attention, so much so that I could,—had such a course not been at variance with the known wishes of the Government,—have distributed, with every prospect of a happy result, many copies among those who would use them.

Unable to give, I yet considered myself at liberty to show the work to those Afghans who came to my house from time to time. The conversation, which generally turned on the subject of religion, afforded me opportunities for showing the Persian N. Testament, and *Mizân-ul-Haqq*, and often I have been entreated to lend this book for a more careful perusal. Next to the New Testament itself, it is the book most likely to be of use amongst Mohammedans. The contrast between Christianity and the religion of Islam is made so strong and in such moderate language, that it seemed to create an anxiety for future inquiry and investigation.

The Jews, too, of Kabul, were generally anxious to obtain copies, and as I considered the prohibition did not extend to them with such force, I on one occasion lent a copy of the work to the head of their tribe, but had considerable difficulty in recovering it, which I soon became anxious to do, on finding the deep interest it excited. To use their own expression, "the *Mîzân-ul-Haqq* put words into their mouth, and enabled them to speak out to Mohammedans, which before they had not been able to do. In my humble opinion, the work is so valuable, that it should be translated into Urdoo, Arabic, and every language in use with Mohammedans."

But it will be asked what effect these productions have had upon the native mind in India? Pfander distributed copies very extensively, with a request that the arguments should be attentively considered, and if possible replied to. The gauntlet, thus thrown down before Mohammedan society in the North-Western Provinces, has been taken up by one or two distinguished opponents, who have hitherto treated with a smile of contempt the puny attacks made against their faith. While we write, the promised refutation of the Shiea Apologist, Maulavi Syud Ali, has issued from the press of Lucknow as a thick octavo volume, not yet seen by us.[1]

A long and protracted controversy was carried on in Urdoo by Pfander with two Mohammedans, Syud Rehmat Ali and Mohammed Kâzim Ali,[2] the latter being the leading writer. It began in 1842, and lasted for two or three years; there are seven epistles, which gradually increase in length, the last containing 147 closely-written pages. The disputant sets out with the text, "I am not sent but unto the lost sheep of the house of Israel"; and asserting that our Saviour here and elsewhere declared that His mission extended only to the Jews, challenges his opponent to prove its universality, and affects virtuous indignation at our missionaries practising so foul a deception as to attempt conversion to an obsolete religion intended only for the Jews. Pfander had here to argue at a disadvantage against the Moslem's preconceived notion that Christ's mission was, like that of other prophets, fully developed during His life; he had to concede that in one sense He was primarily sent to the Jews, and that the universality of His faith was not proclaimed till after His Ascension; still, a number of passages which clearly establish the doctrine, are quoted from our Saviour's own discourses, and the apostles' teaching is added as conclusive on the subject. Kâzim Ali's objections display the perversity and helpless blindness of the followers of Islam. To all assertions of Christ Himself made *before* His Ascension, he objects that they contradict the above verse, and His own directions to the Seventy. To the final command "Go ye, therefore, and teach all nations," he objects that it is immediately preceded by a clause which destroys dependence on it, namely, "but some doubted." The Apostles' declarations are treated as contradictory, and as in-

[1] [An account of it is given at the end of this article.]

[2] These writers are, we believe, *Vakeels* in the civil court at Agra; Kâzim Ali seems to be possessed of some intelligence and sharpness, but his talents do not rise above mediocrity.

sufficient to prove a doctrine which their Master Himself is alleged not to have held. When particularly hard pressed, an easy refuge is obtained behind the charge of corruption, of which the smallest apparent discrepancy is regarded as full and satisfactory proof. The controversy then branches out into the general subject,—embracing the claim of the Apostles to inspiration; the Divinity of Christ; the prophecies applied by Mohammedans to their Prophet, etc. But Kâzim Ali's perversity surpasses that of the most of his brethren: he assumes the most fanciful interpretations, and insists that they can be the only correct ones, however absurd and obstinately perverted they may have been proved.[1] In the same spirit the plainest interpretations are constantly ascribed with irony to Pfander's extraordinary acuteness, and characterised as phantoms of his imagination. Pfander soon perceived what a *bully* he had to deal with, and in his second and third letters threatened to close the controversy if more impartiality were not shewn by his antagonists. Kâzim Ali's fourth letter exceeded its predecessors in irrational bigotry, and its style began to descend to petulant and offensive remarks. Pfander accordingly carried his threat into execution, and refused to reply unless umpires were selected to decide whether certain points had not been satisfactorily proved; to this Kâzim Ali would not accede, and here the matter ended. The Mohammedan argument is conducted with some ability and much subtilty; and a sur-

[1] For instance, "Out of Zion shall go forth the Law and the Word of the Lord from Jerusalem," the law *left* Jerusalem, and where else can it be pretended to have migrated but to Mecca? The passage, "He shall not cry, nor lift up, nor cause his voice to be heard in the street," refers to Mahommed, and it cannot apply to Christ, who "cried" on the cross. In endeavouring to prove the corruption of the Scriptures, he says, "You ask, what object had the Christians in corrupting the notices of Mohammed? What! is it no object to eat pork and drink wine; to avoid praying five times a day, and fast for a month in the year?" Shortly after he says, "I do not mean to affirm that the Scriptures were corrupted in later ages when Christians were numerous and copies multiplied; no, it was in the early ages of the Apostles when there were but few to detect the change": he forgets that the time he alludes to was more than 500 years prior to the existence of the motives and actions he had before supposed.

prising number of passages both from the Old and New Testaments are adduced; but the whole is guided by a determined wrong-headedness, which adopts the most fallacious and inconclusive reasoning merely because it ends favourably, and refuses to see its errors, however plainly pointed out. This controversy must have proved a severe trial to Pfander's temper; and if flippant contradictions, false insinuations, and bitter scoffs, may have occasionally led him to severe remarks,—it is not to be wondered at; on the contrary, we are surprised at the calm and candid manner which he preserved throughout. We should like to see the whole printed with appropriate remarks; but Pfander is, perhaps, wise in keeping back any further publication until he shall have seen his adversaries' replies; then, we understand, he intends to come forward with a general and complete refutation.

Another discussion, contained in a series of twenty-two letters which passed between Pfander and Maulavi Syud Ali Hassan [1] of Agra, has gained greater celebrity, from its having been printed in the *Khair Khah Hind.*[2] As a translation of this controversy (though abounding with mistakes) has appeared in the romanised version of that paper, our notice of its contents shall be very limited. After an amusing parley, in which the Maulavi bargains for the titles of respect by which his Prophet and Coran are to be mentioned, he introduces his argument in the ninth letter, by defining two species of improbability, — logical and experimental; and then he puts this curious question, "If by rejecting an *experimental*, you are forced to believe a logical impossibility,—what course does reason recom-

[1] Syud Ali Hassan is a man of very superior abilities, and holds a high place in Mohammedan society for attainments and learning. He is an officer of some standing in the Sudder Dewany Adalut, N.-W. P.

[2] This is a useful little monthly paper, published in Urdoo by the mission at Mirzapore: as it often languishes for want of matter, why do not the missionaries of other stations contribute an occasional article? it is hard for the editor to be reduced to the necessity of copying the Government *Gazette* into its columns:—much like printing the Acts of Parliament in a missionary periodical or monthly journal.

mend?"[1] Pfander, much against his will, is thus plunged among impossibilities; he acknowledges that where a logical impossibility is really established, it must cancel every supposition involved in it; but he denies the sovereignty of man's reason to determine what are absolute impossibilities; and he demurs to the argument altogether as being foreign to the subject in hand. The Maulavi, however, sticks manfully by his first position, asserting that if the doctrine of impossibilities be not within man's reason, and be not settled at the outset, all attempts at reasoning are absurd. After several futile endeavours on Pfander's part to draw back the Maulavi to the proofs of Christianity, and repeatedly challenging him to impugn the reasoning of his published works, the controversy falls to the ground. The Maulavi's closing letter afforded Pfander an opportunity of adding a valuable note upon the use and abuse of reason in matters of religion. This controversy possesses a peculiar interest, because the line of reasoning taken by the Maulavi is that which even sensible and intelligent Mussulmans generally adopt. Human reason is used or rather misused as a sovereign judge, and the higher possibilities of Divine interference are thereby put aside. The controversy, however, is not closed, for Ali Hassan is now printing a work at Lucknow in refutation of Christianity and in defence of the Coran, at which he has been labouring for fifteen years, and which is, by the way, to contain a full reply to the *Mîzân* as well as to the *Dîn Haqq*.

We must now take leave of Pfander's writings, and we do so with regret and admiration. Let him not forget the singular advantages and talents he possesses, nor abandon his post of champion of Christianity against the Mohammedans. We are sure, if God spare him, that he will soon be again in the field, and we heartily wish him God-speed in this most momentous struggle.

[1] In the fourteenth letter he illustrates his position by the following example:—"If not to credit the fact of a bullock having spoken, imply belief in an infinitesimal series or in the co-existence of contraries, which impossibility must be rejected?" Pfander's faculties must have been sadly puzzled to make out the learned Maulavi's meaning.

The most popular work against Christianity in the North-West Provinces is at present the *Saulat uz Zaigham*, or "Lion's Onset," a rambling, desultory attack, full of spite and animosity, and careless as to the correctness of its premises, but written in a vigorous and attractive style. An abridgment of it in Urdoo has gained great currency among the Mohammedans, and as a reply to it has just issued from the press, our readers will probably be interested to know the character and merits of both books. The *Khulâsa i Saulat uz Zaigham* was written thirteen years ago, but was only printed within the last three years. The object, as described in the concluding paragraph, is as follows :—

In former times when Christians were not in power, and the noisy violence of their abrogated religion was therefore concealed, our Professors seldom turned their thoughts towards its refutation ; but upon the learned of *this* age it is incumbent as a sacred duty, to use every endeavour for overturning their faith, otherwise these people by insidious efforts will gradually mislead whole multitudes. And be not discouraged by the knowledge that such attempts will be thrown away upon the infidels themselves ; for when it became generally known that I had written the *Saulat uz Zaigham*, people began to dispute with the Padres, White and Williams, and with me, and in the end, by God's assistance, I overcame them ; and the effect was that, of their friends, who had turned Christians, two came to me and resumed the Mohammedan faith. Then praise be to God, the Lord of both worlds !

The chief peculiarities of this treatise are the audacity with which lengthened extracts from the Bible are, by the facile use of perverse application, turned into predictions of Mohammed. It is difficult, perhaps, to say how far many of these may not be the *bonâ fide* convictions of a sincere mind searching after the confirmation of what it deems the true faith ; but some of the fancies are so conceited and puerile, some so extravagantly absurd, that the most extensive charity will hardly admit their sincerity. Thus, not only is every mention of armies, fear, terror, conquest, goodness or dominion, intended for Mohammed and nobody else, but the Prophet's very horses, swords and arrows were prefigured,—nay, his love of perfumes and hatred of garlick and onions were not overlooked. The "White stone" of the Revelations must mean the famous stone given by Gabriel to Mohammed, or else it is the Black stone of the Caaba, which once was white; and, who could have been predicted to walk in "white garments," but our Prophet who was so fond of them? The descendants of Ishmael inherit every promise intended for the Israelites; and "more are the children of the *desolate* (*i.e.* of Hagar), than of the married wife," viz. Sarah (Isa. liv. 1). It is *Mecca* that was "forsaken," but is now "an eternal excellency, the joy of many generations" (Isa. lx. 15). Again, in the parable of the sower, the three unfruitful species of seed are the Greeks, Jews and Christians; they that produced an hundredfold, the Mohammedans; the "tares" are the scoffing infidels who were slain in the battle of Bedr, and fell into the furnace of hell-fire; the "righteous" are the Mohammedans, "who shone forth as the sun."[1] In the parable of the vineyard, the husbandmen are the Jews, who are *said* to have killed Christ, who was *called*[2] the Son of God; the garden was therefore taken from them and given to the Arabs; on hearing this, the Jews expressed their astonishment; on which Jesus bade them not to be surprised, for Isaiah had told them this long ago, when he said, "The stone which the builders rejected, *i.e.* the despised Ishmaelites, will become the head of the corner; and thus in Mohammed will be fulfilled the blessing promised to Abraham." Such are the gratuitous assumptions to which the Moslems descend. The disquisition on the *Fárkalete*, or Holy Spirit, are fair specimens of the sophistry of the Mussulmans,—a counterpart of the Jews who opposed Paul "contradicting and blaspheming." Various other topics are taken up, but are all treated in the same arrogant and wayward manner. Indeed, the abusive and insulting language

[1] In the parable of the talents, the king is Christ, the enemies the Jews, and the Christians who made good use of their talents, are those who doubled them by believing on Mohammed. The "morning star," of the Revelations, is the Coran, or perhaps Friday (the Mohammedan sacred day), which is *Sukbar*, or the day of *Venus* the morning star; or Christ may have called himself so, as being the harbinger of Mohammed his Sun!

[2] By the use of the two words in italics, he cleverly avoids the conclusion which might be drawn from this passage of Christ's having been actually crucified, and of his being the Son of God.

made use of in this treatise towards the blessed Saviour, cannot but cut the Christian to the heart.

The reply by Mr. Rankin, of the American mission at Futtehgurh, is a creditable performance. It does not take up the writer's positions in detail, but classes them under several heads. It is good as far as it goes; but the style is monotonous[1] and meagre, and the author wants the vigorous, lucid, and attractive language of his opponent, to gain a favourable audience for his arguments. Nor does he sufficiently descend into particulars. However absurd many of these may be, it is proper that they should all have a reply:—because the work is in the hands of so many, and the ignorance of the vast majority so great, that they will not perceive the fallacies until they are plainly pointed out. The frequent and copious extracts from the Bible which occur in almost every page of the *Saulat*, would have afforded Mr. Rankin

[1] The stops, commas, colons, and notes of interrogation must sadly puzzle the Mohammedan reader, and probably raise a contemptuous smile: and what is the use of them? Good Urdoo is perfectly intelligible without stops, and if the style be bad and obscure, why, then, they only add to the reader's difficulty. The star as a stop is quite sufficient, and even that should be used sparingly. Let us consult the tastes and adapt our writings to the habits and ideas of our readers: if we do not, we only defeat our own object; for inconsiderable as such things may appear to us, the unfavourable effect upon their minds is immense. A late Review on "the French Lake," well described the feeling of repugnance entertained by Oriental nations towards foreign appearances; a smart Frenchman is there stated to be the very quintessence of aversion and contempt of the believer, who points to him in the streets, "Look, my child, to what you would come, if you were to deny the Prophet and become an infidel!" Adopt the native publications as your model: if you cannot afford to lithograph, at all events consult the habits of your readers, and keep as close to their favourite and long-rooted customs as possible; and above all, avoid with the utmost caution, every thing foreign either in style or appearance. If you require *notes*, throw them into the lateral margin, and not to the bottom of the page with distracting marks of reference as in the *Dîn Haqq*. Many excellent publications have issued from the Allahabad press, especially a series of valuable tracts by the Rev. Mr. Wilson, whose introduction to the Coran was noticed in a former number: but most of them labour under the disadvantages we have been noticing. If our adversaries can afford to lithograph, why cannot we? Pfander's publications are a model in their appearance, as well as their contents.

arguments ready to his hand; and the concessions of the adversary in their explanation, would form materials for truthful conclusions. Indeed, we have never seen so favourable an opportunity of closing upon the antagonist with an *argumentum ad hominem.* The passages which he has himself brought forward cannot again be withdrawn by him on the plea of interpolation, and sufficient has been admitted in their interpretation, to overthrow him on his own ground.

In examining this controversy, we have gone sufficiently into details, to show that Henry Martyn's description of the Persian is no less applicable to the Indian Mohammedan; he is a compound of ignorance and bigotry; and all access to the one is hedged up by the other. That we may learn how best to treat this melancholy state of mind, there is no more useful lesson than the careful perusal of these controversial tracts. Besides acquiring a knowledge of the subject in all its bearings, a thorough acquaintance with the Mohammedan ideas and tenets, and familiarity with their modes of polemical reasoning, there is a valuable lesson to be gained, namely, *experience to avoid their faults.* Arguments may reach to demonstration, and yet they may not force conviction: that depends upon causes, some of which may be materially modified by us. Cautious advances, breathing kindness and love, may lessen the prejudices of our opponents, while unguarded expressions and imprudent severity must increase and tend to render them insurmountable. Hence the paramount necessity for all engaged in this work to be intimately acquainted not merely with the rules of logic and requirements of sound reason, but with the human heart,—with all those springs of feeling, interest, affection, and desire, which are so closely blended with conviction. This must be sought for by the patient study of human nature, and much will be gained if each tries his own heart in the crucible of the *Saulat uz Zaigham.* What effect does the haughty demeanour and abusive language of the Moslem have upon you other than to rouse angry and contemptuous feelings? His blasphemy against the Holy Ghost, and sneers at all we hold sacred,—above all, the dishonour which he puts on the Founder of our faith by derogatory insinuations and opprobrious epithets,—does not all this cut us to the quick, and make us cling the closer to those objects which are enshrined in our affections? And must not similar language stir up similar feelings in the Mussulman bosom? We all know what a strong principle nationality is, and how easily it is wounded; now the Mohammedan's is a *nationality of faith*, and is equally injured by opprobrious imputation against his religion. Their prejudices are imbibed with their mother's milk, nourished in childhood by the marvellous tales of their Prophet and their saints, and welded into an impenetrable system by the constantly recurring ceremonies, which are interwoven with their very existence. We must also bear in mind the prescriptive hold which their religion has upon them. How many of our own countrymen profess Christianity for no better reason than that it was the religion of their forefathers; and do we not ourselves feel how much comfort and support are frequently derived from a reflection upon the numberless learned and illustrious characters who have adorned the Christian faith? Now, reverence for *their* cloud of witnesses and fathers must be no less an overpowering consideration and a comfort and support with many, than it is with us. The fact that Islam has not only stood for thirteen centuries, but has expanded and progressed, and has seldom cowered before its present foe, must be a strong and satisfactory reflection to our opponents. Again, we find with them a *religious nobility* founded on the fact that Islam has been the pure and unbroken creed of their ancestors through a succession of generations running up to the time of their Prophet. How deep-rooted must be those feelings of pride, of high and ancient parentage inwrought with a faith deemed by them so noble, so unparalleled; —a faith which affords salvation to all mankind, and which reflects its glory and lustre upon them! If anywhere we are to expect prejudice, anywhere to make allowance for it, surely it must be here. Let all our arguments, then, be framed, all our expressions selected, with these feelings and prejudices prominently in our view; let there be no *unnecessary* wounding of the national feeling, no harsh epithets, no irritating insinuations. We press this point with the greater earnestness, because the provoking insinuations, gratuitous severity, and supercilious language which we sometimes meet with are the most powerful adversaries of conviction. Let us not, however, be mistaken; we are boldly and unflinchingly to declare the message and truth of the Gospel, and the incompatibility of the Moslem faith with it, but it must be done with prudence, with kindness, with love. The missionary of the Cross will find it a difficult thing in the heat of controversy, when his own feelings are wounded in the tenderest point, when his Saviour is afresh buffeted in his presence, to command his temper and his words;—and yet it is absolutely necessary, as well for the exemplification of the Christian character as for success. Finally, there are two lessons we should learn from this controversy. The first is, never to employ a weak argument; for the effect generally is most disadvantageous to our position, and we may be certain that it will not escape the eagle eye of our adversary, who will leave all our stronger reasoning in order to expose the fallacy of the weaker. The second is, never to *force* a prophecy; fanciful and far-fetched interpretations must be studiously avoided by ourselves, if we wish with any consistency to deny those of the Mohammedans: let our conclusions be always the clear, unforced, unquestionable, deductions of reason.

We cannot close the subject without referring to an argument which is strongly urged by all the Mohammedan writers we have been reviewing, and which, if proved, would establish the divine origin of Islam; more especially as one of its most able supporters is a clergyman of the Church of England. Mr. Forster, in his *Mohammedanism Unveiled*, proposes to explain the success of that creed, which he holds has never been satisfactorily accounted for, by considering it the fulfilment of the blessing promised to Abraham for Ishmael's seed.[1] How eagerly would our Maulavis welcome Mr. Forster! Ahmed, Mahommed Ruza, Kâzim Ali, and the author of the *Saulat uz Zaigham*, all adopt the very same line of reasoning, namely, that the blessing of Ishmael is fulfilled in Mohammed, that the twelve princes are the twelve

[1] Gen. xvii. 20.

Imams, and the "innumerable multitude"[1] Mussulman believers. Pfander, Rankin, and all our other writers, deny any *spiritual* fulfilment of the promise, and hold that it was fulfilled in the rapid increase of Ishmael's posterity and the twelve princes mentioned in Gen. xxv. Does Mr. Forster, then, acknowledge the *truth* of Mohammedanism? Oh no; he styles it a "false and spurious revelation," a "baleful superstition," and its author an "imposter, earthly, sensual, devilish, beyond even the licence of his own licentious creed." Let us see, then, how he would make out this *imposture* to be the *blessing* promised by God to Abraham; we shall give his views in his own words, and beg of the reader to remark how he blends a spiritual with a temporal meaning, the accomplishment of prophecy with the fulfilment of a promise:—

"The basis of the present argument is laid in the existence of a prophetic promise to Abraham, in behalf of his sons Isaac and Ishmael. By the terms of this promise, a blessing is annexed to the posterity of each, and on Ishmael as well as on Isaac this blessing is pronounced, because he was Abraham's seed, and as a *special mark of Divine favour*. This last consideration is worth attending to; since a promise to Ishmael, thus connected by Jehovah Himself with his descent from the faithful, seems to lead the mind naturally beyond the idea of a mere temporal fulfilment. *Some sufficient fulfilment*, we are certainly authorised and bound to expect *for each branch of the original promise*. The striking literal correspondence between the terms of its two parts appears to sanction the further expectation of an analogy equally strong between the respective fulfilments: which expectation, moreover, receives fresh warrant from the fact, that the promise in behalf of Ishmael was granted in *answer* to a prayer of Abraham, in which he implored for Ishmael the blessing reserved for Isaac" (p. 87). The promises thus parallel are found actually to have had a parallel "fulfilment, as the facts of the case so strongly indicate, in the rise and success of Mohammed, and in the temporal and spiritual establishment of the Mohammedan superstition. . . . The facts of the analogy are incontrovertible; they require to be solved; and they admit of but the one satisfactory solution. We have only to receive the original promise to Abraham, according to the terms of it, as germinant and parallel in both its parts; and to recognise in Christianity and Mohammedanism its twofold fulfilment, and the whole doubts and difficulties of the question disappear" (p. 89).

In arguing the existence of a spiritual blessing for Ishmael, great stress is laid on its being the answer to Abraham's prayer.

[1] Gen. xvi. 10.

But whatever was the nature of the petition, God vouchsafed only a temporal blessing. Forster's reasoning hangs here upon a very slender thread, and yet upon that is suspended the whole of his argument! he says, the covenant of Ishmael,

"Would seem, as well from the manner of its announcement, as from the general analogy of character plainly intended by the parallel terms of the two covenants, to contain a certain real, though low and subordinate, spiritual application. Indeed that Abraham should have offered up the petition that Ishmael might live in the light of God's countenance, and under a Divine blessing and protection (a petition *certainly* implied by the prayer that he might live before Jehovah, and inherit the promise granted in favour of Isaac), may be received as conclusive and moral evidence on this point; for a blessing of a merely temporal nature was little likely to be *thus* sought by 'the father of the faithful'; in whose eyes things temporal appear invariably to have been held in little estimation" (p. 119).

Assuming thus, the whole point at issue, he proceeds :—

"In the case of Isaac, we know the precise manner and steps of the accomplishment; and in our knowledge of this detail, possess the clue for investigating the analogous accomplishment, in the case of Ishmael. It is requisite only, that the apparent historical fulfilments of the covenant of Ishmael shall be found on examination to correspond with the ascertained historical fulfilments of the covenant of Isaac, and if there be any force in the scriptural analogy established between those brethren, the demonstration aimed at in these pages must be considered complete" (p. 132).

Forster's ideas, however, of a promised blessing, and its fulfilment, are very singular. He assumes that because Hagar was a *bondswoman*, and Ishmael *illegitimate*, the religion of their descendants must partake of the qualities of both; in his own language,

"If from Isaac was to spring the true religion; from Ishmael there might be expected to arise as a counterpart, a *spurious* faith. If the true Messiah, the descendant of Isaac, and who, like him, came *by* promise, was to be the founder of the one creed; a counterfeit Messiah, the descendant of Ishmael, and who, like him, should come *without* promise, could be the only appropriate founder of the other" (p. 90). And again, "Prophecy cannot be supposed to recognise in Ishmael, the child of the flesh, the son of the bondwoman, the illegitimate seed, anything higher than the forefather of a false prophet, and the source of a spurious faith"—"the arch antitype of all preceding false Christs,"—"the spurious Messiah Mohammed" (pp. 164 and 140).

What! a *spurious* faith, a *false* prophet, a *counterfeit* Messiah, the fulfilment of a promised blessing! Is this the mode in which God fulfils His promises? To discover a parallel between Christianity and this "spurious revelation," is the object of the whole book, and it is very ably dealt with by a succession of curious analogies in the prophetical anticipations,[1] morality, doctrine, ritual, scriptures, heresies, crusades, and civilisation of Mohammedanism, Judaism and Christianity. These analogies prove nothing, because the foundation of the argument, as we have shown, is unsound; but they contain a vast fund of useful information, which will well repay the trouble of a perusal.

The nature of Forster's argument is such that upon approaching it, he is always led into confusion or inconsistency. Thus he acknowledges that the lesser blessing of Ishmael was "manifestly of a temporal nature"; yet he hence deduces that, "through the Gospel and the Coran, the *promise* to Abraham, continually advanced towards its *fulfilment*, in the posterity of his sons, until of these two brethren was the whole earth overspread"; we have here the temporal confused with a spiritual blessing. Again he says, "the one was the covenant of the spirit; the other the covenant of the flesh, . . . the arm of flesh therefore was the natural and proper weapon for its enforcement." It is acknowledged to be "a covenant of the flesh," then why attempt to make it spiritual? Again, "the grand feature in the promise concerning Isaac was, *that in his seed all the nations of the earth should be blessed*"; and the responding feature in the parallel

[1] Some of the historical analogies are sufficiently far-fetched; for instance, Christianity rose in *Judea*, while Islam made that one of its earliest conquests. *Jerusalem* was the site of the Jewish temple, and it is that of the mosque of Omar. *Constantinople* was the imperial metropolis, and the cathedral of St. Sophia the central fane of eastern Christianity; but that city is now the metropolis of Mohammedans, and the cathedral a mosque. "*Three* in company in flight to Egypt, Joseph, Mary, Jesus;—Gabriel their conductor: *Three* in company in flight to Medina, Mohammed, Abubeker, Amer Ebn Fohaira;—Gabriel their pretended conductor."

promise respecting Ishmael, that *he should dwell in the presence of all his brethren*"; the former, it is contended, was fulfilled in Christianity, the latter, in Mohammedanism. There is no "responding feature" here; Mohammedanism *may* be the accomplishment of a prophecy, but that is a very different thing from the fulfilment of a promise. Forster would make circumcision to "be equally at the root of both parts of the original covenant, and to be the common bond of a certain spiritual relation,—'to be a God unto thee and to thy seed after thee';—and we can only tell of the force of this application to Ishmael by an investigation of RESULTS." This argument, however, proves a great deal too much, as it would extend to the whole of Abraham's seed, including the children of Ketura,—to whom no special spiritual blessing was accorded. "Isaac becomes the father of the true faith; Ishmael,—of a spurious imitation of it." But a "spurious imitation" is no fulfilment; and if Islam is actually the fulfilment of the promise, it cannot be spurious, but must be acknowledged a divine faith. The fabric is based upon a contradiction.

It frequently falls in with Forster's views to prove Islam a blessing, and then it is curious to observe how he avoids comparing it with the Gospel. Thus he says that when we "submit Mohammedanism to a comparison with Christianity, exclusively of Judaism, we are not trying it by the proper and equitable standard; . . . for it is no more than the barest justice, that the parts of it derived from the law of Moses should be tried by that law, instead of being condemned without reserve or discrimination, by another rule,—the infinitely perfect law of Christ." But surely there can be no reason why his creed should not be tried and condemned by that faith which its founder supplanted, and in room of which he substituted his own. Again, "some of the most objectionable features of his moral law, instead of being, as heretofore, tried and condemned by the perfect rule of the Gospel, would seem entitled to be judged by reference to the *source whence it is derived*, and the *standard to which it appeals*." The source from whence he professes to derive his law is God Himself: why then adopt a lower standard than His word?

Elsewhere he says :—

"The intrinsic merits of Mohammedanism, while utterly beneath comparison with the only true revelation, are yet confessedly superior to those of every other religious system which has obtained among men. . . . As opposed to the Gospel, indeed, Mohammedanism must be considered only as a curse; but as the pre-appointed scourge of heresy and heathenism, as cleansing the world from the gross pollutions of idolatry, and as preparing the way for the reception of a purer faith, it may well be regarded as a blessing."

On a nearer inspection, we fear that he would have modified this praise: their false worship opposes obstacles to conversion, greater even than those of heathenism itself.

As to the *prospective* views of Mohammedanism, Mr. Forster's expectations are glowing in the extreme. After expatiating on the points common to both creeds, he proceeds :—

"Suppose these, and similar positions, plainly deducible from the Coran and its commentators, once brought clearly and conclusively to *elucidate* the authoritative record of Scripture, by men whose zeal shall shine forth on the benighted East, sustained by extensive knowledge, and tempered by a wise discretion, while their walk among men forms that best of commentaries, a living one, on the truth and power of these doctrines;—suppose episcopal Christianity, in a word, one day taught and exemplified in Asia, as it was originally taught and exemplified in the Apostolic times, and who, that reflects on the whole providential history and relationship of the two religions, can doubt the eventful result throughout the Mohammedan world?" (vol. i. p. 400). "And thus out of the most deadly and devastating apostasy with which the justice of Heaven ever visited the sins of men, does the mercy of God seem, all along, to have been secretly, but effectually, preparing the instrumental means for the glorious re-edification of our Eastern Sion, by the final bringing in of Jew, Mohammedan and Gentile, to the church and kingdom of the Gospel" (vol. ii. p. 371).

These are bright visions indeed; and may God of His infinite mercy grant them a speedy fulfilment: but we fear they are not borne out by the premises. Alas! there is nothing in Islam which warrants us in saying that it tends towards Christianity. At first sight, indeed, we appear to have many advantages in the contest; we have no infidel views to oppose; the existence of sin, and its future punishment, are allowed; the necessity of a revelation, and even the Divine origin of the Old and New Testament dispensations, are conceded; the most of the attributes of God, the immaculate conception of Christ, and the miracles which attested His mission, are all admitted. The Mohammedans believe a Gospel, but it is not ours: they worship a God, but not the God and Father of our Lord Jesus Christ: they acknowledge a Jesus, but not Him who was so called, because He should save His people from their sins. Hear Mirza Ibrahim:—

"For we are not sure of the miracles of *that* Moses and Jesus, of whom the Jews and Christians speak; and who as they say did not believe in the mission of our Prophet; but we speak of the miracles of that Moses and Jesus, who have given their testimony to the mission of Mohammed: and how great is the difference between them when viewed in these different lights! Let it not be said that the persons are the same in both cases. We believe in these prophets, in consequence of their being described in the Coran, and not as described by the Jews and Christians."—(*Cont. Tracts*, p. 33.)

Yes,—it must be borne in mind, that it is *simply* as they are mentioned in the Coran, and only *because* they are mentioned there, that the Moslem believes in the prophets and the Bible; and the misrepresentations of the Coran not merely destroy their identity, but by cancelling and overturning all preceding revelations, take from us the only means we have of proving the imposture false. Could the counsels of the Evil one have devised any more perfect plan for frustrating the Gospel and grace of God?[1]

It is true, indeed, that the Coran has taken much from the Bible, and abounds therefore with approaches to the truth; and it might have been hoped that these would have proved as foundations upon which to build, as a *fulcrum* whereon to ply our argument. But it is a melancholy truth, that a certain amount of light and knowledge often renders it only the more difficult to drive the bigot from his prejudices. Thus the Mussulman is conscious of possessing many truths behind which he proudly entrenches himself, persuaded that he has the whole truth and nothing but the truth. The supposed advantages then, the points common to both, are thus turned into a barrier against us, into a thick impenetrable veil which effectually excludes every glimmer-

[1] Having quoted a verse from the Coran, Forster adds, "this assuredly is none other than the voice of *Satan* speaking by the mouth of a False apostle"—strange epithets for the promised blessing!

ing of the true light. How delusive, therefore, are such anticipations as these of Mr. Forster:—

"*Since we find among the followers of Mohammed, such favourable prepossessions, and established doctrines,* AS WILL RENDER EASY THE APPROACH TO THEIR CONVERSION, neither force of obligation, NOR PROSPECT OF SUCCESS,[1] is wanting to encourage our progress, and animate our zeal": and again, he affirms, that the two religions "hold so many great fundamentals in common, that they contain a *natural and necessary tendency to convergence*:—the imperfect scheme, when its providential work shall have been accomplished, becoming absorbed in the perfect, and the moon of Mohammed resigning its borrowed rays, to melt in the undivided light of the everlasting Gospel."

It is certainly a novel idea to speak of Mohammed or his Coran under the simile of the moon; his own people[2] style him the sun, and our Saviour the moon, and they would laugh to scorn any mention of their Prophet's "*borrowed* light" melting into that of the Gospel.

These are melancholy reflections. Have we, then, no more encouraging thoughts with which to conclude this article? Have all our efforts been thrown away, and our cause nowise advanced? God forbid! for, amid discouragement, we can discern pleasing tokens of progress. And first, our friends, it is evident, are closely and carefully examining the Scriptures; the simple fact, therefore, of the perusal of the Word of God is a step gained, and one which will, we yet may hope, lead to favourable results. Again, as the controversy advances, and books on the subject are spread abroad, the mistaken views hitherto entertained of our leading doctrines, will be removed, and scriptural knowledge substituted in their stead. This should sweep away many of the strongholds built on erroneous notions of Christianity;—and then rejection of our faith will be in the face of the clearest light. We trust, too, that Christian character is now more generally exhibited to the view of our adversaries; and its excellencies and graces cannot fail (if we are but true to our profession) to aid their conviction of the truth of our religion. And, lastly, we look with anxious hope, to the influence of the native Christians from amongst our Orphan

[1] The *italics* and *capitals* are Forster's own.

[2] As in the *Saulat uz Zaigham*.

asylums and converts generally, and to the effect which appeals thus sounding from among themselves, and addressing their feelings and reason with native home-drawn arguments, will have throughout the country.

But of all human means we trust most to those exhibitions of earnestness and anxiety, which Christian love is now prompting its professors to put into active motion. Yes; it is a matter of congratulation that the attitude which Europe and America are now assuming, is just that which is likely to strike conviction into the impassive heart of the Mohammedan. When he sees Christians so vitally alive to the infinite blessings their religion is calculated to impart, so tenderly concerned for the perishing condition of their brethren, and so filled with zeal to make them sharers of their own blessings, as cheerfully to undergo loss and suffer privation ;—*this* is a practical argument, the most likely of any to convince him of the reality and Divine nature of the Gospel. God be praised that Christianity is beginning gradually to assume her rightful position; and no sooner shall she have fully done so, than a light must break forth establishing before the world her truth and the unspeakable difference between it and every false religion.

In conclusion, we would earnestly press the necessity which lies upon all of removing, as far as their ability extends, the ignorance of the Mohammedans; and the responsibility those are under who possess the requisite qualifications, of affording them access to the numerous spheres of learning, a knowledge of which is presupposed in most of our religious discussions. Let us attend to Dr. Lee :—

"In ancient History and Scripture, the Persians are necessarily very ignorant,[1] the best means they have of obtaining either being the fragments

[1] As an instance of their ignorance of History, there is a passage in the *Saulat uz Zaigham*, where the author adduces the fall of Babylon as the accomplishment of ancient prophecies in favour of Mohammed. He says that Isaiah and Jeremiah successively predicted the destruction of this city, but had it fallen in their times that its overthrow would not again have been foretold by St. John in the Revelations. At last, he tells us, the priest *Sátih* predicted it to Noushirvan, as about to follow the establishment of Mohammed's creed. It will be difficult to disabuse them of the idea that we

found in the Coran or the traditions; nor is there much probability of their improving in this respect, until they shall possess a good translation of the whole Bible, with some such works as the connections of the Old and New Testaments by Prideaux, the connections of sacred and profane History by Shuckford, and some good commentary on the Text of Scripture" (p. cxxii.). And again: "It would be well to translate into the Persian some of our standard books on the apparent contradictions of the Scriptures, with Paley's *Evidences of Christianity*, or the recent work of Mr. Sumner."

Translations, however, to make them useful, should be adapted and remodelled, leaving out much that would be unsuitable to an Oriental, and supplying much that would be superfluous to a European reader.[1] We would urge this duty, not upon our Indian Society alone, but upon the learned of England. Islam is not, like the religion of the Hindoo, a subject foreign to the European; for twelve centuries it has been his near neighbour; it effected a footing in Spain and Italy, and it now reigns in Turkey; from the stores of its learning was the darkness of the Middle Ages first enlightened; and our libraries are full of learned and controversial works in defence and in defiance of both religions. Why then have we not more instances of our countrymen treading in the steps of Dr. Lee? The stimulus of a *prize* is sufficient to entice the learned inmates of Oxford and Cambridge to combat the remote and dimly distinguished tenets of the *Hindoo.* And shall not the interest and proximity of the subject, its close connection with Europe, and the ample resources at hand for obtaining a knowledge of the principles of Islam, be sufficient to tempt our learned countrymen to come forward in the Mohammedan contest; and thus, without the labour or the banishment of

are deceiving them in representing John's as a *spiritual* Babylon, without a considerable knowledge of History on their part.

[1] A thousand such works are urgently required. When will our philanthropic spirit prompt us to supply our native fellow-subjects with a theological library? A running commentary on the whole Bible, but especially on the New Testament, is urgently needed. Brief notes, lithographed in the margin, would prove invaluable; such a work should be executed so as to accommodate the native taste. Take the Lucknow Coran with its running marginal Urdoo notes as the model. A wide margin and smaller writing for the notes, will afford ample room for all that needs to be said. We trust soon to see some work of this description.

a missionary life, to forward the Christian cause by aids more valuable than thousands of silver and gold?

We would also impress upon those who are unable to help by writing, the duty which the more heavily devolves upon them of furnishing means for printing and circulating books already provided. We understand that Pfander's works are nearly out of print; and we strongly recommend that *five*, or, if possible, *ten* thousand copies of *Mîzân-ul-Haqq*, and two thousand of the other treatises, be struck off in Urdoo, with a reasonable proportion in Persian; for this, no doubt, extraordinary funds will be required, but surely the Christian public, when awakened to a sense of the magnitude and urgency of the object, will not be backward in furnishing them. At all events, in thus prominently directing public attention to the subject, we have discharged a duty towards one of the worthiest of men and one of the noblest of causes. Of Pfander or his writings, many of our Indian residents may probably have never heard. And if what has been written shall prove the means of leading any of them so to esteem the author, and appreciate the value of his works, as to stir them up to lend effective aid in circulating them throughout the Mohammedan world, one great object which we had in view in this review will have been gained. Dr. Pfander is an ordained minister of the Church of England; and it is by the multiplication of such agents, that this or any other branch of the Christian Church can expect to obtain a secure footing and a permanent ascendancy among the hitherto unreclaimed realms of heathenism.

SUPPLEMENT REGARDING THE *Kashf-ul-Astâr li Kasri Miftâh-ul-Asrâr;* or, "Key of Mysteries Shattered."

Since writing the above article we have perused the work published by Syud Ali Hassan, the Mujtahid of Lucknow, to which reference is made at page 33. At its close is printed correspondence which passed between this eminent Apologist and Pfander, who had forwarded his books to him in 1842. The Mujtahid replied, as before stated, in a very courteous manner, complimented Pfander on the uncommon merit of his productions, and informed him that he had set one of his pupils to furnish a reply.[1] The author of the present work, therefore, is not the Shiea Apologist himself, but his nephew, Syud Mahommed Hâdi, whose father and the Mujtahid are sons of the famous Syud Dildar Ali, who gained celebrity by his travels in Arabia, Persia, and other countries; and, being a pillar of the Shiea faith, and a man famed for his attainments, became the spiritual guide of the King of Oudh, and the Mujtahid of Lucknow. The office would thus appear to be in some measure hereditary, and the incumbent is said to be enriched by the free-will offerings of the Oudh nobility; so that the position is not only a dignified but a lucrative one.

The work is entitled: "Key of Mysteries (*Miftâh-ul-Asrâr*) Shattered." The full title is: "The Curtain drawn aside, to shew the 'Key of Mysteries' (*Miftâh-ul-Asrâr*) shattered, and the Conceits of a certain Ecclesiastic refuted." It is written in very high Persian, and abounds with Arabic phrases; the author, indeed, frequently breaks into whole sentences and even pages of Arabic, especially where he reduces his reasoning to a logical form: he may, no doubt, have found that the technical and laconic language of the Arabians enabled him at times to express his ideas with greater exactness and precision, but the general effect is to give an appearance of pedantry and display. The arrangement is much the same as that recommended above for a reply to the *Saulat uz Zaigham*. A quotation is first made from the *Miftâh*, comprising generally a whole chapter or division, headed in large letters, "Thus writes the Christian." At the close follows his reply,

[1] At the same time he forwarded for Pfander's perusal five tracts in refutation of the Christian religion; of these, one is a reply to the *Dalâil Wâfiah*, a tract noticed in *Saulat uz Zaigham*, but which we have not seen. Another is an account of some controversies with the Rev. William Bowley, of Chunar, —who, no doubt, is the same referred to in the *Saulat* as "William Padre." A third is a disputation with "Padre Joseph Wolff," who is stated to have visited Lucknow, and proclaimed the advent of our Saviour as about to take place in fourteen years, a topic which is more than once mentioned with exultation as a proof of the liability of Christians to err in the interpretation of their Scriptures.

begun similarly with the words, "I say in reply, and from the Lord I seek assistance." After general remarks, if he has occasion to notice any particular passage, it is introduced with the title, "Again he says" (quoting the passage), and then proceeds to give his answer as before. This mode of reply is recommended for imitation on similar occasions. The headings mark the alternations of text and commentary as clearly as any division into chapters could, and the whole is a most convenient as well as strictly Oriental mode of composition.

The line of attack shows the subtilty and skill of our adversaries. The Mujtahid, in his letter to Pfander, assumes that the turning-point between us is the doctrine of the Trinity. Rather, the turning-point is the genuineness and integrity of our Scriptures; when that is proved, the truth of the Christian religion and falsity of Mohammedanism follow quite independently of the Trinity or any other Christian doctrine. These form, indeed, valuable subsidiary points, for they prove the Coran to oppose previous revelation, but they are all involved in the soundness of the Scriptures; and till this is proved on our side, or disproved on that of the Moslems, the arguments must remain incomplete and unsatisfactory. To have rendered the present attack in any degree a fair one, the author was bound either to have acknowledged the genuineness of the Bible, or proved its corruption; instead, he passes over the *Mîzân* with the sneer that its arguments had been formerly refuted, and that it might more aptly have been called the *Mizân i Bátil*,[1] and proceeds to analyse and discuss the contents of the *Miftâh-ul-Asrâr*. He is thus enabled to take up at pleasure the most profound and mysterious doctrines of Revelation; he appeals to reason to attest their impossibility, and hence he deduces the corruption of our Scriptures. Further, he denies that the Scriptures, even as they stand, contain the dis-

[1] That is, the False or Foolish Balance, as opposed to the "Balance of Truth" (*Mizân-ul-Haqq*). He says, however, in the course of his book, that he meditates a reply to the *Mizân-ul-Haqq*, and we hope he will accomplish it. The integrity of the Scriptures is the ground upon which our closest struggle must take place, of which the Mussulmans are very shy; they hardly ever approach it fairly and openly, but delight in covert attacks.

puted tenets, and, by throwing into the shade the stronger passages adduced by Pfander, by describing others as metaphorical, by applying a few to his own Prophet, and explaining away the remainder, he in appearance destroys the amount of cumulative evidence which before appeared irresistible. But the most unjust and gratuitous portion of his books is that which rejects *in toto* the Acts and Epistles, and assumes that the Four Gospels alone are to be regarded as inspired, the rest being of no more value than the *Hyát-ul-Culúb,*[1] or other Mohammedan histories. Taking up such ground, and assuming to himself such unbounded licence of dispensing with our evidence, it is not to be wondered that the Divinity of Christ and the Trinity are dogmatically rejected by the writer as unfounded and absurd, and pronounced to be the fabrications of a heated imagination. We shall now notice some of his chief lines of reasoning which may prove interesting to our readers.

The grand feature of the book is, that reason being the supreme Judge, the Divinity of Christ and the Trinity are *absolute impossibilities.* On both doctrines, while directly at issue with Pfander, he simply assumes his own position as axiomatic, and proceeds to draw his inferences from them. His work is therefore beside the point, and cannot be regarded as a reply to the *Miftâh* until he strengthens his premises by argument and proof. Revelation, he argues, must be communicated through a prophet, whose mission cannot be established until the existence of the Deity by whom he is commissioned be ascertained; and that can be done by reason alone; therefore, reason is prior to revelation, and to imagine anything proved by revelation which is contrary to reason is to imagine a thing to be proved by itself, which is absurd; and hence he deduces that revelation must bend to reason, and that anything in the former which opposes the latter must be explained as metaphorical, or abandoned altogether. From such premises he concludes, that were the Trinity, or any other impossible doctrine, contained even in an acknowledged revelation, it must

[1] "Life or History of Hearts." When the Acts are adduced in support of a doctrine, he applies to us the proverb, "The fox saw his own tail," implying that they are a fabrication of the Christians, and therefore useless as evidence.

be rejected; consequently its existence in our Scriptures would simply prove their corruption, not the truth of the doctrine. Our opponent being determined to resist the utmost amount of evidence, it was needless for him to have advanced further. With a mind so bent against the reception of evidence, what advantage could be anticipated from discussion?

To the argument that our reason is feeble, and that a thousand things about us are as incomprehensible as the Divine mystery, he replies, that these things are involved in *creation*, and are therefore nothing to the point. Every thing that we can think of, he divides into three classes:[1] (1) the *absolute*, whose existence is beyond change or question; (2) the *impossible*, whose existence cannot be conceived; and (3) the *possible*, of which the existence and non-existence are both imaginable. The mysteries of nature belong to the third class, and, liable to change and composition, cannot be regarded as analogies of the Divine nature; but real *trinity in unity* is included in the second category, and, therefore, the mysteries of nature, however incomprehensible, cannot affect its impossibility. He thus asserts that the doctrine in dispute is not incomprehensible, but impossible; and he accuses Pfander of confounding that which it is impossible to comprehend with what we comprehend to be impossible. Thus, by begging the question, he renders his reasoning inconclusive.

The Maulavi feigns surprise that Pfander, having once renounced reason, should again at pleasure use it to his service. Reason, he pretends, is abjured by us only for the occasion; in one sense, indeed, we do reject our own reason, by taking up with that of the devil! He taunts his opponent: "At times affecting the extreme of piety, you abandon your reason and follow only *the Word*; at others, you hold the most extravagant absurdities, fabricated out of your own head, and even in opposition to the Scripture!" Thus he takes Pfander to task for speaking of the planets as *hung in the air*; assuming from the Old Testament the creation of a material Heavens, he accuses his adversary of substituting in their stead an empty space on the hypothesis of our

[1] In the original: (1) *Wâjib al Wujûd*; (2) *Mumtanâ al Wujûd*; (3) *Mumkin al Wujûd*.

star-gazing philosophers, and in direct contradiction to the voice at once of Astronomy and Revelation.[1] The Maulavi apparently cannot distinguish between the *use* and the *abuse* of reason. He can not, or will not, see that we may employ reason to ascertain the existence of the Deity (without presuming to search out the mysteries of His nature), and then to guide us in recognising His revelation; here reason must stop, and henceforth her only legitimate office is to search into the contents and discover the meaning of the Divine record. Until this principle be admitted we have little to hope from Moslem discussion.

In pressing his argument from Scripture, the Maulavi opposes to Christ's assumption of Divine attributes His own express avowal of subordination. Such attributes cannot be proved to exist in His nature *independently* and *absolutely* (which alone would imply divinity), for they are generally spoken of as derived from the Father, and this dependence is inadmissible in the idea of the Divine nature.

His union with the Father is stated to be a union of spirits like that which subsists among believers, and the word "forsaken" pronounced upon the cross, is adduced as clearly proving the absence of any closer connection. He holds that there are two applications of the word *God*, one of which was in the Old Testament used towards prophets and princes, and in the New to Christ; and he dextrously adduces our Saviour's quotation, "I said ye are gods," as conclusive upon this head. The argument of obeisance and adoration he treats in the same way, but does not explain how Thomas came to join them together in his act of worship. The "*word*" and "*spirit* of God" are explained in much the same way as that of the authors we have already considered. The *Word* means the imperative "Be," by which all

[1] Not long after the publication of this book, Pfander received a note regarding it from a learned Hindoo resident of Lucknow, well versed apparently in Arabic philosophy. He discards the views of the Maulavi, and holds that, according to Grecian and Hindoo philosophy, there is no material Heavens, and that a sect of Mohammedan philosophers profess the same belief, though the remainder are bound to the opposite doctrine as a part of their religious system.

things were created, and especially Christ, who was born without a father; "the word Be was in the beginning before all creation, and the word was God," that is, by an ellipse, "was the word of God"; and "the word became flesh," that is, was the cause of Christ's birth![1] To the catholic interpretation of this passage he opposes the dictates of reason regarding the impossibility of the incarnation of God; and he asserts that Pfander has mistranslated the words "dwelt among us"—the Arabic version having in this place, "he entered into us" (halla fi nâ), which involves the doctrine of transmigration or communication of the Divine essence to another (hullûl), a tenet regarded by orthodox Mussulmans with peculiar horror. Had the Maulavi consulted the *original*, he would have found that the words ἐσκήνωσεν ἐν ἡμῖν were most aptly rendered as above. Indeed, the Maulavi is too much in the habit of throwing grave suspicions on the integrity of Pfander's views and translations, merely on the authority of Arabic

[1] Of his frivolous perversions of the sacred text, a few examples may be noticed. "No man hath ascended up to Heaven, but he that came down from Heaven"; this, and similar passages as "I am from above," apply equally to Elijah, who also "ascended up," and must therefore have also "come down from heaven." The last clause, "even the Son of Man which is in heaven," is denied as an interpolation, and a curious tradition is mentioned of Imam Riza having publicly stated before a Christian minister called *Hathuliq*, who could not deny the correctness of the quotation, that the verse originally ran thus: "Verily, verily, my disciples, I say unto you that no man shall ascend into heaven but he that descended from heaven, except the camel-mounted, the last of the Prophets,—he, indeed, will ascend to heaven, and again descend," referring to Mohammed's *Mirâj* (ascent to the seventh heaven); and this tradition he says is a thousand times more deserving of credit than all your corrupted Gospels put together. Even admitting the present reading, he says, "who is in heaven," does not mean actual presence there, but alludes, by a common mode of speech, to his residence in heaven as being close at hand. The power of raising the dead, which Christ assumed as inherent in Himself, he describes as referring to the approaching miracle of Lazarus, and as implying no higher virtue than Elisha possessed. His presence, promised to the disciples to the end of the world, is explained metaphorically, "I shall be so aware of the state of each, that, as it were, I shall be always in the midst of you"; or if it does mean spiritual presence, it is nothing more than what we believe of other angels, and extends at most to the Judgment Day,—intimating that then, like other men, he must die.

translations. This may for a time acquire for him some credit with his unlearned brethren, but as soon as the untenableness of his positions become generally known, it will end only in confusion. We recommend the Maulavi to become a student of Greek and Hebrew at the Lucknow Martiniere, and to make himself thoroughly master of those languages, before he again ventures to call in question the renderings of competent persons.

The proofs from the Old Testament he treats with still less fairness. Some of the most important passages are passed over, and many others are advanced on the ground that they apply to Mohammed.[1] He then produces what he considers two irrefragable arguments in substantiation of his Prophet's mission. The first, the perfection of his religion as a code of morals and devotion; the second, that Mohammed must have been either a true prophet or a madman. He proves by his many virtues and talents that he was not the latter, and triumphantly asserts that he must have been the former.[2] He forgets that the same argument would apply with even greater weight to the apostles; for

[1] Like Kâzim Ali, he applies the glorious promises of Isaiah to Mohammed; though with greater candour he allows that the introductory verses, "He shall not cry," etc., refer to Jesus. He holds that part of the second psalm applies to Jesus, and part to Mohammed; but does not show how to distinguish between the two. He denies that the 53rd of Isaiah can refer to Christ, because it is said, "He shall see his *seed*"; on the contrary, he holds that the promise of "a portion with the great and spoil with the strong," is an evident token of Mohammed, forgetting the remarkable words that follow, "because he hath poured out his soul unto death," etc. The commencement of the chapter could not designate Christ, because the Prophet speaks in the *past* tense, "he *was* despised, and we *esteemed* him not"; it can, therefore, only mean that "we despised and rejected Ishmael," and, by a common figure of speech, his descendant Mohammed in him. The "root out of a *dry* ground" is a reference to Hagar, who, to worldly appearance, was an unlikely source for a prophet;—or more probably to the arid plains of Mecca, noted for their dryness and sterility.

[2] The learned Hindoo of Lucknow, before referred to, attacks the Maulavi on this point; he asserts that he has omitted a much more likely supposition, namely, that of having been a false prophet and imposter. It is pleasing to see the subject so soon attract the notice of the Hindoos and elicit so very pertinent a criticism.

with them we have many claimants to inspiration, instead of one—we have pure morals, and an entire absence of worldly motives.

In taking up the chapter on the Holy Ghost as third Person of the Trinity, he leaves almost unnoticed the strongest passages from the New Testament, and dwells upon others which Pfander himself acknowledges are no more than allusions. He mistakes the *gift* and *influences* of the Holy Ghost, for the Divine spirit itself; and asserts that our doctrine would lead to the supposition that Christ was in the womb of Elizabeth and Mary at the same time; for "John was filled with the Holy Ghost from his mother's womb." He holds that the epithet here means the gift of repentance or spirit of faith, which was imparted by the apostles to those who believed. The Athanasian creed, as translated into Arabic by Sabat, is now criticised, and by applying the attributes and nature of one Person in the blessed Trinity to another, as he affirms he is warranted to do upon the supposition of real Unity, he reduces the doctrine *ad absurdum*, and holds it up in a variety of lights, as involving contradictions and impossibilities. He omits, throughout his reply, the orthodox doctrine of the two natures of Christ which, had he approached the subject in a proper spirit, would have extricated him from many of his dilemmas.

The examples and analogies from nature are rejected because, while the unity is that of figure or substance, the plurality consists in parts or qualities. He does not fail to take Pfander to task for the examples of the *circle*, etc.; but his language is perhaps less strong and improper than that of others noticed before. One's sense of the disadvantage of these illustrations is, if possible, strengthened by the Maulavi's remarks. The disadvantage of metaphysical reasoning on this vitally important subject is strikingly shown in several passages, where it is assumed by our opponent that we consider the Son and the Holy Ghost to be *manifestations* of the Divine essence; the former being the attribute of *wisdom* or *intelligence*, the latter, of *power* and *love*. Such views, however carefully the language may be chosen, are undoubtedly prone to denude the blessed

Persons of that individuality which the Bible attributes to them.

The Maulavi exults that his adversary has been driven for examples of the Trinity to the tenets of idolatrous nations and heathen philosophers, and quotes the proverb, "The drowning man clutches at every straw," to intimate that he could only have adopted so dangerous an expedient from the badness of his cause.[1] He warns him that religion is a serious and a delicate subject, and that we are not here, as in worldly matters, to seek assistance from all by force or by fraud.[2] These remarks show how totally he misunderstands Pfander's argument, which is to prove the consistency of a species of plurality in unity with human reason: now, the Grecian philosophers, for instance, had certainly by nature as strong and sound a faculty of reason as our adversaries or we possess; and since it is upon reason, *unaided by revelation*, that the Mohammedan hangs his cause, it is surely reasonable in us to adduce the evidence of impartial reasoners, whose minds, unwarped by any of our supposed prejudices, directed the intensest thought towards the discovery of the mode in which the Divine Being exists: such deductions, surely we may safely oppose to the simple *ipse dixit* of our adversaries, without being suspected of any intention to countenance the doctrines themselves. The *Sufies* are abused by the Maulavi, as unbelievers still worse than ourselves, but he will not admit that their views in any degree assist us; because, first, they hold a greater variety of manifestations than mere *intelligence* and *will*, and the analogy, therefore, proves too much; and, secondly, their doctrines are not allowed by the orthodox Mussulmans. He likewise accuses Pfander of inconsistency in first representing these Sufie philosophers as believing in a trinity,

[1] He throws the proverb in our teeth, "Idolatry and infidelity are but one religion," as implying that we and the idolaters are much alike in error.

[2] He denies that the Hindoos hold plurality in unity regarding their deity; asserting that Brahma, Vishnu, and Mahesh represent the angels Asrafäel, Michael, and Azrael, and are in fact only the ministers of the Deity; and he makes large extracts upon this subject from a Persian writer. He, accordingly, denies that they hold the incarnation of the *Deity*.

and afterwards asserting that absolute metaphysical unity would land its professor in the Sufie error of regarding the Divinity as a mere existence, and all creation his attributes. He distinctly denies that they or any other Mussulmans look upon the Deity as a rigid metaphysical unity,—but as a being endowed with attributes and perfections, although absolutely one in person and individuality.

Pfander's most important and concluding chapter he treats with contempt, and allots but six pages to its reply. The knowledge of God can be obtained only in accordance with reason and revelation, both of which he affirms point to unity and not to trinity. That the salvation of man is dependent upon these doctrines, he ridicules as the height of absurdity, because we hold that Christ actually descended into *Hell*, a shocking blasphemy which no other people ever dared to affirm of their prophet.[1] The all-important doctrine of Christ's vicarious suffering he treats with scorn, and applies to us the proverb—

"They flee for refuge from the rain,
And stand for shelter 'neath the drain,"—

that is, in seeking to escape from a *slight* misfortune, viz. the punishment of our sins, we run into the greater danger of charging God with injustice by inflicting the punishment of the guilty upon the innocent. Having thus abandoned the atonement, he satisfies himself with saying that the faith in Christ, to which pardon is promised, is nothing more nor less than the faith and obedience which every prophet has insisted upon, and in return for which he has promised the same blessings.

Upon the whole, there is nothing to discourage us in this production. The fallacy of the greater part of the reasoning must be recognised by the majority of thinking Mussulmans if they choose to reflect with impartiality; and though it may for a time throw dust unto the eyes of the less candid and intelligent portion of the community, still, as Pfander's entire[2] work is

[1] This popular delusion the Mohammedans have probably picked up from the Apostles' creed; it certainly appears to be very generally promulgated among them.

[2] The eleventh page alone is omitted, we cannot see with what object.

quoted chapter by chapter, we cannot but rejoice that so great a portion of truth is placed before the Mohammedan reader (if he will but attend to it) as an antidote to the poison. We understand that Pfander, at the close of the controversy with Ali Hassan, which he is about to publish, intends to add a few remarks in refutation of the Volume we have been considering in this supplementary addition to our article.

SECOND ARTICLE

BIOGRAPHIES OF MOHAMMED FOR INDIA;

AND

THE MOHAMMEDAN CONTROVERSY

From the "Calcutta Review," 1852

1. *Life of Mohammed.* Bombay Tract and Book Society. Bombay, 1851.
2. *The Life of Mohammed.* London: Religious Tract Society.
3. *Life of Mohammed.* By Washington Irving. London: Henry G. Bohn, 1850.
4. *Moulûd Sharîf.* "The Ennobled Nativity." Lucknow, 1562 Heg. Cawnpore, 1267 Heg. Agra, 1268 Heg. (1852).
5. *Kitâb i Istifsâr.* ("Book of Questions.") Pp. 806. Lucknow, 1261 Heg. (1845).
6. *Hall ul Ishkâl.* ("Solution of Difficulties.") "A Reply to *Kashf-ul-Astâr*, and *Kitâb i Istifsâr.*" Agra, 1847.

Within the last ten or twenty years, the mind of Christian Europe has been directed, with more studious earnestness and dispassionate inquiry, towards the rise of Islam, than in any preceding period: and the progress made in searching out the truths of that crisis in the world's history, is characterised by corresponding success. Indeed, the amount of facts carefully collected, and of data philosophically weighed, within this short term is, perhaps, of greater value than all the labours of Christian writers during the twelve preceding centuries.

5

It is only necessary to mention the names of Weil, of Caussin de Percival, and of Sprenger,—and very many more might be adduced,—to call up to recollection the depth of study, philosophy, and Oriental learning which have been brought to bear upon the subject. Some portions of these labours have already been cursorily reviewed in this journal. But they deserve, and will we trust yet receive, a far deeper and more extended survey. The task is one to which an Indian periodical may well be devoted. The facilities for the study are, probably, greater here than in any other part of the world; and the discovery by Sprenger of the invaluable Wâckidi, gives promise of, perhaps, still further treasures purchased from the West at some remote period by the riches of Indian conquerors and Ameers, being still extant in the land. However, if the exertions of Sprenger had resulted only in bringing Wâckidi to the light, he had deserved, for that task alone, the gratitude of all the lovers of Mohammed's biography.[1]

But our labours must not dissipate in literary phantoms, in the mere charms of antiquarian research, or even in the substantial acquisition of remote historical truths. Dear as these are to us, they are but baubles in themselves. It is because they bear upon the faith and the superstitions of millions of Mohammedans about us, that these investigations are possessed of an unspeakable value and importance.

Hitherto, we have been able to address the Moslem only in the language of the West; we have told him of the disquisitions of Maracci and of Prideaux, and he has looked with contemptuous incredulity upon our words. In truth, he might well do so: for they are but poor authorities, who ventured with no tempered weapons into the momentous strife. They were possessed neither of the native records, nor of the cool

[1] [This same copy of Wâckidi was given to me by its possessor after the Mutiny. It was transcribed at Damascus A.H. 718 (A.D. 1318); the chain of copyists attesting its accuracy runs up to the Secretary of Wâckidi himself. I have placed it in the India Office library. It is worth inspecting for the beauty of its antique writing. A beautiful copy of the same has also been deposited in the Edinburgh University library. —W. M.]

judgment and philosophy, requisite for closing hand to hand with Moslem adversaries.

But now we can boldly take our stand with the best of our opponents. We have free access to their most authentic sources, —Ibn Ishac, Wâckidi, Hishamí, Tabari. And we can, without fear, confront them with an array of hostile weapons drawn from their own armouries.

How then, it may be asked, are we bringing these new advantages to bear upon their Prophet's life and doctrine? The answer is one of shame and humiliation. Besides a few tracts, generally of a questionable composition, the only vernacular treatises likely to affect the Mohammedan mind, are the admirable works of the Missionary Pfander, which we have in a former Number passed under examination: but even these have little reference to the historical deductions of modern research, and deal more with the deep principles of reason and of faith.

The first treatise at the head of this Article, professes to be a direct step towards the object we have in view. It is a *Life of Mohammed* intended by the Bombay Tract Society for translation into "the vernacular tongues." The preface, after dwelling on the inapplicability of *European* biographies to the "Asiatic public," thus states the object of the treatise: "It was, therefore, thought advisable to prepare another *Life of Mohammed*, with special reference to the state of mind and circumstances of the people of this country. This is now presented." We looked to see advantage taken in this Biography of the investigations regarding the rise of Islam which have been prosecuted with such success in France, Germany, Austria, as well as here in India. But our expectation was speedily disappointed by the following statement: "Many works have been consulted, "but the following, and especially the first three, are those which "have been most copiously used, viz. :—

Bush's *Life of Mohammed.*
Washington Irving's *Life of Mohammed.*
Religious Tract Society's *Life of Mohammed.* London.
Sale's *Coran* and *Preliminary Treatises.*
Gibbon's *History.*"

Of the three works thus chiefly relied upon, we have no knowledge of the first. But the second and third do not possess any pretensions whatever to critical accuracy, being simple digests, popularly constructed from the current histories on the subject. From such sources a treatise adapted for the uncritical portion of the European public might, perhaps, have been well compiled, but it was a wrong step to lean upon such authorities, in the preparation of a biography intended for the natives of India.

The Biography of their Prophet, it is true, is not a favourite study with the Mohammedans of the present day; it forms no part of the usual course of scholastic study or theological reading; and is only taken up by those whose religious or antiquarian tastes attract them to the subject. Still the main facts of Mohammed's life are generally known; and the natives of India can, at any rate, readily ascertain them by reference to the historical works scattered about the country. Lives of the Prophet by Christians will challenge the closest examination. If errors be detected in them, their effect will not simply be neutralised: their tendency will be positively injurious. The natives will be impressed with the idea that our sources of information are imperfect and erroneous, and will conclude that our judgment of Mohammed and of his religion, founded upon these, is imperfect and erroneous. They will thus be fortified in their scornful rejection of Christian evidence, and in their self-complacent reliance on the dogmas of Islam.

This is, therefore, not a mere speculative criticism, in which the Reviewer may be accused of searching for faults merely for fault-finding's sake. The most apparently trifling misrepresentation has a real and important bearing on the controversy with the Mohammedans. It is a subject in which every Christian man has a deep interest at stake. And as such we take it up. Let us therefore look for a moment at the two authorities from which the *Life of Mohammed*, published by the Tract and Book Society of Bombay, is mainly constructed.

The *Life of Mohammed*, by Washington Irving, does not aim at being more than a popular treatise. "The author lays no claim to novelty of fact, nor profundity of research." His work "does not aspire to be consulted as an authority, but merely to be read as a digest of current knowledge, adapted to popular use." Yet even in such a biography, rigid accuracy as far as his authorities went, the public had a right to expect; but in this treatise the truth is too often lost sight of amid the charms of a romantic style and an enchanting narrative. This is not owing to any unfair bias in the historian's mind. For the conclusions drawn from his facts are generally such as do credit to his feelings as well as his judgment. It is owing to imperfect knowledge, arising apparently in part from want of diligence in using authorities actually at his command, and in part from the disadvantages which all writers must labour under who approach the subject without a knowledge of Arabic and acquaintance with the early Arabian authors.

In one respect this is the more inexcusable, because Washington Irving confesses, in his preface, to have "profited by recent lights thrown on the subject by different writers, and particularly by Dr. Gustav Weil, to whose industrious researches and able disquisitions he acknowledges himself greatly indebted." From such authorities he has, indeed, enriched his pages with many facts hitherto new to the English reader, and with many a story delightfully told. But he has not used them invariably as he might. Had he studied with diligence the invaluable work of Dr. Weil, he would have avoided many of the mistakes and imperfections which must seriously detract from the value of his biography. Another objection, and one that runs throughout the book, is, that the author writes too much for effect. The style is beautiful. A charm of romance is thrown around the topics so poetically portrayed. But truth is sometimes sacrificed to effect. And thus the very essence and only worth of an historical treatise is, in great measure, lost. It is true that very often, if not always, this may be owing to the indistinctness or imperfection of the author's knowledge. But the fault itself is not the less to be regretted.

A most prejudicial result of this uncritical and rhetorical style is, that the fabricated stories of supernatural and miraculous events, which the pious credulity of later days engrafted on the biography of Mohammed, have been wrought into the history, while no means are afforded to the reader for discerning the real from the fictitious events; nor amongst the latter, for discriminating which originated with Mohammed himself, and which were long afterwards without grounds ascribed to him. The beautiful portrait of Mohammed, placed at its commencement, is a fit emblem of the whole work. The countenance beams with intelligence, struggling between sensuousness and lofty resolve; while in the background is the Kaaba, with its sombre hangings; and a crowd of followers are seen flourishing their scimitars and daggers with angry gesture at each other. A charming picture! But not that of the real Mohammed in his Arab garb; for here he is sumptuously arrayed in an ermine-bound robe; in one hand he holds an open volume, and the other is stretched aloft, to enforce his earnest address. Now Mohammed never preached from any book; the Coran was, in fact, not even collected during his lifetime, but remained recorded in scattered shreds. So much for the delighful but fancy sketches of Washington Irving: pleasant, perhaps profitable, for the English reader, but in no wise suited for Mohammedan lands.

The biographies of the two Tract Societies equally abound in misstatements which it would be fatal to publish in the proposed translations. It may be well to quote a few instances.[1] Here is the first paragraph:—

> Mohammed was left in his childhood to the care of his grandfather, who, at his death, intrusted the orphan to his son Abu Tâlib, on whom the *honours* and the *wealth* of the family then devolved. The uncle trained the youth at a proper age, to the business of a merchant traveller. He continued in the employ of his uncle till he was twenty-five years old; and this is all that is known of his early history.

Now Abu Tâlib, instead of being wealthy, was extremely indigent. A *portion* of the honours of the family did, indeed, devolve upon him, but his poverty forced him to abandon them to his brother Abbas. Thus Weil:—

[1] [The original Article contains several pages of such erroneous statements; but as the works under review are no longer in use, only two or three instances are here retained.—W. M.]

After Abd Al Muttalib's death, the right to entertain the pilgrims passed over to his son Abu Tâlib, who, however, soon became so poor, that he left it to his brother Abbas, who received also the political charge of the temple.

It was, in fact, Abu Tâlib's poverty which obliged him to suggest that his nephew should seek for a livelihood in Khadîja's service. Thus Wâckidi:—

When Mohammed reached his five-and-twentieth year, Abu Tâlib thus addressed him:—"I am, as thou well knowest, a man without substance, and the times deal hardly with me. Now here is a caravan of thine own tribe about to set out for Syria, and Khadîja, daughter of Khuweilid, needeth men from amongst our people to send forth with her merchandise. If thou wert to offer thyself in this capacity, she would readily accept thee."

On a previous occasion, when Mohammed was a boy of twelve, Abu Tâlib carried him on a mercantile trip to Syria: but this was simply because the orphan lad clung to his paternal protector. So Wâckidi again:—

When Abu Tâlib was on the point of starting, Mohammed was overcome by affection and by grief, at the prospect of being separated from him: and Abu Tâlib's bowels were moved, and he said, "I will take him with me, and he shall not part from me, nor I from him, for ever."

These are the only two mercantile expeditions ever undertaken by Mohammed. What then becomes of the "training at a proper "age, to the business of a merchant traveller, and continuing in "the employ of his uncle till he was twenty-five years old"?

Equally wrong is the following passage, regarding the evidence for the miracles of Mohammed:—

By some of the more credulous of Mohammed's followers, there are, it is true, several miracles attributed to him, as that he clave the moon asunder; that trees went forth to meet him; that water flowed from between his fingers; that the stones saluted him; that a beam groaned to him; that a camel complained to him; and that a shoulder of mutton informed him of its being poisoned; together with several others. But these miracles were never alleged by Mohammed himself, *nor are they maintained by any respectable Moslem writer.*

On the contrary, these miracles are maintained by every Mohammedan writer of the present day, whether respectable or not. Even the honest Wâckidi, as Dr. Sprenger well styles him, gives the whole of the miracles (excepting the first) specified above, and very many more besides. Indeed, a Mohammedan would not be regarded as orthodox, who denied any of these miracles.

An anonymous but carefully prepared Urdoo *Life of Mohammed* (written apparently at Dehli) contains particulars of the following, among a multitude of other miraculous works. A dirty handkerchief cast into an oven, came out of the flames white and unsinged, because it had been used by Mohammed. His spittle turned a bitter well into a sweet one; removed a scald; cured the ophthalmia; restored sight to a blind man; mended a broken leg, and healed instantaneously a deep wound. A man's hand was severed in battle from his arm; he carried it to Mohammed, who, by applying his spittle, rejoined it as before. Catâda's eye was knocked entirely out; the Prophet placed his hand upon it and healed it. A dumb boy was cured by drinking the water the prophet had washed his mouth and hands in. He laid his hands upon a lunatic child, who was cured, a black reptile being immediately discharged from his body. A great variety of animals opened their mouths on different occasions, and gave testimony in his favour. He laid hold of a goat, and the mark of his fingers, impressed on its ear, descended to its posterity, and still remains a living evidence! Notwithstanding that the book contained these and scores of other equally ridiculous stories, an intelligent Mohammedan, intimately acquainted with the early Arabic biographers, declared to us his conviction that it was throughout credible, and based on well-founded traditions!

The same author abuses a set of heretics at Dehli, who, he says, do not receive "the miracle of the foot," viz. that stones received the impression of Mohammed's step, while it left no mark on soft or sandy ground. These are his words:—

It is a matter of extreme astonishment, that a lately established sect, notwithstanding their claims to learning, deny the miracle of the Blessed foot. And what is still stranger, they prohibit the mention of the Holy nativity, the Mirâj, the miracles, and the death of the Prophet;—some calling it abominable veneration of the creature, others heresy. They seem not to know that to make mention of Mohammed, is tantamount to making mention of God Himself, a duty enjoined in the Coran. Such people may well tremble, lest they draw down upon themselves the wrath of the Lord, and a fearful punishment.

Considerable pains are then taken to prove from the Coran and tradition, that the mention of the Prophet is equal to the mention of God, and that it is lawful to invoke the Prophet in prayer, saying, "O Mohammed!" a practice reprobated apparently by these Wahâby (*Protestant*) Moslems.[1]

The Moslems are as proud of their victories as they are sensitive of their disasters; we therefore give an example of each. And first the grand field of Bedr. The accounts of this battle are singularly inaccurate both in Irving and in the other biographies. It is assumed that the Medina force interposed between the caravan of Abu Sofiân and the Meccan army; while, in reality, the caravan had already passed safely some days before either of the armies reached Bedr. The following paragraph is full of errors:—

The spies of the Prophet informed him that their rich and apparently easy prey was within his grasp. He advanced with a few followers, in pursuit of it; but before he could overtake the unprotected band, Abu Sofiân had despatched a message to his brethren at Mecca, for a re-inforcement. . . . Mohammed was posted *between the caravan and the approaching succour* with only 313 soldiers. . . . The troops were persuaded to engage the superior forces of the enemy, abandoning, for the present, the tempting prize of Abu Sofiân's wealthy caravan. . . . A slight entrenchment was formed, to cover the flank of his troops, and a rivulet flowing past the spot he had chosen for encampment, furnished his army with a constant supply of water. . . . At the commencement of the battle, the Prophet, together with Abu Bekr, mounted a kind of throne or pulpit, earnestly asking of God the assistance of Gabriel, with 3000 angels; but when his army appeared to waver he started from his place of prayer, *threw himself upon a horse*, and casting a handful of sand into the air, exclaiming, "confusion fill their faces!" rushed upon the enemy. . . . This sum (the ransom of the prisoners) would compensate, in a measure, for the escape of the booty; *for, notwithstanding the defeat, Abu Sofiân managed*

[1] The people here reprehended are called *Wahâbies*, and their origin is no doubt connected in some way with the *Wahâbies* of Arabia. Equally with them, they reject much of the marvellous foolery and superstitions of the modern Moslems, and have learnt to submit the current notions received from their fathers to the judgment of reason. Are they not hence prepared, in some measure, to appreciate and to welcome our criticism of the early historical sources? It would be interesting to know something more of these Dehli Wahâbies.

to effect a decent retreat, and to arrive safely at Mecca, with the *greater part* of the caravan. The spoils, however, arising from the ransom of the prisoners, *and the partial plunder of the caravan,* amounted to a considerable sum, the division of which very nearly proved fatal to the victors themselves. . . . A furious altercation ensued, etc. (pp. 60–63).

The facts are these. While still in Syria, Abu Sofiân heard of Mohammed's design to attack the returning caravan as it passed Medina, and despatched Dham Dham (not Omar, as Irving has it) to rouse the Coreish and bring an army to his succour. Approaching Bedr, Abu Sofiân rode forward to reconnoitre the spot, and by the fountain came upon traces of Mohammed's scouts, whom he recognised as such by the peculiar shape of the date-stones in the dung left by their camels.[1] In dismay he hurried back to his caravan, left the main road, and by forced marching along the seacoast was soon out of danger. He then sent back a messenger to the Coreish army, by this time on its way to Bedr, to inform them of his safety, and recall them; but they preferred to try the issue with Mohammed. On the other hand, when the Medina army arrived at Bedr, Mohammed was still ignorant that the caravan had passed, or even that the Coreish were advancing to attack him; and their watering party was seized and beaten in the vain hope of finding that they belonged to the caravan. It was after this that the battle occurred.

We see thus how grossly inaccurate is the account of Mohammed's army "being posted between the caravan and the approaching succour"; of "partial plunder of the caravan"; and of Abu Sofiân, "notwithstanding the defeat, managing to effect a decent retreat, and arriving at Mecca with the greater part of the caravan." The notices of a "rivulet" at Bedr, where there were

[1] Irving's inaccuracy here deserves notice. "At length he came upon the track of the little army of Mohammed. He knew it from the size of the kernels of the dates, which the troops had thrown by the wayside as they marched." Mohammed's army, in point of fact, had hardly yet left Medina. The date-kernels were not thrown by the way, but were found by Abu Sofiân in the camels' dung; and the traditions are particular in describing how he took up the dung and crumbled it to scrutinise the kernels.

only wells; of the Prophet mounting a "kind of throne or pulpit"; of his "throwing himself upon a horse"; and of disputes about the spoil "very nearly proving fatal to the victors themselves," are altogether without foundation. An unpardonable error is that Omar was left behind to defend Medina,—the more unpardonable as the names of the famous 303 warriors are all recorded by careful tradition. The only follower who really was left behind (besides Abu Lubâba for the city's defence) was Othman; and he stayed to watch the deathbed of his wife Rockeya, the Prophet's daughter.

These errors are the more to be regretted as the Moslems regard the victory of Bedr with greater than even their usual pride. Let us now take an instance of one of their defeats. The expedition to Mûta against the Greeks, three years before the Prophet's death, is represented by the Tract Society as ending in a triumph; it is added, "The account of this victory so delighted Mohammed, that he bestowed on Khaled the title of being 'One of the swords of the Lord.'" Irvine, going still further wrong, says that the Greeks "were pursued with great slaughter. Khaled then plundered their camp, in which was found great booty." But the facts of the case are, beyond question, in an entirely different direction. The defeat of the Moslems was complete, and the carnage fearful. It was only by the most masterly generalship that Khaled managed to save any portion of the army; and when the remnants that escaped returned in disgrace to Medina, the inhabitants assembled to meet them, and cast dirt in their faces, with taunts such as these, "Ah, ye runaways! shame upon you, that ye dare to turn your backs when fighting for the Lord!" Mohammed stilled the people, and comforted the fugitives, saying, "Nay! they are not runaways: but they are men who shall return again unto the battle, if the Lord will."

Not to weary the reader with the inaccuracies which abound everywhere, let us take just one more from the closing scene:—

After the death of the Prophet, "the body *was placed in a magnificent tent*. . . . When these preparations were completed, his family *led the funeral procession*, followed by the surviving companions of his flight, by the principal citizens of Mecca, and by a silent crowd of men, women, and children."—(Bombay *Life*, p. 109; London *Life*, p. 84.)

This is pure imagination. The body was never removed from the little chamber in Ayesha's house in which the Prophet died, and there it still lies below the spot on which he breathed his last.

Our chief object in the above review has been to show the inexpediency of publishing any vernacular version of the "Bombay Life" in its present state. Much it contains that is admirable and well suited to the natives of India; but it requires careful revision; and the numerous errors must first be rectified before it is presented to the Mohammedan and the Hindoo public. It is, indeed, high time for us to bestir ourselves, and give to our Native fellow-subjects a vernacular life of the Prophet of Arabia. We have as yet presented them with nothing of the kind, and their own current biographies of Mohammed are the veriest inanities which, by any possibility, could be imagined.

To give some idea of the recent Biographies by Native writers, extracts will now be given from a treatise in Urdoo, which has met with a favourable reception, and is much sought after by Mohammedans. It is called *Maulûd Sharîf*, "THE ENNOBLED NATIVITY," though not confined to the birth or childhood of Mohammed. Three editions now lie on our table, the first printed at Lucknow in 1265 Hegira (1843); the second at Cawnpore in 1267 Hegira (1845); the third at Agra in the present year, much enlarged (pp. 94). No less than ten or twelve editions have already been printed at Lucknow. The author is Gholâm Imâm Shahíd, a polished and ornate writer of some celebrity, and formerly an officer of standing in the Court of Sudder Dewany.

The work is composed of so-called traditions and stories, each new story being introduced by the words "It is related," or "There is a narrative to the effect that," etc. It is interspersed with pieces of poetry, generally in Persian, sometimes in Urdoo, lauding Mohammed, and appealing to the hearts and affections of devout Moslems. The great bulk of the tales are of late fabrication, to be found nowhere in any early biographies such as those of Hishâmî and Wâckidi. Not a single old authority appears to have been consulted, but only such late Persian works as the *Rowzat ul Ahbâb*, the *Madârij ul Nubûwat*, etc. The Maulavi of course ignores criticism in any shape.

The legends recorded in this biography are incredibly extravagant. The improbabilities are so great that the most childish intellect, honestly exercised, would not for a moment entertain them. And yet all is told—the visits of angels and their conversations, scenes of heaven and hell both past and prospective, and above all, that wild fiction of Mohammed's existence cycles of years before the creation,—all told with unhesitating credence, as mere matters of fact. The first eight pages trace the progress of the "Light of Mohammed," from its first creation to the conception of the Prophet. After the usual introduction, the work opens thus:—

> Ye that are lovers of the face of Mohammed, and ye that be enamoured with the curls of Ahmed, know and be well aware, that the light of Mohammed is the origin of all existing things, and the essence of every thing that hath a being; because that when it pleased the great Creator to manifest His glory, He first of all created the light of Mohammed from the light of His own Unity; and from the light of Mohammed produced every existent being. Now, this glorious personage was made the last of the prophets, solely on this account that, as the rising sun chaseth away the splendours of the moon and stars, so doth the glory of the religion of Mohammed supersede all other religions; so that, if that pre-existent light had displayed its brilliancy from the first, then would all other prophets have shrunk into obscurity, and been shorn of their apostolic dignity.

After tracing this light into the form of a star, its history is interrupted by some stories such as the following:—

> A tradition runs that, in the days of the children of Israel, there was a sinful and flagitious man who, for the space of 200 years, wearied every one by the enormity of his offences; when he died, they threw his corpse upon a dunghill;—no sooner done than Gabriel coming to Moses, spake thus;—Thus saith the Almighty God, "This day my friend hath departed from the world, and the people have cast his corpse upon a dunghill. Now let that corpse be dressed and prepared for burial without delay: and ye shall speak unto the children of Israel, that they forthwith recite the burial service over his bier if they are desirous of pardon." Therefore, Moses marvelled exceedingly, and inquired why forgiveness was required; and God answered thus:—"The Lord well knoweth all the sins which that

inner hath, during these 200 years, committed; and verily he never could have been pardoned. But one day this wicked man was reading the Towrât, and seeing there the name of the blessed Mohammed, he wept and pressed the page to his eyes. This honour and reverence shown to my beloved was pleasing unto me, and from the blessed effects of that single act, I have blotted out the sins of the whole 200 years." Lovers of the blessed Mohammed! rejoice in your hearts, and be assured, that love for the holy Prophet, the Lord of the creation, is in every possible condition the means of salvation (p. 3).

A tradition follows regarding the Judgment Day, the proceedings of which are so to be conducted as to show to Mohammed how much the Lord forgives for his sake. Again, when Adam sinned and fell, the sentence went forth to expel him from Paradise. He begged for pity, appealing in every variety of way to God's mercy and to the promise of future prophets. But of no avail; after every entreaty, the command was repeated for the angels to carry him away. At last, as they were dragging him off, the blessed word passed his lips, "Have mercy on me for the sake of Mohammed"; instantly the Lord commanded the angels to let him go, and even treat him with reverence, "for he hath taken hold of a great intercessor, and his sins are forgiven for Mohammed's sake."

Where such absurd legends are received as facts, to what a state of superstitious credulity must the spiritual and intellectual faculties of the Mohammedans be reduced! Another example will suffice. Satan used every day to receive from an angel a blow upon his face, so severe that the effects remained till the following day. When the Lord of Creation, the Prophet of Islam, appeared, Satan besought that he should not be shut out from the benefits of his advent, seeing that these are promised in the Coran to all creation: the Lord therefore commanded that from that day forward the blow should be discontinued. "Oh Moslems, consider this! If the rejected Satan was delivered from these calamitous blows, by the appearing of the blessed Mohammed, what wonder that his followers shall be kept safe from the pains of hell-fire?"

The history of the "Light of Mohammed" is then resumed, of which the following is the briefest sketch. God wishing to manifest Himself, formed this Light of Mohammed a thousand years before the creation; and it performed in the heavens the duties of circuit and obeisance for a long space of time. Then formed into a substance, it was divided into ten portions, viz. the throne, the tablet of decrees, the sun, moon, etc.; and, last of all, the SPIRIT OF MOHAMMED. This spirit spent 70,000 years in adoration around the throne of God, and 5000 upon the footstool. Gabriel and other angels then descending, obtained, by order of the Lord, a small portion of our earth; and the earth, hearing the name of Mohammed, split asunder and produced from the Prophet's grave a white fragment like camphor. Wrought up with aromatics, it became the essence of Mohammed's being, and was carried round the world by Gabriel, who sounded the glad tidings to all creation, "This is the earth of the beloved of the Lord of all worlds, the intercessor for the guilty," etc. Long before the creation of Adam, the precious emblem remained suspended like a lamp or sparkling star from the highest heavens. It was, in fact, the "Faith" which, according to the Coran, was offered to all creatures; but shunned by all. Rash man alone accepted the responsibility. The "Light of Mohammed" thus given to man, beamed forth from the forehead of Adam. It descended from generation to generation, through a favoured chain, and at last shone in the brow of Abdallah, the Prophet's father.

The prodigies related of Abdallah may be imagined from the extravagancies of such a narrative. At times a brilliant lustre encircled everything around him: the earth saluted him as "The Light of Mohammed"; at his approach the withered trees revived, and again drooped as he departed; idol demons entreated him not to come near for their destruction; while his grandfather, Abdal Muttalib, prophesied, saying, "Hail, Abdallah! From thy loins shall be begotten the lord of the prophets," etc. Then follows the transfer of this light to Amina, Mohammed's mother. The night of Mohammed's conception was marked by prodigies in heaven and in earth: 200 damsels of the Coreish died of envy: the din of the angels' joy was heard even on earth: Gabriel affixed a green crescent to the Kaaba, etc. At last comes the birth of Mohammed, and pious Mohammedans are stirred up by hymns and prayers to rejoice and to bless the Prophet. The prayers are composed of stale repetitions, but the hymns are curious, and might help us to a model Christmas hymn adapted to the native taste. [With this view in the original article two of the Native hymns were added; and, as such, are worth while referring to at p. 18 of the *Calcutta Review* for 1852. The jubilant tone might well become our Urdoo hymn-book. One opens thus:—

From the bearers of Heaven's Throne, a voice:—
Raise high the majesty of Ahmed!
Born, hath been the mighty King!
Born, intercessor of the Judgment Day!
Born, the Prince of both the worlds!

And so on. The other:—

Islam, O Sun of Law and Truth!
Islam, O help of helpless poor!
Islam, O source of earth's creation!
Islam, O best of guides and souls' delight!
Refuge I vainly seek elsewhere.

And so on.][1]

Here are a few of the wonders that followed the birth. Amina was terrified by a fearful noise, when immediately a white bird came, and, laying its wing upon her bosom, restored her confidence; she became thirsty, and anon a cup of a delicious beverage, white as milk and sweet as honey, was presented by an unseen hand; heavenly voices and tread of steps were heard around her, but no person was seen: a sheet was let down from heaven, and a voice proclaimed that the blessed child was to be screened from mortal view: birds of Paradise, with ruby beaks and wings of emerald, strutting along, regaled her with surpassing warbling; aromas from mid-heaven were scattered all around her, etc. No sooner was the infant born than, prostrating himself on the ground, the little creature raised its hands to heaven and prayed earnestly for the pardon of his people. Then, swept away in a cloud of light, he was carried to the four quarters of creation, that all

[1] [These hymns are printed in the Urdoo character, and therefore not inserted here; but they are worth looking at in the original by those familiar with the language.—W.M.]

things might recognise the glories of Mohammed, and know that in him every excellency of previous prophets centred,—the vicegerency of Adam, the beauty of Joseph, the grace of Jesus, etc.

Safia, Mohammed's aunt, was present at his birth, and testifies to six memorable incidents. *First*, the new-born child performed obeisance, and prayed with a slow and distinct voice, "Oh Lord, pardon my people, pardon my people!" *Second*, in clear and eloquent tones, he repeated the Creed, "I bear witness that there is no God but the Lord alone, and that I am his apostle." *Third*, the light of Mohammed obscured the lamp. *Fourth*, she was about to wash the babe, when a voice from the unseen world said, "Oh Safia, trouble not thyself, I have sent forth the blessed Mohammed washed and pure. *Fifth*, he was born circumcised and with his navel cut. *Sixth*, on his holy back the seal of prophecy was visible in letters of light, more resplendent than the morning star, viz. "There is no god but the Lord," etc. Three persons, brilliant as the sun, appeared from heaven. One held a silver goblet; the second an emerald tray; the third a silver towel; they washed him seven times, then blessed and saluted him with a glorious address as the Prince of mankind.

Abdal Muttalib was, at the time, in the Kaaba, where a number of prodigies and voices from the holy temple apprised him of the wonderful event. He instantly repaired to Amina, and finding that the light had departed from her, insisted on seeing his grandchild. She informed him that its invisible guardians had ordered that no one should see it for three days. Abdal Muttalib thereupon fell into a rage, and threatened to kill either himself or her. She was about to produce the child, when one with a drawn sword stepped between, and exclaimed, that no mortal should set eyes upon the babe, until all the favoured angels had visited him. Abdal Muttalib was affrighted, and let the sword drop from his hands. All the kings of the earth were struck with dumbness, and remained inarticulate for a day and a night: the vault of Kesra was rent; fourteen of its battlements fell to the ground, etc.

After much of this description, there succeeds in great detail the story of Halîma, the Prophet's nurse. This legend, in its earliest recorded form, is given by Sprenger with a sufficiency of fabulous matter; but Ghulâm Imâm's version advances incomparably further. A few of the marvels of the Prophet's childhood may be added here :—

There is a tradition, that the Lord of the universe, the blessed Mohammed, used to advance as much in one day, as other children in a year. When two months old, he made himself understood by signs and beckonings; in the third month he arose of himself and stood upright; in the fourth he began to walk, taking hold of the wall, and in the fifth, without assistance; in the sixth month he could walk fast, and in the seventh he could run; in the eighth month he could talk, and in the ninth speak with the most perfect eloquence. After the tenth month he contended with the boys in archery, and when in his second year he appeared like a full-grown youth.

Halîma adds, that the first words which issued from his blessed mouth were the Creed: that he never took up anything in his hands without saying, "In the name of the Lord": that his infantile gear was never dirtied as is usual with children, nor ever required to be washed, etc.

Mohammed himself, in after years, related to his uncle Abbas that when an infant, his nurse happened to tie his hand rather tight, and that he wept sorely. But the moon addressed him thus, "If a drop of thy tears falls to the earth, it will never again be green and fresh, until the judgment day; so for the love of my people, I refrained from crying, and the moon talking with me kept me engaged with her in prattle, lest I should cry." Abbas expressed his astonishment that his nephew should remember incidents that occurred when he was six weeks old, when Mohammed only added to his wonder, by telling him that he perfectly recollected events which happened when in his mother's womb, as the noise of the eternal pen on the tablet of fate, and the sound of the sun and moon making obeisance before the Almighty!

After a long description of the Prophet's person and manners, this curious passage follows :—

Mohammed Husein, manager of the *Mohammedy* press, respectfully urges upon all those who love the Prophet of the Lord, that they transfer to the mirror of their hearts, this ennobled description of the personal appearance of the Prophet, which is a literal translation from the traditions of Tirmidzy;

in order that, if perchance in a true vision they should see the blessed Prophet himself, they may know the vision to be a real one, and give thanks to the Lord for it. Because, according to his own words, "whoso hath seen me, hath seen the truth"; that is, "whoever hath seen me in a vision, hath really and truly seen me, the blessed Mohammed," and such an one shall escape the deceptions of Satan: for Satan is unable to assume the glorious appearance described above, but ofttimes shows himself in other forms, and claiming to be a prophet beguiles ignorant worshippers, in their visions and reveries.

The legend of Mohammed's chest being opened, follows in great detail. But the rest of his early history,—the death of Amina and Abdal Muttalib; Abu Tâlib's guardianship; Mohammed's marriage; his throes of inspiration; conversion of his first disciples, etc., are all disposed of in a couple of pages! On the subject of miracles our author finds a more congenial theme.

To give one hundredth, or even a thousandth part of the famous miracles performed by the holy Prophet—even if the waves of the ocean were turned into pens, its waters into ink, and the expanse of heaven into one vast scroll—would be utterly impossible. The least of them are as follows;

The absence of shadow (which is followed by a most blasphemous application [1]): the splitting of the moon: that birds would not fly over, nor flies alight, on him: evidence given by a corpse interred 100 years before, by the stones, by a porpoise, and by a golden peacock which issued from the rocks;—all this is stated to be too notorious to require further description. The Mirâj, or heavenly ascent, occupies eleven pages of the strangest absurdities and extravagancies.

Passing over the rest of his career, both at Mecca and Medina the author hastens to the last scenes of the Prophet's life, which we deems it necessary to introduce in an apologetic strain, as if it here a matter of astonishment that he, for whom Adam, nay, for whom 18,000 worlds, were created, should be required to die.

1 "Ah! ye who love the blessed Mohammed! a beautiful thought of the amorous class, here occurs to me, which will be pleasing to the pure-hearted Súfies. It is this, that God Almighty declareth Himself to be in love with the great source of love (Mohammed): but the lover doth not like to see his beloved accompanied by a shadow:—

"No shadow near thee let me see,
Lest love beget fond jealousy!"

On his deathbed, Gabriel comes with messages of condolence and inquiry from the Lord, and offers him life and health, should he desire it. Again he comes, accompanied by Azrael the angel of death, whom Fatima, taking to be an Arab, refuses to admit. Gabriel tells the Prophet that Azrael was to obey his every order, and either take his spirit or retire at once, as he preferred. Mohammed, in consternation, applies for counsel to Gabriel, who pictures to him the glories of Paradise, "the black-eyed houries adorned from head to foot, waiting in expectation of his glorious approach." Mohammed, re-assured by these exciting prospects, gives command to Azrael, and dies.

Till the hour of his burial, a thick darkness overspread Medina, so that one could not see his hand or his neighbour's face.[1] When Abbas lifted up the winding sheet, the lips of the deceased were seen to move and to repeat the same prayer for his people, as that which issued from his lips when newly born. The angels offered to convey his body to Paradise, but Mohammed preferred not to be separated from his fellows whom he had come to save; a fact which is thus improved:—

Ye lovers of Mohammed! consider for a moment the wonderful compassion and grace which showered such favours upon us, unworthy handfuls of the dust! verily, it is incumbent upon us to sacrifice our very selves for the sake of such a compassionate Intercessor, and to become ennobled by visiting his glorious tomb and sacred resting-place.

We have already trespassed too far, but one other extract we must add:—

In his last illness Mohammed entered the Mosque of Medina, which was filled to overflowing; and as his final request, besought that if any one had suffered wrong or injury at his hands, he would there without ceremony declare it, and taking retribution for the injury done, thus enable him to go to heaven with an easy conscience. Hearing this, Okâsha exclaimed, "Oh Prophet of the Lord, on a certain stage when marching with thee, thou once without due cause scourgedst my back. I should never

---

[1] The traditions of Wâckidi speak of the *gloom* (social) cast over Medina by Mohammed's death: this was transformed into a *physical* gloom; and that again magnified into *thick darkness*. "Anis (Mohammed's servant) said that no day was so light as that in which Mohammed entered Medina, and none so dark and dismal as that in which he died." The metaphor grew to be a fact.

have desired retribution, but when thou so straitly commandedst, I felt it incumbent upon me to declare the matter." The Prophet answered: "The Lord have mercy upon thee, Okâsha: Dost thou desire retribution?" "Yea: apostle of God!" Then the Lord of the universe, the blessed Mohammed, commanded Balâl to go to Fatima's house, and "Bring with thee," said he, "that scourge, which I used to take with me in the wars." Balâl, in consternation and distress, proceeded to that noble lady's house and brought the scourge. Then the Prophet made it over to Okâsha, and sitting in the courtyard of the Mosque, said, "The mercy of the Lord be upon thee, Okâsha! Take thy retribution without fear or favour." Okâsha receiving the whip, prepared himself to administer stripes upon the Prophet. But a mighty noise, like that of the judgment day, arose from the assembled throng. The Prophet's companions, one after another, stepped forward, and expostulated with Okâsha on the fearful temerity of scourging Mohammed, the Messenger of God, who was moreover in so infirm a state, and close upon his heavenly journey. They offered to receive upon their own backs a thousand lashes in his stead; but Okâsha replied, that vicarious retribution was not permitted by the Lord. At last Mohammed, becoming impatient, said, "Perform thy work quickly, oh Okâsha; God forbid that death should rob me of the opportunity, and that this claim should remain against me to all eternity." Okâsha replied, "Oh blessed of the Lord! when thou scourgedst me I was naked, and thou art at this time clad in raiment." The blessed Prophet thereupon took off his raiment, and forthwith the whole assembly burst into the wildest grief and passionate lamentation; and the angels nearest to the Throne poured forth their deprecations, expostulating with the Lord, etc. At last Okâsha arose, and kissed the seal of prophecy,—the signet of apostleship: and then he spake as follows: "Oh beloved of the Lord! It was my earnest desire that at thy last breath I should be ennobled by looking upon the seal of prophecy. And by this stratagem of retribution, I have obtained the blessed fortune. Neither didst thou, most holy Prophet, ever touch me with the scourge, nor could I have had the temerity to demand retribution."

The Prophet invoked a blessing upon Okâsha, and retired to his own abode.

From beginning to end the tale is a pure work of fancy, early tradition containing not a vestige of it.

Here, once more, is a common type of the childish legends by which later traditionists have endeavoured to discredit our Scriptures:—

A narrator relates that there was, in the kingdom of Syria, a Jew who, while busily engaged one Sabbath day in perusing the Old Testament, perceived the name of the blessed Prophet written in four places; and out of spite he cast that leaf into the fire. On the following day, he found the same name written in eight places; again he burnt the page. On the third day he found it written in twelve places. The man marvelled exceedingly, saying within himself, "The oftener I cut out this name from the Old Testament, the more do I find it written therein. If I go on at this rate, I shall soon have the entire Scriptures filled with the name." At last he became desirous of visiting the Prophet, and, filled with this anxiety, by day and by night he travelled, from stage to stage, till he reached Medina. When he arrived, Mohammed had been dead three days. His followers concealed the fact from the Jew, fearing it might stagger his faith. At last, learning the truth, he tumbled senseless on the ground, and, beating his head, called out: "Alas! alas! my journey is in vain. Would I had never been born!" He then entreated to be shown the clothes Mohammed wore, and they were brought forth from Fatima's house, patched in seven places. Immediately he smelled the fragrance of them, and clasping them to his eyes, exclaimed, "Let my soul be a sacrifice to the sweetness of thy fragrance, oh Mohammed! Alas, that I missed the sight of thee!" He then repaired to the tomb, repeated the Creed, and prayed thus: "If my cry be accepted in the court of heaven, then call me, this very moment, to the presence of my beloved!" He fell to the ground, exclaiming, "Oh Mohammed! oh Mohammed!" and expired in the arms of his love.

It may be thought that far too much attention and space have been allotted to this pitiful work. But a little reflection may justify the pains we have devoted to it.

For, first, the book is a type and reflection of the Mohammedan mind of India;—credulous beyond belief. It is an important illustration of the position laid down in a previous number of this *Review*, that although Mohammedans are captious and pseudo-critical to the utmost when attacking other religions, they are incredibly simple and superstitious, it may be wilfully blind, in reference to their own.

This biography has also been favourably received by the mass of the people: it has been eagerly bought up, and has gone through repeated editions.[1] It therefore bears the stamp of popular approval. Further, its author is a man of letters and intelligence: for many years he held a ministerial office in our highest court of

[1] The last edition was forwarded to us by the publisher at Agra, just as this article was going to press, with the following note: "The work *Maulûd Sharîf*, composed by our patron Ghulâm Imâm Shahîd, is well known throughout every kingdom and district. In such demand is it, that ten or twelve editions, and thousands of copies, have been printed at

judicature; and was there promoted to an honourable post, implying that he possessed more than usual intelligence and ability. The work of such a man may fairly be viewed as a guage of the religious mind of Moslem India. And hence, as an index of the ideas and dogmas against which we have to contend, too much stress cannot be laid upon such writings. It is incumbent upon us to know well our adversaries' ground; and it is only by such inquiries as the present, that we can hope to reconnoitre it.

It is very sad to find, amongst educated men, such an utter want of the faculty of historical criticism, as we see here. With persons of this class, our great difficulty will lie in placing before them the means for discriminating the grains of truth from the masses of fabricated traditions. The Bombay biography has but alluded to the subject. Even for the unbiassed mind and intelligence of the European, the work of disentangling truth from falsehood in these latter-day traditions, is one encompassed by great difficulties: how much more difficult then to lead the Mohammedans themselves to true principles of criticism! It is however a task towards which much has been contributed already, by the studies of our learned men; and we should not shrink from its further prosecution.

The study is also useful in pressing upon us the necessity of extreme care, that the historical details placed before our fellow-subjects are thoroughly correct. Under the best possible auspices, they will receive our advances with distrust and our criticisms with incredulity. But if we give to them such histories as our English *Lives of Mohammed* have generally been, we shall put ourselves in an incomparably worse position. Perceiving want of accuracy in our narratives, and imperfection in our means of information, they will naturally doubt all our assertions, and summarily deny our conclusions. But if, on the contrary, we carefully avail ourselves of the original sources which the

Lucknow, and are still being printed. There will be found hardly a village or town in the country whither the book has not reached." This is, no doubt, somewhat exaggerated, but it is still proof of immense popularity. The new Agra edition is considerably enlarged, containing ninety-four quarto pages. A great deal of Urdoo poetry has also been added to it.

investigations of a Sprenger and a Weil have placed in our hands (authorities as good as any open to themselves, and far better than those to which they are in the habit of referring), they will be compelled to give credit to our facts and listen with deference to our conclusions. If we can, *from their own best sources*, prove to them that they are deceived and superstitious in many important points, and can thus establish the untenableness of some of their positions; while we at the same time admit all statements that are grounded in fact;—we shall have gone a great way to excite honest inquiry and induce the sincere investigator to follow our lead.

The native mind is at present not insensible to the subject. The Urdoo biography of Ghulâm Imâm is by no means a solitary instance. There are many others. One of the most remarkable is, perhaps, that which appears weekly in an Urdoo newspaper, the *Asad ul Akhbâr*, published at Agra. Ever since its commencement in June 1847, the life of Mohammed has formed the leading article of this paper, and the subject is not yet concluded. This biography is consequently much more extensive and elaborate than Ghulâm Imâm's "Nativity," and goes with great detail into the historical traditions and legendary narratives, translated mostly from the late and credulous Persian biographers of Mohammed, whose narratives are possessed of no historical weight whatever.[1]

That an article on the biography of Mohammed should have regularly appeared for the last five years as the leader in a miscellaneous Urdoo newspaper, is certainly not one of the least remarkable signs of the times, and warrants the hope that intelligent and thinking Mohammedans are turning their attention

[1] The editor, Kamrúd-deen is not very familiar with Arabic, but even had he been qualified to consult the ancient Arabic authorities, it is doubtful whether he would have done so, as the Persian writers, with their marvellous additions, are the authorities generally referred to by natives. The earlier portion of these articles is translated from the *Madârij ul Nubúwat*, the later from the *Rowzât al Ahbâb*. Kamrúd-deen was long employed by Pfander, and assisted him in translating his works into Urdoo. He is therefore thoroughly acquainted with the Christian arguments. His style is elegant and attractive.

to the historical evidences of their faith, and are comparing them with those of Christianity.

These stirrings, however, of the native mind bear but indirectly upon Christianity. Let us inquire what has been done of late directly towards the MOHAMMEDAN CONTROVERSY. And first it may be stated, that large reprints of Dr. Pfander's treatises, both in Urdoo and Persian, have been published during the last few years. This has been effected by the contributions of the public (to whom an appeal was, not in vain, made in a former number of this *Review*), and by the ever liberal aid of the noble London Tract Society.

The long threatened work of Pfander's opponent, Syud Ali Hassan,[1] made its appearance in A.H. 1261 (A.D. 1845). It contains 806 large octavo pages; and is denominated "KITÂB I ISTIFSÂR," or the "BOOK OF QUESTIONS." It is written in an easy but desultory style, rambling from one subject to another, with little logical precision or arrangement. The first four "Questions" (46 pp.) are devoted to the refutation of the doctrine of the Trinity. The next ten (137 pp.) attack the genuineness and authority of the Bible. The main argument here is deduced from variations in the different Oriental versions, each variety in the translations being triumphantly adduced as evidence of variety and corruption in the *Original*! The word of man thus is mingled with the word of God, throughout our Scriptures; and, unlike the Coran, there is no proof that every writer was inspired. There is further no proof of the continued existence of the several

[1] See a former Article (No. VIII.), where it is noticed that Ali Hassan "is now printing a work at Lucknow in refutation of Christianity, and in defence of the Coran, at which he has been labouring for fifteen years, and which is, by the way, to contain a full reply to the *Mîzân* as well as the *Dîn Haqq*." It was stated in the same article, that this author, as well as Ghulâm Imâm, was an officer in the Sudder Court at Agra. After publishing his book, and holding his controversy with Pfander, he was promoted to the independent post of Moonsif, or native Judge;—a fact which must have satisfactorily proved to his countrymen that, under the Company's government, every man is free to hold, and publicly to maintain, his own religious views, without prejudice to his worldly prosperity or official standing.

books, from the time of their alleged authors to that of their publication; *e.g.*, from the time of Ezra to Ptolemy, and from that of the apostles to Constantine. The fifteenth Question asserts that the miracles of Mohammed are the only ones of any prophet that can be proved by testimony, those of all others being dependent upon his evidence (pp. 183–245). The sixteenth holds that, notwithstanding the corruption of the Bible, it contains more prophecies in favour of Mohammed than in favour of Christ. This subject is treated at great length, and with much casuistry (pp. 245–385). The seventeenth and main proposition is that the same objections may be brought against Moses, Jesus and the other prophets, and their books, as against Mohammed. Under this head is embraced the refutation of the *Mîzân*, and *Dîn Haqq* (pp. 385–709). The eighteenth proposition closes the book, with a chapter on the beauties and excellencies of Islam.

The work is written in pleasing language, and in a more respectful style than generally characterises such productions: but this praise is only comparative, for bigotry and pride often overbear the author's natural good feeling, and dictate passages respecting Christianity which the dogmas, even of Islam, should have led him to shrink from. Added to the usual materials brought forward by Moslems on such occasions, there is an ostentatious display of some shallow English learning and ideas which the author has picked up from translations and conversation. On the whole, the spirit of the work, though abounding with the usual blasphemies which make the ears of Christians to tingle, is better and more reasonable than we usually find. A few specimens, taken pretty much at random, will, perhaps, be interesting to the reader.

Thirteen pages are spent in labouring to prove that Mohammed is "the Prince of this world" spoken of in the New Testament. In disposing of the objections to this view, he endeavours to explain away the text,—"the whole world lieth *in wickedness*": and finding that other versions translate the latter words "in the wicked one," he adds:—

Behold! Two copies give it one way, and three the other. To which shall the preference be given? How conclusively the corruption of the original text is here proved! This is what I call corruption (*tahrîf*) (p. 336).

In treating of the variations, or, as he will have it, corruptions of the MSS. of the Bible, such arguments as the following frequently occur:—

Urbanus VIII., of the Romish Church, Sergius Harûnî, and other learned Christians, admit that in the original manuscripts, both Hebrew and Greek, some degree of corruption has crept in, and that words and modes of construction, opposed to the genius of the original languages, are found in these books. See now, how my case is proved even by confession of the defendants! There is this attempted explanation, indeed, that these errors originated in the carelessness of the writers, or want of ability in the translators. But such a fanciful theory cannot impugn the confirmation afforded by the concession to my claim. Again, they say that the Holy Ghost, and the prophets themselves, were accustomed to write in the same strange and erroneous manner (*ghalat palat*). But this is in effect my very argument, that (in the words of the Coran) "they write passages with their hands, and then say this is from the Lord," *i.e.* they say of what they themselves composed, that is the word of God. Now to attribute such errors to the Holy Ghost and to the prophets, is the same as attributing them to God (p. 433).

He endeavours to rebut Pfander's argument, that the Bible being from an early date in the hands of multitudes throughout the world, it was impossible all should have united in corrupting it, in the following manner:—

Twelfth proof. It is evidently *possible*, that any book, say the *Shah Nameh*, might be in the hands of every man throughout the whole world, and that every man might, in his own place, make the same alteration therein. This is not an intellectual impossibility; at the very most it would be a miracle. Seeing, then, that this is not a logical impossibility, the proof of it might be established by the same species of evidence as that by which the mission of Moses or Jesus is established:—that is to say, by him (Mohammed) who was endowed with prophecy and showed evident miracles,—and as the last of the prophets hath evidenced both facts equally by an inspired declaration. Copies of the Bible, however, at that early epoch, were not spread abroad to so great an extent as is now the case, but remained for the most part in the hands of those alone whose perfidy was foretold by Jesus and his apostles; and since these afterwards reached you through the hands of people whom you yourselves testify that for centuries they held an undivided power and authority over the book;—it results that its corruption would not amount even to a miracle, and must consequently be admitted on the testimony of the Prophet of Islam. Under any circumstances, the assertions of such corruption cannot be regarded as reflecting on the prophetical claim of Mohammed (as if he had advanced an intellectual impossibility). And the great injustice and departure from right which ye commit, is this, that ye do not regard the assertion of a logical impossibility to be an argument against a claim to prophecy, while you here hold the assertion of a simple miracle to be so. That is to say, the assertion of the incarnation and manifestation of God, and of the equality of that which is produced to that which produces it (doctrines which you hold with regard to Jesus on the authority of the Bible), is not regarded by you as falsifying the claim to prophecy; and yet ye hold a statement regarding the corruption of the Bible, which would not amount even to a common miracle, to be a disproof of the prophetical rank of the blessed Prophet of Islam. Verily, this is a marvellous thing (pp. 438–440).

Pfander had referred to the evidence of the Coran itself as proving that our Scriptures were not altered prior to Mohammed's appearance, and to the evidence of ancient manuscripts that they had not been altered since; and here is an example of the way in which Ali Hassan avoids the conclusion:—

According to the above interpretation of the passage,[1] it might indeed be held that the *prophecies* regarding the last of the prophets were not corrupted until his appearance, else why were the people in expectation of his coming, and ready to believe upon him? My reply is, that even supposing this argument to be correct, all that would be proved therefrom, would be that only those passages containing predictions of Mohammed remained uncorrupted until his appearing; not by any means, that throughout the whole Bible no other passage had been corrupted. The Padre's deduction that the *entire* Bible remained intact, thus falls to the ground.

And if any one say that the passages which contain those predictions (asserted in the Coran to have been altered after Mohammed's appearing) are still identically the same with the corresponding places in the ancient manuscripts to which the Padre has referred; my reply is that the naked claim of the Padre, as to the existence of manuscripts thirteen or fifteen hundred years old, is not worthy of being listened to, especially as his stories contradictions and bigotry have already been fully exposed. That paper and writing should remain so many ages, and yet be legible, would be miraculous indeed. Some Pope, or other such personage, in order to cast

---

[1] Sura xcviii. 3: "Neither were those who possessed the Scriptures, divided among themselves, until after the clear evidence (Islam) had come unto them."—See Sale's note.

suspicion on the Mussulmans, must have produced forged manuscripts, and declared they were older than the time of Mohammed. It is moreover very unlikely that the character of such a manuscript could be even deciphered by any one nowadays (pp. 448, 449).

To Pfander's account of the ancient manuscripts of the New Testament, the Vatican, Alexandrine, etc., and his explanation of their value, Ali Hassan makes the following reply :—

It is evident that the Padre Sahib is not on terms of intimacy with any of the distinguished gentlemen who preside in our Courts, otherwise he would have known that if contending parties adduce ancient documents in favour of their claims, no reliance whatever can be placed on the mere ancientness of the paper, and of the date. If then in worldly matters the oldness of the paper is no test of the age of the writing, how shall it become a test in religious affairs ? And, especially, is this to be doubted, when we recollect that the heads of the Christian religion in those days, were not such as we find the English gentlemen now to be, but were very perfidious and deceptive in their faith, such as they whom they call "*Pope*" and "*Papa*." Therefore, until due proof be advanced, I cannot concede the ancientness of these manuscripts, as assumed by the Padre. And the more so, as such a conclusion would be in opposition to the commentators of the Bible, Urbanus VIII., etc., for if these ancient manuscripts be really genuine, whence and how came the corruptions of the text, which they admit to exist. But all this reasoning would only then be necessary, if it were really admitted, that the Padre spoke the truth, and that these manuscripts really do exist, bear the date of completion inscribed on them, and are clearly legible ; otherwise, the whole statement seems to me to be unfounded (pp. 454, 455).

With respect to the writings of the fathers, and the quotations from the Scriptures contained therein, the following is one of his replies :—

It is evident, from the way in which the Reverend gentleman speaks, that these books are not written like our commentaries in which the entire text is quoted verse by verse ; but that the words of Jesus appear in them as in our scientific or religious works, where the Coran and the traditions are often referred to. But have I ever held that the whole of the Old and New Testaments has been altered, or that the pure Gospel was not written by some of the apostles ? Thus even admitting, which I do not, that these books are really true and correct, and the authority of their writers acknowledged, their correspondence with the manuscripts handed down, would neither injure my argument nor benefit yours (pp. 458, 459).

The Maulvi's remarks on the advantages of conquest, and its legality, as a means of spreading Islam, are very curious, especially as he makes many references to occidental history, to the spread of Christianity in Britain under Edgar, and to its present favourable prospects under the prestige of British victory in India.

In concluding his answer to the *Mîzân-ul-Haqq*, our Author explains why he has not quoted his adversary at length, and answered him word for word. "If these unprofitable disquisitions," he says, "were confined by the Padres to two or three treatises, and they were themselves such sort of people that when the groundlessness of their assertions had once been proved, other Padres would hide their heads, and English gentlemen would keep them back from advancing such absurdities in future,—then, indeed, there were some object in replying to their arguments word by word. But such is far from being the case: nay, thousands of Padres earn their bread by this very trade, and their livelihood consists in attacking the religions of other people,—quite apart from the consideration of whether those religions are supported by reason or not. They are constantly writing and printing new treatises, without any sort of rational ground; but simply in order to support their families, they labour night and day at this work. Besides, if you prove never so well the unreasonableness of a Padre's statements, it seems to have no effect whatever upon others, for we find no one endeavouring to persuade such a writer to give up these irrational arguments. Seeing therefore that it does not constitute *our* livelihood to spread abroad religion, and that English gentlemen, though they be lovers of fair argument, yet maintain only their own Padres in such service, and give nothing to the professors of *other* religions for the same purpose;—Say, how can it be expected of us to reply word for word to the arguments of these Padres? Indeed, we ought to regard ourselves as fortunate in not being hindered by the Officers of the Sirkar Company, from replying to our adversaries' objections; and such of these Officers as are of a philosophical turn of mind, can themselves appreciate a well-framed refutation. The real objections, too, are confined to narrow ground; it seemed, therefore, sufficient to reply only to them" (pp. 605–607).

Ali Hassan does not treat the *Dîn Haqq* with so much respect even as the *Mîzân-ul-Haqq*.

Know, says he, that whatever grounds of reasonable dispute,—such as they are,—the Christians have against the Moslems, are (along with much unreasonable matter) contained in the *Mîzân-ul-Haqq*. Now, as to the other treatise,—the *Dîn Haqq ki tahqîq*, wherever in some little measure it is the shadow of certain portions of the *Mîzân-ul-Haqq*, it is upon the whole reasonable. But the remaining, and by far the greatest, portion is much more unreasonable than the unreasonable portions of this *Mîzân*.

A single instance will suffice. The *Dîn Haqq*, after quoting the Prophets, and also secular writers, Jewish Christian and Roman, in respect of Christ's death, proceeds to say that if Mohammed had possessed the slightest acquaintance with history, he would never have written of the crucifixion as in the Coran he has. The Maulvi denies the prophecies, and then proceeds:—

The Padre does not perceive that the Coran itself admits, nay expressly asserts, the fact that both Jews and Christians hold the crucifixion of Jesus; and yet he writes, that the author of the Coran was unacquainted with this historical fact! Such a babbler shall have his answer from the Lord. Reflect for a moment, and hide thy face with confusion. Say;—What advantage could he who gave forth the Coran have had in view when he asserted in opposition to vast and influential multitudes that Jesus was not slain, but had ascended to heaven in his mortal body! Had he made his assertion to accord with the views of these immense multitudes, then indeed he had gained an object, viz., the lessening of their opposition, and he had obtained likewise an argument to strengthen his opposition to the Divinity of Christ, that, namely, drawn from the fact of his mortality (p. 637).

He then goes on to say that the Gospel is perfectly correct, because the *semblance* of Christ was actually taken and crucified; "but there is no replying, to the argument you bring against us, viz., that where we agree with the Bible, it is plagiarism—where we disagree, it is false!"[1] No less than eighteen pages are de-

[1] It is curious to observe in what light this Maulvi regards the practice of dancing. He turns the tables against the *Dîn Haqq* in which certain indelicate passages in the Coran are censured, by asserting that *we* are in the habit of justifying indelicate practices by the authority of the Bible. "Miriam's dancing with cymbals is adduced by Christians as

voted to the explaining away, with extraordinary evasions and ingenuity, the plain declarations of the Gospel on the subject of the crucifixion; but it is needless to multiply examples of this style of reasoning. It has rather been our object to give specimens of the more sensible and less unreasonable portions of the book.

In 1847, Pfander published a treatise called HALL UL ISHKÂL, or Solution of Difficulties; *being a reply to* KASHF UL ASTÂR *and* KITÂB I ISTIFSÂR. The *Kashf ul Astâr* has already been noticed at some length in this *Review*. Pfander's rejoinder is brief and pertinent. It is followed by a translation of the remarks on the *Kashf ul Astâr* which appeared in this *Review*. Then follow ten questions put to Pfander by a Maulvi Syad Abdallah Sabzwari of Lucknow, with their replies.[1] After these comes the reply to Ali Hassan's *Kitâb i Istifsâr*, the work we have just been reviewing. The chief points of the Maulvi's desultory attacks are ably noticed and well refuted. The book concludes with the whole correspondence which passed between Pfander and Ali Hassan, and which has been previously described in the article referred to above. Dr. Pfander has not, since the publication of this volume, entered into any further written discussions with the Mohammedans. But although this

proving the innocency of any kind of dancing: and supported by this and other instances in the Bible, your countrymen take their wives, daughters, and sisters to dancing parties, and regard the custom as one approved by religion: nay, you look upon the kissing of the grown-up daughters, sisters and wives of other people, and passing the hand round their waists, pretty much in the same light as we do for men to shake hands with each other, or to fondle little children;—*i.e.*, as right and proper. If it be really thus as I have heard, and such things are, in truth, not held by you to be forbidden by the Divine law, then it is deep disgrace to you" (p. 622).

This passage (of which from necessity we have softened and modified some of the expressions) shows that either the Maulvi's informants or his own bigotry have greatly misrepresented our social practices; still it is matter for reflection whether there may not be some of our practices offering to the Mussulmans a vulnerable point of which they are not slow to avail themselves in their attacks upon our faith, and self-conceit with their own.

[1] A translation of these appeared in the *Christian Intelligencer*, and was the cause of some correspondence in that journal.

controversy is for the present suspended,—and it is perhaps well that it should be so for a time,—it must not be supposed that the native mind is inactive, or that the attention of intelligent and thinking men is withdrawn from the subject. The following extracts from the report of the Agra Tract Society for 1852 will be read with interest, as giving satisfactory evidence on this point:—

At Dehli copies of the Scriptures, and Christian books of a controversial character, have been in great demand in consequence of the controversy between some Hindoos and the Cazee mentioned above. Many Mohammedans seem to have been aroused from the slumber of their blind confidence in their Prophet and his Book by the astounding fact now presented to them, that they are attacked not by the Christians only, but even by the Hindoos, and that with a result not in any way flattering to themselves. To prepare for the battle, they have betaken themselves to reading our books, many, no doubt, with a desire to find arguments against us. But still this excitement amongst them can only be viewed with interest, and we cannot but hope that it will have a beneficial result in some way or other.

A Hindoo friend at Dehli, through whom many Mohammedans have received tracts and books, writes on the subject: "I beg to inform you that I have received the books you forwarded to me. They have all been given away to learned Mussulmans, who required them very earnestly. At their own request, I made over to them all copies of the *Mîzân-ul-Haqq* I had; I have even been obliged to give them my own copy. But they require still more copies, and, consequently, I beg that you will send me another supply at an early opportunity."

In another letter he remarks: "In my opinion it would be very desirable to publish a great number of small pamphlets, containing that part of the *Mîzân-ul-Haqq* which shows that Mohammed performed no miracle, and that also the Coran is no miracle. This will bring numerous Moslem readers to one point, a point which is quite sufficient to show that they have no firm ground to stand upon in defending their creed. It is this point in which the Mohammedan religion is most palpably vulnerable. The ignorance of this very subject, in my opinion, makes the majority of the Mussulmans think that Mohammed was as good a prophet as Moses and Christ."

In a subsequent letter he writes: "A learned Mohammedan of Kurnaul has written a large work, of about 960 pages, the chief object of which appears an attempt to show that the same objections which Christians make to the Coran, can be reverted to the Bible. He has studied, I believe, with great care, all procurable translations of the Bible in Arabic, Persian and Urdoo, and all controversial works, and he is very probably sincere in his inquiries. As to his book, part of which I have read, I think he will find that he is highly mistaken."

"The other day I saw two Mohammedans disputing among themselves about the objections contained in the *Mizân-ul-Haqq*, regarding the miracles of Mohammed. One of them was endeavouring to solve the difficulties; but the other was altogether dissatisfied with his explanations."

The same intelligent Hindoo, with another Hindoo coadjutor (both of them, by the way, specimens of the good effects that may be produced by the system of education pursued in our Government Colleges), has himself entered the lists with the Mohammedans. The following account of a controversy held by them with the Cazee of Dehli, is extracted from the same report:—

A Controversy between a Hindoo and the Cazee of Dehli. — This is a very interesting argument: it is the one referred to at page 12 of last year's report, and was made over to the Committee by the Hindoo, who is desirous that it should be printed. It is entirely aggressive on the part of the Hindoo, who carries the battle into Mohammedan territory; the chief ground occupied, being the insufficiency of the evidences or the miracles alleged to have been wrought by Mohammed. The argument opens with a short paper by the Hindoo, who states his doubts, especially as regards the "splitting of the moon," and asks for evidence. The Cazee answers in a paper of considerable length, endeavouring to bolster up the tottering edifice of traditions, and explain away the damaging admissions which pervade the Coran. The Hindoo rejoins in a long paper, in which he completely demolishes the Cazee's argument, proceeds to impugn the morality of the Coran, and closes with a decided expression of preference for Christianity and its evidences. The Cazee made no reply.

The Committee are preparing a short paper by way of conclusion, and opportunity will be taken to add something on the insufficiency of the historical evidence in support of the Mohammedan traditions. The Committee trust that this publication will be received with acceptance by the Hindoo community, and with interest by all.

The above work is now in the press: and a most important document was placed in the hands of the Committee in time to be added as an appendix. It consists of twenty-three questions sent by a Mohammedan of Kerach to his brother Moslems, with the view of eliciting any possible proofs of the truth of Islam. The paper opens thus:— "I was born a Mohammedan and, at my twenty-fourth year, am still of the same religion: but I now perceive by the exercise of my intellect, that the Mohammedan religion is false, and the Christian true: because there is no proof whatever of the inspiration of Mohammed." He proceeds to state that he considers Islam to be wanting in miracles and in other evidence; that there can be but one true religion in the world given by God, and that if he neglects that, he incurs the perils of the lost. "Therefore I am urged by the fear of future punishment to ask the sages of Islam, if their religion be really true, to prove it to me. And it is their bounden duty either to prove or to forsake it. With this view I have prepared a few questions for my own peace of mind, and entreat a fair and reasonable answer, such as shall aid me in reaching the truth. May the Almighty direct me to Himself, and let Him not be displeased with me!" We believe this to be the genuine effusion of an anxious, burdened spirit, and heartily join in its concluding prayer. The twenty-three questions embrace the grand points of controversy discussed in the *Mîzân-ul-Haqq*: and are short, but conclusive.

Such appearances are encouraging. We receive them as types of the intellectual inquiry and spiritual thought now at work both among Hindoos and Mohammedans. A few singular cases have risen to the surface and attracted our attention. How many similar instances may be occurring, deep and unknown, among the masses of the people, we have no means of knowing. It is undoubted, however, that more correct and extensive knowledge of Christianity is gradually permeating all classes of our fellow-subjects, and that a slow, but sure, advance towards enlightenment is in progress. It is true that, in the view of human agency, there are more hopeful tokens among the Hindoos than amongst the Mohammedans; but that should not discourage us from our controversy with the latter, which indeed must exercise a powerful, though indirect, influence upon the Hindoos also. This important fact has been established by the controversy at Dehli. The Hindoo, sickened by idolatry, turns to the other two religions which surround him, and inquires into their respective claims; and we must be ready at hand to meet him with the proofs of our most Holy faith. It is interesting to watch on such an occasion the convincing effects of a comparison between the *morality* of the Gospel and of the Coran, apart from all questions of external proof. The Hindoo, who has cast off his hereditary idolatry, is bound by no family shackles or national prejudices to Islam; and, if his conscience be really awakened, the comparison of the two religions, Christianity and Mohammedanism, cannot fail to be of essential service and, under God's blessing, to lead to practical results.

We must not then grow weary in following this noble vocation. Britain must not faint until her millions in the East abandon both the false Prophet and the Idol shrines, and rally around that eternal truth which has been brought to light in the Gospel. At every point of contact with Islam, Christianity has the temporal ascendancy. The political prestige of Mohammed is departed for ever. The relation of France to Africa, and of Russia and Austria to the Turkish and Persian dynasties, evinces in a striking light the depression of Islam. But it is to be feared that the *spiritual* influences brought into play by these European powers are comparatively puny and ineffective. The corruptions of the Greek and Roman Churches cannot but injure the usefulness of any efforts made by Russia or Austria, if any such be in progress;[1] while the Government of the former, by

[1] A late journal illustrates the practical effects of this corruption in a very painful manner. After describing the long-standing disputes between the Greek and Roman Churches, for the Sacred places in Palestine, the rivalries and hatred which not unfrequently end in "bloody battles even within the interior of the Churches," and inspire the Mohammedans with contempt and disgust,—the writer proceeds:—

"The quarrel of these monks and pilgrims has lately reached its greatest height. Diplomacy ensued. On the one side the chair of Rome, and France, supported the demands of the Latins. On the other side the cabinet of St. Petersburg defended the cause of the Greeks. . . . The negotiations lasted a long time. The Ottoman Porte was very embarrassed by these opposing claims, and knew not how to reconcile them. At length the disputes appear to have been arranged. This was the decision. First, the Latins shall have the outer key of the grand church of Bethlehem, and the two keys of the side gates, etc. . . . Thus all the noise that has been made, these strifes, battles, negotiations, diplomatic despatches, and long deliberations of the Ottoman Porte, concerned—what? The restitution of

their expulsion from Shushy of Dr. Pfander and his band, have cast aside the missionary teaching so generously afforded them by Germany. Little is to be hoped for from the Roman Catholics of France, and of the proceedings of the Evangelical Churches there we have no information. They have a noble field opened for their endeavours in Algeria, and ought not to be slow in occupying it.

From this review the mind reverts with pleasure and with hope to the efforts now made in British India. Let these be prosecuted with patience, with vigour, and with dependence on the Divine blessing, and in due time that blessing will be vouchsafed.

two or three keys, the fabrication of a silver star, the participation in such and such a compartment of an old edifice; what puerility! what pity!"—*Evang. Christendom*, April 1852.

This is the Christianity displayed before the Turks, these are the efforts made by the Greek and Roman Churches, such the contrast between our political ascendancy, and the spiritual humiliation to which aberrations from our faith have subjected us!

THIRD ARTICLE

VALUE OF EARLY MAHOMETAN HISTORICAL SOURCES

From the "Calcutta Review," 1868

1. *Das Leben und die Lehre des Mohammad, nach bisher grösstentheils unbenutzen Quellen, bearbeitet von* A. Sprenger. Berlin, 1865.

   The Life and Doctrine of Mahomet from Sources hitherto for the most part unused. By A. Sprenger. 3 Vols. Berlin, 1865. *Essay prefixed to Vol. III. on the Original Traditional Sources of Islam.*

THIS is really a great work, the fruit of prodigious learning, and of a life the greater part spent in India in the unwearying search after materials for the early history of Islam, and in their study. Some twenty years ago, Sprenger published at Allahabad a *Life of Mohammed* in English; but, compared with the present, it was bald and meagre, and also incomplete since it stopped short at the Flight from Mecca. It was also marked by a love of paradox, and tendency to strike out theories based on but slender grounds. The present work labours, to some extent, under the same defect. For example, from an expression (Hanîf) used in the Coran by Mahomet to signify that he followed the pure and catholic faith of Abraham, Sprenger assumes the existence of an important sect of "Hanîfites," and of Hanîfite works made use of by the Prophet; and having made the assumption, he proceeds to use it as the premise for still further conclusions. His estimate of the Prophet's character is also essentially inadequate; for, a man of a weak and cunning mind, as Sprenger describes him, could never have accomplished the mighty mission which Mahomet wrought. But notwithstanding such blemishes, the work displays incredible research, and is a perfect treasure-house of materials for the study, not only of the lives of Mahomet and his contemporaries, but of the religious, social, and literary development of the early Moslem empire.

It is not our intention, on the present occasion, to review this treatise as a whole, but simply the Essay prefixed to the third volume, in which the nature and value of the materials for the life of Mahomet, and specially of Tradition, are discussed. The work abounds throughout with prelections and digressions which, though valuable in themselves, often check and disturb the flow of the history. But the Preface we are now to consider forms a detached and independent piece, filling 180 closely-printed pages. And it appears to us to be perhaps the most valuable portion of the whole work.

We make no apology in presenting the subject to our readers. It may be dry to most, and (from our imperfect treatment) heavy. But the origin and development of the faith of so many millions around us, and the traditional basis and evidence of the things most surely believed among them, cannot be devoid of interest, and, though perhaps difficult to treat attractively, should not on that account be cast aside.

The materials bearing on the rise of Islam are divided by Sprenger into five classes: the Coran; Biographies of the Prophet; the Sunna or Tradition proper; Commentaries on the Coran; Genealogies. There is a sixth, namely, Original documents copied by the Collectors of tradition; but these are known to us only by means of Tradition, and do not properly form a separate class. The genuineness of the CORAN, and its bearing on the life of Mahomet, have already been discussed at length in this Periodical, and need not therefore again be dwelt upon.[1] But the other subjects, which are also of the deepest interest, we propose to bring under the notice of our Readers.

The peculiar treatment of Sprenger may be illustrated by one

[1] [The Articles here referred to, have to a great extent formed the basis of the preliminary chapters of my Life of Mahomet.—W.M.]

or two of his theories. He holds, for example, that Mahomet at the first fulminated denunciations of temporal judgment impending over his unbelieving people; and then, having been, like Jonah, disappointed in the fulfilment of the menace, and jeered at by his fellow-citizens, he covered his retreat by the threat of judgment in the world to come; and finally, in order to hide the manœuvre, arranged the passages of his revelation so that the latter were interpolated among the former, and the colouring of a future life thus given to the whole. But there is no ground for this imputation. The two classes of denunciations, present and future, were intermingled in his preaching by Mahomet from the very first; or, if one had the precedence in time, it seems clearly to have been the latter. When the Meccans hardened their hearts and stiffened their necks, then the promise of a nearer and a swifter vengeance was pronounced. And then, as in the days of Isaiah, these mysterious denunciations called forth the scoffs of the people, who challenged their fulfilment like the ancient Jews:—"Let Him make speed and hasten His work, that we may see it; let the counsel of the Holy One of Israel draw nigh and come, that we may know it."

Another characteristic assumption Sprenger bases on the term *Mathâni*, or "reiterated passages," applied by Mahomet himself to certain parts of his book. These our Author distinguishes from the rest of the revelation, which was styled the "blessed Coran." His theory is, that Mahomet at first did not pretend to deliver a new Scripture, but only to *reproduce* by Divine aid, in an Arabic form, the revelations of the Jewish and Christian periods. To this rehearsal of existing Scripture, he for a time confined himself; till, after several years, breaking through his scruples, he commenced the delivery of a direct and independent revelation. The idea is ingenious, but that is all. Whatever the term "reiterated" may signify, it is certain that the recitation of patriarchal passages and incidents belongs to a comparatively late stage in the composition of the Coran; in the earlier portions there is but little reference to them.

The history of Zeid's collection of the scattered Suras (named *The Coran*), and of its official recension under Othmân, is ably traced, and is important to the Christian advocate as accounting for the otherwise marvellous purity of the text. But this is ground on which it is not necessary for us here to enter. We proceed to describe Sprenger's account of the nature and growth of the SUNNA, that is, of Tradition proper so far as it relates to the practice and precepts of the Prophet;—points that are imperative, as laying down the law and ritual of Islam.

By *Sunna*, says Dr. Sprenger, is meant Usage, or the Law of custom. There is, he thinks, among Oriental nations an irrepressible craving, unknown to us in the West, after "the positive"; they must have, not only their religious duties, but the law civil and criminal, and even the commonest details of life—eating, drinking, dress, etc.—prescribed for them by Divine command.[1] The Coran failed to fully satisfy this need; and so resort was had to the precepts and practice of the Prophet himself; and hence the authority of the *Sunna*, which professes to hand down the tradition of Mahomet's utterances, habits, and actions.

We must pause for a moment to say, that the *rationale* here propounded is quite insufficient to account for the growth of the vast ceremonial of the *Sunna*. There exists, it is true, an enfeebling and deteriorating element in the human mind, always prone to rites and ceremonies. But it is as strong in the Western as in the Eastern nations; perhaps, indeed, stronger, for the Church of Rome has gone far greater lengths in this direction than the Eastern Churches. Even with Protestants, who had apparently clean escaped from subjection to human ordinances, "touch not, taste not, handle not, which all are to perish with the using," we must sorrowfully confess how it needs but little to turn multitudes "again to the weak and beggarly elements, whereunto they desire again to be in bondage,"—a mock and ossified counterfeit of the living Faith!

Indeed, it was not the bent of the Asiatic mind, but *the spirit*

[1] "Die Orientalen, besonders die Perser, fühlen ein viel grösseres Bedürfniss nach etwas Positivem als wir, und sie wünschen nicht nur über eigentlich religiöse Dinge, sondern auch über Civil- und Criminal-gesetze und Gewohnheiten des Lebens, z. B. wie man essen und trinken, wie man sich kleiden soll, von Gott ausgehende Weisung" (vol. iii. p. lxxvii.).

and system of the Arabian Prophet, which developed the *Sunna*; just as it was the ceremonial element in the Mosaic law which, exaggerated and distorted by the legal letter-loving spirit of the Jews, led to the endless washing of cups and pots, the tithing of mint and cummin, and all the mazes of rabbinical tradition. Unlike the Christian Scripture which, prescribing principles, leaves their application to the circumstance of the day and the conscience of the individual, the Coran contains minute instructions on rites and ceremonies, and on social and domestic obligations. It was the ceremonial spirit of Mahomet and his Coran, which stamped its formal and ritualistic impress on the Moslem world, and thus gave rise to the *Sunna*. After the Prophet's death, new relations and contingencies were continually arising, for which the Coran had provided no directions; conquest and growing civilisation added daily to the necessity for fresh rules, and for new adaptations of the old. To supply this need, resort was had to the actual or supposed sayings and practice of the Prophet; these were eagerly sought after from the lips of the Companions of the Prophet, or of any who at second hand could trace a tradition to one of those Companions; and thus by the aid of analogy and of fictitious traditions, was provided an exhaustive treasury of precedents for every possible case.

It is true that Mahomet never claimed for his own opinions or actions infallibility. But if he erred on any material point, a dream, an intimation from Gabriel, or a verse revealed for the purpose, was supposed to correct the aberration; so that, as Sprenger shows, the aberration was in point of fact only temporary. He might have added that the image of the Prophet, after he had passed away, was soon encircled with a divine effulgence which he never anticipated; and that his commonest sayings and minutest actions became eventually invested with a celestial sanctity which he would probably have been the last himself to countenance.

Sprenger thinks that the Moslems of the earliest era were freer and bolder than those of later times in expressing their views, and in interpreting the sayings of Mahomet according to the spirit rather than the letter. This may be doubted. The thraldom of Islam was as powerful, the sword of its inquisition as sharp and prompt, in the days of Omar, the Companion of Mahomet, as in those of the intolerant Omar II. The truth seems to be that every day narrowed the field of subjects open to discussion, and on which new traditions needed to be advanced. Judgments professing to proceed from Mahomet, or to be founded on principles enunciated by him, were gradually framed and promulgated for every kind of case transpiring in the daily concerns of life. The system became fixed and stereotyped. And, moreover, the Companions of Mahomet, who alone could authoritatively declare his practice and judgment, one by one dropped off from the scene: and with them ceased the creative freedom and freshness of the earliest era.

A few examples will illustrate the origin and growth of tradition. Mughîra laid claim to a certain property on the strength of an utterance attributed to Mahomet. The Caliph, Abu Bekr, refused to admit the claim until the statement was corroborated by witness; Ibn Maslama testified that he had heard the Prophet affirm the claim, whereupon the Caliph gave judgment in Mughîra's favour. Again, during Mahomet's lifetime, Sobaya lost her first husband, and, shortly after, began to deck herself out in a manner which plainly implied that she already entertained thoughts of attracting a second. A discreet and pious Moslem, scandalised at her conduct, told her that she should tarry four months before thinking of another marriage; but she, regarding this unreasonable, repaired to Mahomet, who confirmed the precept. When, after the Prophet's death, people began to gather up his sayings, a certain collector of tradition wrote to a friend to visit Sobaya, and record from her own lips an exact account of her interview and of the Prophet's precept; and hence the *Sunna* regarding it. On one occasion, Muâvia, while engaged in the Syrian campaign, referred a doubtful point connected with the rules of warfare to Aly, as the person most conversant with the views of Mahomet. So likewise, the son of Abbâs, a renowned traditionist, was consulted on the question whether women and slaves accompanying the army were entitled to share in the booty; his decision, based on the analogy of the Prophet's practice, was that as women and slaves used to be present for the care of the wounded, they had grounds to expect a gift as of favour, but possessed no legal title to a "share." Such are specimens of the way in which tradition, direct and by analogy, grew up.

Each tradition is in a separate independent form. It consists simply in a statement of the Prophet's dictum or his act; in a question and his reply; or in the brief narrative of a conversation, or action which constitutes a precedent for all time to come. It is given, in the direct form of speech, on the authority of the Companion who tells the story; and the names in succession of every witness in the whole chain through whom it has been handed down, and who vouch for its authenticity, are carefully prefixed to it. In process of time this string of authorities becomes of immense length, until it stops at the period when (as we shall see) a written record of the tradition and its authorities supersedes the system of oral communication.

According to Sprenger, tradition was developed into a regular science by the civil wars which broke out upon the murder of Othmân. These, at any rate, imparted to it the powerful impulse of faction; and the force of that impulse will be understood if we remember that the prize in contest was no less than the Caliphate itself. Each party anathematised the other, and based its denunciations upon the authority of the Prophet. The faction that followed Aly held him and his successors in the Imâmship to be as infallible as the Prophet. Their opponents, on the other hand, acknowledged but two sources of infallible authority—the Coran, and the precept or practice of Mahomet. To place the certified precedents of their Prophet upon an authoritative basis, and to preserve them from the possibility of unauthorised additions, the Sunnies, or vast body of orthodox Moslems, reduced tradition to a fixed form, namely, the *Sunna*; by it and by the Coran alone they have ever been guided, and hence their name.

The rapid and exuberant growth of tradition is truly marvellous. Sprenger thinks that the collection of traditions was not taken up as a regular profession till A.H. 40, or some thirty years after the Prophet's death. From the Companions who died before that time only such traditions were preserved as the contingencies and requirements of the day called forth in the way of precedent and direction. But afterwards, while everybody continued more or less a tradition-monger, it became the special business of a numerous class to record from all quarters whatever recollections of the Prophet still lingered in the memory of the people. Mecca and Medina, of course, were specially ransacked, while every spot, however distant, was visited in the hope of meeting some one from whom the fragment of a reminiscence might be gleaned. We have consequently a much greater body of traditions from the Companions who survived to this busy time, than from those who died before it. Abu Horeira (*d.* A.H. 58), himself a Companion, collected no fewer than 3000 traditions regarding the Prophet, from the lips either of eye-witnesses or of those who had received them from eye-witnesses.

At such a distance of time there could be no great scrupulousness or exactitude either as to the expressions or the subject-matter thus handed down. Penetrated by an irresistible fanaticism, the traditionist "placed subjective truth far higher than objective." It was the ideal of the Prophet, and the glory of Islam, which tradition set forth, rather than any accurate and historical statement. At all events, it was only such reports as coincided with the spirit of Islam that maintained their currency; and hence we find tradition to be necessarily partial and one-sided. The strife of sect and party, it is true, acted to some extent as a check upon misstatement, but only in so far as sect and party were concerned. In the glorification of the Prophet and exaltation of Islam all were interested and all agreed.

One cannot fail to be struck by the uniformity of style and construction which pervades the whole mass of tradition. The form and type throughout are one. Sprenger thinks this remarkable similarity to be the work of the professional traditionists who shaped and *formularised*, according to the recognised model, all traditional matter which fell into their hands. Thus, an imperfect fragment would be set in the frame of question and answer; or the prolix story of some aged descendant of a Companion would be compressed and as such dressed up in the traditional shape. Then, as new points of usage or law from time to time came forward for settlement, these, reduced into the proper interrogatory form, would be put to every person likely to have traditional cognisance of the matter.

By the end of the first century of the Hegira, our author thinks that by far the greater part of the traditions of the Mahometan world were in the hands of the professional traditionists, and had been already formularised by them. But each Collector as yet possessed only his own separate and limited store. By degrees these were brought together in the course of the second century, and, as rills converging from all quarters, formed the mighty stream of tradition. Men still compassed sea and land in search of something new; and here and there one might have the good fortune to light upon a fresh tradition. But as time rolled on, such sources all dried up. The competition and jealousy of the traditionists subjected new matter to the severest tests; and if a recently found tradition broke down under the scrutiny, the propagator lost his character for veracity. It was thus that Ibn Ishâc and others fell into disrepute among some of their contemporaries.

Tradition, as above described, is not confined to details belonging to the lifetime of Mahomet. The childish habit was contracted of putting the relation of every trivial fact and story into the popular form of a tradition with its string of authorities; and there is consequently a great mass of quasi-traditional matter on the early progress of Islam subsequent to the Prophet's death. Excluding this, and confining our view solely to what belongs to the lifetime of Mahomet, it is remarkable that the original sources, the recognised "Sheikhs" or Fathers of tradition, are comparatively few, great numbers having been rejected by the Collectors as inadmissible. Thus Hâshid (*d.* 258) relates that he had heard the recitals of 1750 Sheikhs, but adopted in his collection the traditions of but 310; he had collected separate traditions to the number of one million and a half, but accepted only 300,000. Wâckidi, again, amassed probably a couple of millions, but the number of Sheikhs he relied on was small. Setting aside repetitions of the same occurrence, he retained in his collection not more than some 40,000 traditions, of which perhaps not half are genuine; and even of these, many relate to one and the same subject-matter.

The distinguishing feature of early Mahometan tradition is, that it was essentially *oral*. Even if committed to writing, the tradition acquired no new authority from the record: it must still be transmitted by word of mouth, the record counting absolutely for nothing. The canons of tradition formed a distinct science, and had a literature of their own. It was found necessary to relax the strict Mahometan law of evidence in its application to tradition: thus, a single credible witness (instead of the legal two) sufficed, if only the links of oral transmission were otherwise complete. An exception was also made in favour of *epistolary* communications, which at a very early period were admitted as trustworthy without oral attestation; but under all other circumstances, the test by word of mouth was rigidly insisted upon, as essential to the validity of each step in the transmission. Thus the possessor of the notes or memoranda of a Sheikh could make no recognised use of them unless he was able to say that they had been *orally* vouched for by the writer of the manuscript; and indeed the entire rehearsal of each tradition by the person transmitting and the person receiving it, in the hearing of each other, was insisted upon as an indispensable condition of trustworthiness.

Where the traditions of a Companion were handed down in various channels, we have special means of testing the accuracy of transmission. Thus Abu Horeira had 800 pupils to whom he communicated his learning, several of whose names survive in the traditional chains; now, since some of these lived at a period when it was customary to commit a tradition to writing,—hence, by comparing the text of the same tradition as given by the different authorities, we have a strong guarantee that the words of Abu Horeira himself have been correctly preserved. But the same cannot be said of most of the Companions of the Prophet who were the youngest and survived the longest. There was among them great latitude for fabrication. A collector of tradition often stood in a specially intimate relation to some one of the Companions (as Orwa to Ayesha, Ikrima to the son of Abbâs, Abu Ishâc to Barâ), and became thus the chief and often sole medium for transmitting the traditions of the Companion to whom he was thus attached. Such monopoly was no doubt often greatly abused; and from the nature of the case there was no means of checking it. The seclusion of the Harem also exaggerated the evil; and Sprenger is of opinion that Orwa, for example, has recited many a tradition on the authority of Ayesha which she never dreamt of. The traditions, emanating from such suspicious sources, were sometimes found to run counter to the received and orthodox views; hence arose the canon that no *Ahâd* (ἁπαξ λεγομενα one might call them) or traditions vouched only by a single authority, were to be received. But history lost more than it gained by such arbitrary exclusion; for whenever a tradition of this nature was (like the *Mirâj*, or Heavenly journey) in conformity with the spirit of the age, other authorities were easily invented for its support; while important facts, if thought discreditable to the Prophet's memory (as his relapse into idolatry) or opposed to received dogma, were dropped out of sight and lost. Happily, the Biographers did not hold themselves bound by the strict canons of the *Sunna*; they have preserved traditions sometimes resting on a single authority, or otherwise technically weak, and therefore rejected by the Collectors of the *Sunna*; and they have thus rescued for us not a few facts and narratives of special interest, bearing internal marks of authenticity.

Sprenger next discusses the important question of the Time at which tradition began to be reduced to writing. And, first, as to the material. Egyptian paper, though freely exported to Constantinople, could have been little known in Arabia, at all events not in sufficient quantities for ordinary use. We read in the *Fihrist*, that the flax paper of Khorasan was introduced under the Omeyyad or the Abbasside Caliphs. "In the first century, the Moslems wrote their memoranda upon tablets of wood and slate; for more permanent records, they made use of leather and parchment." The gazelle skin, tanned in early times with unslaked lime, was hard and stiff. Later, at Cûfâ a preparation of dates was used, and the parchment thus manufactured was white and soft. By this test the antiquity of the very early MSS. (such as the exemplar of the Coran at Homs) can be satisfactorily ascertained. The writing was often washed off, as in the case of early classical manuscripts, to make way for more recent compositions; and many valuable works have thus been lost to us.

The traditions which ascribe to Mahomet a prejudice against writing, appear to have no good foundation. They originated, no doubt, in the circumstance that he himself had little, if any, knowledge of the art. It was the pious fashion to follow his example and practice, to the minutest particular; hence Ibn Masûd, Abu Horeira, and others of the more scrupulous believers, hesitated to commit the Prophet's sayings to writing, and the report of his having forbidden the practice thus gained currency. On the other hand, we have evidence which makes it highly probable that even during the lifetime of Mahomet there were persons whe kept up memoranda of his utterances. At any rate, there is frequent notice of the custom shortly after his death. Thus we find mention of the son of Abbâs (the uncle of Mahomet) having left behind him a camel load of manuscripts, from which both Ikrima and Ibn Ocba made copious extracts. Aly copied out certain precepts of the Prophet regarding the ransom of prisoners, etc.; and, in order to have them constantly at hand, tied the roll round the handle of his sword. Another hero made use of his boot as a receptacle for the same purpose. It is related of an early Collector of tradition, that he carried about with him a portfolio filled with pages of leather; and the famous Zohri, when other material failed, made notes of what was told him upon his yellow boots, and copied them out in order afterwards. The practice increased so rapidly, that towards the end of the first century, Omar II. (with a view analogous to that which induced Abu Bekr to direct the collection of the Coran) issued orders for a complete compilation of all recorded traditions; but he died before the work was accomplished. According to the strict canon of the *Sunna*, the object of written collections was not to supersede, but only to assist, the *memoriter* preservation of tradition; for oral repetition was still the inexorable rule. Indeed, the prejudice against *recorded* collections even yet ran so high, that instances are given of Collectors committing their treasures to the flames (not without regret when the loss was found irreparable), or leaving instructions to their executors to destroy them after their death. Still the superior check and authority of a record must in practice have gradually superseded reliance on unassisted memory. Collections of the earlier traditionists fell somtimes into the hands of later authors, and we find Wâckidi and others making use of these treasures in a manner inconsistent with the canons of the *Sunna.*

Sprenger states the following as the successive stages of record: (1) Notes or memoranda; (2) School or college collections; (3) Regular books. Our previous remarks refer exclusively to the first, that is, notes professing to be used simply for the refreshment of the memory. Towards the end of the first century, the second class, or School collections, began to be in vogue. Orwa and Zohri, for example, used such records in their prelections. The pupils were at liberty either to trust solely to their memory, or to make copies of their Master's collection; but so rigidly was the oral canon still followed, that the copies thus taken had no authority until they were first rehearsed by the scholar in the hearing of his Master; and the date of each rehearsal (árz) was usually noted upon his manuscript by the copyist.[1]

The third class of documents, answering to our *published Books*, was of much later rise. A Mahometan authority tells us that Ibn Jureij and Ibn Abi Rabia, who both died about the middle of the second century, were the first who wrote books. Mussulman writers themselves understand this passage as meaning that these persons were the first to make use of manuscript tradition in any shape. But this appears a mistake: the simple purport being that these were the first to put forth "Books," or collections of tradition, *which carried their own authority with them*, the condition of oral repetition being no longer required. It had become a question of accuracy of manuscript and edition; no longer pure accuracy of recollection.

The use of books gradually displaced the old and cumbrous

[1] The collections were generally in "parts" (*juz*) of 40 pages, each of which could be read at one sitting; the date of the rehearsal being entered in the margin. The earliest instance we have seen of such rehearsal, is the old MS. of the Secretary of Wâckidi (noticed elsewhere), which gives the date of reading of the original copy, in the year A.H. 146.

system. But the prejudice against them lasted so long that, even before the end of the second century, we meet with aspersions cast on authors who made use of manuscripts wanting the stamp of oral tradition. With just severity Sprenger comments on the childish pedantry which for two whole centuries clung by the absurd paradox that memory was a more trustworthy authority than the pen. Yet this much excuse may be urged, that without an oral attestation at each step in the tradition, there would have been absolutely no guarantee whatever against forgery and interpolation.

Even when books came into vogue, the collection of a Master was freely subject to alteration at the hands of his pupil, who, performing as it were the functions of an editor, selected or omitted passages at pleasure, and even added (but always with his name) new matter of his own, and sometimes collections of fresh traditions from other sources. The work, notwithstanding these alterations, was still known under the Master's name. It is thus that we find different versions of such compilations, as that of Bokhâri, to vary both in the number of the traditions and in the subject-matter. It is also sometimes not easy to trace the original work from which quotations are made. Tabari, for example, who composed his annals almost entirely of extracts copied *verbatim* from previous collections, makes little mention of the Author from whom he borrows: it is the name of some obscure Sheikh under whom he read the work which, under the pedantic rules of tradition, figures as his authority; the name of the real author (Ibn Ishâc, for instance) occurring in the middle of the long string of vouchers, as a mere link in the transmission. When he had read a collection under more than one Sheikh, he makes a parade of his learning by quoting now under the name of one, and now of another. And to carry the system to the extreme of absurdity, where he had read only part of a work with a Master, he quotes the part he had not so read under the fiction of a *letter* from his Sheikh; letters being admissible as evidence, but not a manuscript or book!

Towards the end of the second century, a crowd of systematic Collectors of tradition sprang up with the view of fixing the *Sunnie* doctrine. Such collections not unfrequently contain statements at variance with one another. Inference from analogy (Qyâs) here came into play; among differing traditions, that one was adopted which symbolised most closely with the axioms of the Collector's theological school. Thus each school had its special collections (musnâd), composed of a selection of those traditions which best supported its tenets. One of the earliest is that of Muätta, who died A.H. 179. Besides traditions, these works contain the opinions of the author expressed in the form of brief decisions which, though primarily directed to legal or theological questions, have sometimes also a material bearing on the province of history.[1]

While Theologians thus selected traditions with a special view, thousands of Traditionists were busy in making collections with little or no specific purpose other than that of mere collection. Their object was simply to mass together as many traditions as they could, and for a long period they were guided by no fixed critical rules. Bokhâri was the first of the general Collectors to adopt rules of (so-called) critical selection: he proposed to himself the task of confining his collection to "sound" or authentic traditions.[2] He was moved, it is said, to this duty by a dream in which he seemed to be driving away the flies from Mahomet, interpreted to signify that he would dispel the "lies" which clustered around his memory. The canons which guided him, however, hardly deserve the name of criticism. He looked simply to the completeness of

[1] The received collections of Shâfi (*d.* 204), Abu Hanîfa (*d.* 150), and Ibn Hanbal (*d.* 234), represent the views of so many different schools. Prior to these, although the different sects had their special collections, they were confined to notes and memoriter traditions. In Bokhâri, on the other hand, and in other *general* collections like his, we have all such traditions, and others of a general character, the whole thrown together indiscriminately, without reference to the tenets of any theological school. By a comparison of the several collections we can trace the variety of theological views and the history of dogma; and this inquiry Sprenger thinks necessary to a correct conception of the intellectual efforts of each age.

[2] When we speak of "criticism," it must not be supposed that there ever was any such in the strict sense of the term. That was stifled by the blind and intolerant teaching of Islam. Any attempt at the free exercise of reason and common sense would have been cut short as impious apostasy by the sword.

the traditional chain, and the character of the witnesses composing it; and as one of his rules was to refuse every tradition at variance with his own ideas of orthodoxy, it by no means follows that any statement rejected by him is really untrustworthy. His collections, however, differ from the "Musnâds" in not having respect to any school of theology, but solely to the character and supposed *soundness* of the traditions. It also takes a wider range and embraces statements on the exegesis of the Coran, the ancient prophets, the campaigns, etc. It contains 7275 separate traditions; or, excluding repetitions, somewhere about 4000.

The great rival of Bokhâri is his pupil Muslim, whose object it was to complete and improve his Master's collection by adding fresh traditions and new chains of authorities. His work thus contains some 12,000 traditions, but if we exclude repetitions, the contents hardly exceed those of Bokhâri; the arrangement, however, is better, and hence the collection more valuable. Bokhâri is the standard authority in Asia and Egypt; Muslim in Northern Africa, and formerly also in Spain. Four other collections, but of less authority, are recognised by the Sunnies, making the canonical number altogether six.[1] There are many others, but these are alone authoritative.

To the *Shiea* collections Sprenger devotes but half a dozen lines. He justly describes them as of little worth. The Shiea Collectors began the work later than the orthodox party; they also hold Aly and the Imâms (successors of Aly) as infallible, and their precepts as sacred as those of Mahomet himself; and "they have at all times sought to bolster up their doctrine by lies and falsehoods." Sprenger himself is a decided Sunnie, and his language is strong; but to one familiar with Shie-ite tradition it can hardly be called unjust.

[1] The minor collections are those of Abu Daûd (*d.* 275); Tirmidzy (*d.* 279); Nasar (*d.* 303); for the fourth some adopt Ibn Mâja (*d.* 273), others Ibn Khozeima (*d.* 311). Besides "sound" traditions, these contain likewise statements based on "tolerable" authority: they also busy themselves more with theology than the two leading collections. Of the various non-canonical collections, some profess to be supplementary to Muslim and Bokhâri, others aspire to give exhaustive collections of their own.

We come next to the BIOGRAPHERS. In many respects Sprenger does them justice; although we shall find, upon the whole, that he entertains a strong prejudice against the class.

We have already seen that, not being bound by the stringent rules of the *Sunna*, the Biographers have preserved to us interesting narratives and valuable clues to truth, which the professional Collector cast aside because they did not answer to the technical requirements of traditionary evidence, or square with his own theological notions. Another distinguishing feature of their writings is, that they often supply us with a connected narrative, to produce which the traditions forming it are fused into one another, and the authorities for the whole given at the beginning of the story. This, however, is not always the case; the greater part of Wâckidi, for example, is composed of separate traditions each with its separate string of authorities, and with the same formalities as in the regular collections.

Some of these consolidated narratives take the form of an Episode or Romance; and Sprenger, though perhaps pushing his theory too far, has given us an ingenious clue to their origin. It is the practice of the Moslem world, during the first ten days of Rabî I. (the month in which Mahomet was born) for the faithful to meet in their family circles, and listen to recitals of his birth, miracles, and death. In opulent houses there is often retained for the purpose a professional Bard, who repeats his story from memory, or extemporises it in the style of the ancient rhapsodists. To aid the reciter, we have a mass of popular works, the most noted being that of Bakry (A.H. 763). They are called *Moulûd Sharîf* ("The Ennobled Nativity"); one of these, written in the Urdoo language, was reviewed in this periodical.[1] They are filled with childish tales, and resemble fiction so much more than history, that, as remarked even by a Mahometan writer, they abound with names of persons, places, kings, and kingdoms, which never existed. We do not know when such annual recitations commenced; but we are assured by Kazrûni that the festival of the birth of Mahomet has been celebrated from the earliest times. Now, if we compare, for instance, the narrative of the Prophet's

[1] No. XXXIV. (First Series), pp. 404 *et seq.*

childhood, especially the "charming idyl" of the nurse Halîma as given by Ibn Ishâc, with the most ancient models of the *Moulúd Sharîf*, we find the same spirit and style pervading both, the later being merely a development of the older. And this again points back to the still earlier rhapsodies made use of by the Biographers. "I doubt not," says Sprenger, "that Ibn Ishâc's narrative has been derived from the earliest (Moslem) *Gospels of the Infancy*."

Such works unveil the early tendency of the Moslems to glorify their Prophet, compiled as they are on Shafy's maxim—"In the exaltation of Mahomet *to exaggerate is lawful.*" This principle is conspicuous in the culminating legend of the "Heavenly journey,"—the grand proof to the credulous believer of the Prophet's mission. It originated at the same period as the other legends,[1] possibly a little later; and it can be traced up, in almost identical expressions through distinct traditionary channels, to three of the pupils of Anas the servant of Mahomet; we have it, therefore, in almost the very words in which a contemporary of the Prophet used to recite the story.

To while away the time by repeating tales has always been a favourite recreation in the East; and to this practice Sprenger attributes the episodic form of many passages in the life of Mahomet. The habit survives in the professional story-tellers who in our own day recite romances like that of Antar; and they do so with a histrionic power for which, compared with that of European actors, Sprenger avows his preference. These romances are committed to memory, and, as occasion requires, repeated in a shorter or longer form; but, however varied and in different shape, when the expressions are compared with the original model, there is found a substantial agreement to prevail.

[1] Sprenger holds that we can often fix the period of the origin of a tradition by the class of persons it was intended to edify;—thus, predictions and prophecies were invented for the Christian; stories of genii, idols, and soothsayers, for the Arab heathen; announcements regarding Chosroes and the East, for the Persians,—the advancing limits of the kingdom of Islam requiring suitable evidence for each people. The argument is not worth much. The real evidence of Islam was the sword. Legend grew up around the Prophet naturally, as the halo round the pictures of our Christian saints.

And so we may suppose it to have been with the leading passages in the life of the Prophet. His infancy, the Heavenly journey, the deputations from Arab tribes, the fields of Bedr, Ohod and Kheibar, his deathbed;—each formed, apparently, a separate episode, amplified by the rhapsodists who had learned the outline. In the course of repetition such episodes gradually acquired a shape that symbolised with the spiritual requirements of the day, and, like the tale of Antar, became stereotyped; and thus, assuming the form of a tradition, were handed down with the usual string of authorities. These episodes, Sprenger thinks, were for the most part not wilful falsehoods, but the invention of a "playful fantasy," which filled up with bright and suitable colouring the ideal outlines of the Prophet's life. Cast in a poetical mould, animated by the dramatic effect of dialogue and sometimes of verses put into the speakers' lips, they contain, he thinks, as little basis of fact as the mere romances of the pseudo-Wâckidi. Indeed, the narratives relating the miracles of Mahomet, which are told with all the gravity of an eye-witness, Sprenger designates "as little less than wilful lies."

Of such essentially worthless and spurious material Sprenger asserts that the biographies are almost entirely composed:—

"This narrative" (the tradition of the Heavenly journey) "gives us a fair idea of the trustworthiness of the dogmatic biography. I need only add that these legends have supplanted nearly all authentic reports of the life and struggle of Mahomet prior to the Flight. The only real historical material consists of personal narratives regarding his followers" (vol. iii. p. lviii.).

"After these remarks, if we read the book of Ibn Ishâc, which my sagacious predecessors with some pomp cite under the title of 'the most ancient source,'—as if this could satisfy criticism,—we find that, with the sole exception of the 'Campaigns,' it contains nothing but the legends and historical romances of the first century. Such traditions suited so well the author's taste that, even when he was possessed of better information, he preferred them. His love for invention and his disregard of the truth ruled so strongly, that he embodies in his work verses which one of his friends put into the mouth of an actor in the scene."

In a note, we are told that our author cites the example of Ibn Ishâc, as being the earliest of the Biographers, and that even Ibn Sad (the Secretary of Wâckidi) indulges in similar legends, each with its proper string of authorities (vol. iii. p. lxi).

Again:—"Legends, elaborately composed episodes, and marvels, form the sole matter which, during the first four or five decades after Mahomet's death (*i.e.* to A.H. 50 or 60), were formularised out of the history of the Prophet. And, once more, speaking of *Campaigns*: 'these form the kernel of the chronological history of Mahomet, and constitute almost the only historical material furnished us by the systematic biographers, such as Ibn Ishâc'" (p. lxiv.).

Now these views appear erroneous and misleading in several respects. They altogether ignore the merit and value of the Biographers, which in other places are fully admitted by Sprenger himself. It is not the case that their works are entirely composed of legend and romance, to the exclusion, or nearly so, of fact. The marriage of Mahomet, the birth of his daughters, the persecution and consequent flight to Abyssinia, the Prophet's "lapse," the long-continued ban and its cancelment, the death of Khadîja and Abu Tâleb, the marriage with Sauda and betrothal to Ayesha, the visit to Tâyif, the meeting with the citizens of Medina and the contract made with them;—surely these and many other incidents, all prior to the Flight, are based on fact and not on fiction. The truth appears to be that the Biographers made use of whatever material they found to their hand, and, free from the shackles of the *Sunna*, they adopted the current legends and marvellous episodes with the rest; but, far from confining themselves to these, they constrained into their service every kind of tradition pertinent to their subject: and it is thus that Wâckidi and his Secretary are specially commended elsewhere by Sprenger, for their diligence in the collection of traditions, and care in verifying them by the requisite authorities. Like the whole race of early Mahometan writers, the Biographers endeavoured (and that not seldom by questionable means) to glorify Mahomet and magnify Islam; but there is no reason to doubt that otherwise they sought honestly to give a true picture of the Prophet; that while they admit some legendary tales excluded from the *Sunna*, their works are to a very great extent composed of precisely the same material; and that they are, moreover, less under the influence of theological bias than were the collectors of the *Sunna*.

Further, in respect of the episodes themselves, these are not always absolute fictions, as represented by Sprenger. The repetition by rhapsodists of "mere fantasies," is a theory which will not account for the uniformity, both as to subject and expression, which we find in the different versions of the same episode. The story, he says, was repeated over and over, till at last it assumed a form suitable to the spiritual requirements of the age, and so became fixed in the same as its permanent form. But the efforts of mere fancy would not of themselves crystallise into any such uniform shape; rather, repetition in different lands, and by various rhapsodists, would produce an infinity of form and colour. To account for the sameness of the episodes, therefore, we must assume something common in their origin.

The common material was no doubt that which it professed to be, namely, the statement of some one of the Companions. Indeed, as respects the Heavenly journey, the most extravagant of all the episodes, Sprenger has satisfied himself (as we have seen) that it can be traced back to the very narrative of Mahomet's own servant; and he deduces the conclusion, that early origin affords no criterion of a story being founded on fact.[1] On the contrary, we hold that early origin does afford a strong presumption that there was at bottom an element of fact, a kernel of reality—small it might be, but still real—which devotion has seized on as a centre around which to cast its halo of the marvellous and supernatural. That there is such a nucleus even for the Heavenly journey, *i.e.* for Mahomet's having told a story of the kind, is proved by the mention of it in the XVII. Sura, and by the scandal occasioned thereby at the first, even among his own followers. And so with the tales of the miracles of Mahomet,—puerile fabrications as they evidently are,—we can generally trace in tradition some real incident on which they were engrafted, which prompted the idea, and gave to fancy a starting-point for its fairy creations and illusive colouring.

The early date at which episodes took fixed shape must afford a certain measure of security that the tales they tell are not altogether legendary. They proceeded from witnesses more or less acquainted with the real facts, and were promulgated in a manner which challenged contradiction from other competent

[1] Vol. iii. p. lix.

witnesses. It is true that the whole Moslem world was impelled by the same tendency to magnify Mahomet without regard to reason or consistency. None would have dared to question a miracle for its inherent improbability, or on a critical conclusion as to the insufficiency of the evidence; the attempt at so dangerous a precedent would have placed the critic in jeopardy of his life. So far, then, as relates to the exaltation of the Prophet, there would have been none to question. But almost every tradition is connected also at some point with an individual, a family, or a tribe, whose memory was affected for good or evil by the story. And here the factions and jealousies which pervaded the very earliest Mahometan society would come into play as an important check upon any deviation from the truth. We may be very certain that no tradition affecting Abu Sofiân or Abbâs, Othmân or Aly, would escape the narrowest criticism by some opposing party, in so far as its interests were concerned. And since every communication with Mahomet handed down by tradition casts a halo around the Companion so honoured, we have in this fact alone a very important restraint upon the licence of legend and episode,—a restraint effective in proportion to the earliness of the period at which the tradition first took fixed shape. Hence in point of fact it is generally possible, with more or less of certainty, to separate the grain of fact from the husk of overlying fiction in which it has been handed down; and through the divine effulgence encircling the Prophet, to distinguish, dimly it may be but yet with some assurance, the outlines of the man.

From this digression we return to trace the development of Biographical research. The study of the *Sunna*, embracing as it did the habits and usage of the Prophet, had already broken ground in this direction, when in the second half of the first century we find persons devoting themselves entirely to the events and chronology of his life. Orwa, born within fourteen years of Mahomet's death, a near relative of Ayesha and a copious narrator of her traditions, was the first who systematically attempted the task. We have remains of his letters on the subject; but it seems doubtful whether he wrote any regular treatise. We next meet with his pupil Zohri, and some others who died early in the second century, engaged in the same work. Zohri attempted the task of writing a history of Mahomet's campaigns, which formed a separate subject of study, and which, as we have seen, Sprenger holds to be the only reliable portion of the biographies. From the public character of the Prophet's warlike undertakings, it is natural to expect that they could be ascertained with more exactness and detail than matters affecting his ordinary life. Yet even in the campaigns, there is abundance of romance: and many episodes regarding the battle of Bedr, for instance, or the exploits of Aly at Kheibar, bear to the full the marvel-loving stamp of the rhapsodist.

The first regular biography of Mahomet of which we have any notice is that by Ibn Ocba (*d.* 141), but it is not extant. The earliest which remains to us is by Ibn Ishâc (*d.* 151), and this we have only in the corrected and amplified version of Ibn Hishâm (*d.* 213). In a former article an account has been given of these early Biographers;[1] it is, therefore, unnecessary here to do more than extract the opinions of Sprenger on the value to be attached to the works of Wâckidi and his secretary, Ibn S'ad:

> Wâckidi, who was born at Medîna, died in Baghdad, A.H. 207 (A.D. 803), aged 78. He spent in the purchase of books 2000 dinars, and he had two slaves constantly employed in copying manuscripts. He left behind him 600 chests full of books, each requiring two men to lift it. With such rapidity had traditional literature increased. . . . He possessed dozens of versions of one and the same tradition, and these he arranged in chapters under appropriate headings. To turn this mass of tradition to advantage, Wâckidi set about the sifting of the mass. The plan of his work consists of biographical notices arranged in chronological order, and embraced all traditionists of note up to his own time. The latest he mentions is Muâvia, whom he met on a pilgrimage. It is related of each traditionist with what persons he had come in contact, and from whom he received and propagated traditions, and the measure of reliance to be placed on him.
>
> Wâckidi chiefly occupied himself with the biography of Mahomet, and he applied a new style of criticism to the work. He wrote various monographs on special subjects connected with the Prophet's life:—one on his Divine mission, a second on his wives (extracted by the Secretary), a third on the chronology, and a fourth on the campaigns, which last is still extant.

---

[1] No. XXXVII. (First Series) of this *Review*.

The criticism of Wâckidi does not consist in the collation of existing works, or in the endeavour to amplify and correct these by the help of new material. Neither he nor any other writer of the time was addicted to the use of reason and argument. The sole ambition of each was to collect the largest number of traditions, to transmit them with exactness, and at the most, after presenting a number of conflicting statements, to add, "According to my view, this or that is the best grounded." Most give no judgment at all, leaving that to the reader. . . . He seems to have taken as few traditions as possible from the *Sunna*, and even of these he gives other versions resting on independent authorities. His great learning enabled him often to assign ten different authorities for a single tradition, with as many varying texts of the same; and to supply many interesting anecdotes which had escaped Ibn Ishâc and his other predecessors. If we admit that he was not always fair or honest, it must be added that his principles were those of an impartial and scientific criticism; and that his zeal and method succeeded in bequeathing to us an important means of forming a judgment on the value of the original authorities.

Of his secretary, Ibn S'ad, who died A.H. 230, Sprenger writes:—

He improved the arrangement of his Master's biographical works; and, after abbreviating them and supplying deficiencies, published the whole, under the title of *Tabacât*, in 12 (or 15) large volumes. His biography of Mahomet, which occupies the greatest part of the first volume,[1] is the most solid work we possess on the subject. The "Campaigns" form a separate chapter, devoted exclusively to the wars of the Prophet. He departs here from his usual practice of citing with each tradition the string of authorities on which it rests; he contents himself with stating in the introduction that his authorities for the whole chapter are Ibn Ishâc, Ibn Ocba, and Abu Mashar, and then he pursues his narrative without again quoting their names. Thus he practises in this part of his biography, historical composition in our sense of the term. The multitudinous different reports had been already duly weighed, contradictions reconciled, the dates fixed by computation, and the whole narrative put on an independent footing. Following Wâckidi almost exclusively, he appears to use the other three authorities only by way of check. His Master's text he condenses in a masterly manner, and introduces here and there valuable geographical notes. At the close of the sections which narrate the most important expeditions, he cites such traditions as had escaped Wâckidi and his other predecessors;—

---

[1] A valuable manuscript of this volume is extant in India. It is described in Art. XXXVII. of this *Review*, before quoted.

[The volume, as elsewhere noticed, is now in the India Office, and copy in the library of the Edinburgh University.]

some of these contain new matter, others are merely variations, or old traditions supported by better authorities than those already known.

The chapter of most value for us is that on the "Deputations." The chief authority here relied on by Ibn S'ad is Ibn Kalby, the Commentator (*d.* 146); but Wâckidi is so constantly referred to, that we may presume he wrote a monograph on that subject also. This chapter, and indeed the Secretary's whole work, excepting the "Campaigns," resembles closely in its composition the *Sunna*; the authorities for each tradition are recited with the same punctiliousness of detail, his own opinion being rarely given, and then only in an extremely short form. The greatest portion of the materials is taken from Wâckidi: but many very valuable traditions of his own collecting are added by the Secretary.

According to the canons of traditional criticism, Wâckidi is reckoned untrustworthy, partly because he was not orthodox (he inclined to the Shica doctrine), partly because he was uncritical in the choice of his authorities, and not himself invariably true. His Secretary, Ibn S'ad, on the contrary, is held so trustworthy that many adopt the traditions of Wâckidi only when attested by his pupil, quoting in this way:—"the following is from Wâckidi, supported, however, by Ibn S'ad." He seems thus to have sifted the materials collected by his Master, and in the process, no doubt, cast much aside.

The merit of Wâckidi and his Secretary does not in the least consist in their rejection of legendary matter, or in their narrative having less the colour of the age than that of Ibn Ishâc. If they put aside certain improbable traditions, because founded on no better authority than Ibn Ishâc, they have, on the other hand, embodied many legends which escaped that author, and given new authorities more ancient than Ibn Ishâc himself, for many of his stories. Their real worth consists chiefly in the additional matter which they supply. By giving (which the Sunna-collectors also do) the more ancient and rudimentary versions of the legends, they aid us in searching out their origin, and thus enable us to demolish the dogmatic biography (III., p. lxxvi.).

We are now in a position to receive, but with some reserve, the conclusion of Sprenger. "According to my judgment," he says, "*the* Sunna *contains more truth than falsehood, the Biographies more falsehood than truth.* Further, the numberless versions in the former, of one and the same tradition, serve as a means of criticism. Hence I hold the *Sunna*, after the Coran and original documents of which copies have been preserved, to be the most trustworthy of our sources" (III., p. civ.). But the main difference, as we have seen, is, not that the Collectors of the

Sunna brought into play more reasonable and efficient canons of criticism than the Biographers, but that they made use of their technical and unreasonable canons in a more servile manner. The less stringent rule of the Biographers, while admitting, no doubt, many fictions and legends, has presented us with much which was excluded from the *Sunna*, and which, if not absolutely true, affords nevertheless very significant indications in the direction of truth. As to the existence of the legendary and marvellous element in all tradition that concerns the Prophet, there is really little choice between the *Sunna* and the biographical works. Our conclusion then is, that Sprenger in the judgment quoted above has unduly lauded the Collectors of the *Sunna*, and depreciated the value of the Biographers.

The works of Wâckidi's Secretary, Ibn S'ad, are the latest which contain any fresh historical matter worthy to be so called. The names of several other Biographers of the same age have been handed down, but they are never quoted by later writers, and their labours are hopelessly lost to us. Tabari (*d.* 310) may, indeed, be held in some small degree an exception, since he has preserved here and there materials (such as the letters of Orwa) not to be found elsewhere. After him there is absolutely no work which contains any independent historical substance. The so-called historians of later times, so far as they deal in history at all, blindly follow Ibn Ishâc, supplementing his statements occasionally by a reference to Wâckidi. To call any of these, original sources, is a mere abuse of the term.

We next come to the Commentaries on the Coran. Besides the desire, natural in a pious Moslem, to expound his Sacred book, explain its difficulties, and illustrate its excellencies, there were two causes which led to the growth of Commentaries; the Coran contradicts the previous Scripture, and sometimes contradicts itself. When such inconsistencies are irreconcilable, then the latest passage is held to cancel the earlier. Thus in the Coran itself a divine command is not unfrequently repealed by the substitution of another. And, on the same principle, the whole body of previous Revelation is superseded by the Coran, at least in so far as the Moslem world is concerned; for there are not wanting intimations in the Coran that, at least in the earlier stages of his teaching, Mahomet enjoined the continued observance of the Tourât and the Gospel by both Jews and Christians.

But besides simple contradictions, there are various inconsistencies in the Coran which the believer understands as only apparent, the deeper and real sense being in harmony. Indeed, an under-current of spiritual truth, in proportion as hid from ordinary perception, is held to be one of the chief glories of the Revelation. "In such cases," says Sprenger, "the student marvelled neither at the acuteness, nor yet at the audacity, of his Master; he marvelled rather at the wisdom of God which could draw forth such mysterious interpretations. Theology, in fact, had now made such happy progress, that men looked on common sense as a mere human attribute,—the reverse being that which they expected from the Deity!"

The Arabs were themselves unread, excepting in the rude literature of the desert. But the victories of Islam soon brought within its pale a multitude of Jewish and Christian tribes more or less versed in Scripture and traditional lore. Of this, the Christian portion was dropped almost untouched. Between Christianity and Islam there was little in common. The Coran itself contains no doctrine peculiar to Christianity, if perhaps we except the Resurrection from the dead, and the Life to come; and even these are travestied and cast into the mould of rabbinical legend. Mahomet's notion of the Messiah was largely conceived under the influence of Jewish prejudice; and the very rare and obscure references to such subjects as the descending "Table" or Supper of the Lord, and the Seven sleepers of Antioch, are after the same legendary type. Thus the points of contact are apparent rather than real. The convert from Christianity must needs cast away his old associations and all that was peculiar to the Christian religion; his traditions and his literature disappeared with his conversion. It was not till, in the obscurity of the Middle Ages, Christianity became dialectic, that it showed any affinity to Arab literature; and then only with that school among the Mahometans, which had engrafted its teaching upon the Greek philosophy.[1]

Far otherwise was it with the Jewish faith. By reason of his hostile relations with the Jews at Medina, it is true that Mahomet hated and denounced the whole race with a bitterness which he never displayed towards the Christian. But his book and his system were not the less cast in a thoroughly Jewish type. The histories and legends, the precepts and ceremonial, of the Coran are largely adopted from the Old Testament and Rabbinical tradition. Islam, thus sympathising closely with Judaism, was capable of copious illustration from it. Indeed, a large portion of the Coran cannot be properly understood without some knowledge of the biblical and rabbinical sources which inspired the Prophet. The Jewish converts, then, were not severed, like the Christian, from all sympathy with their old traditions. And these, easily accessible to the Mahometan commentators and genealogists, were eagerly devoured and reproduced by them, often in a distorted form so as to suit their own ends and the national taste. Hence the flood of Jewish tale and legend which forms a distinguishing mark of the literature of Islam.

This important consideration is well known to the Mahometans themselves. Ibn Khaldûn thus writes :—

The Arabs were a people without literature or science, rude and unlearned. When that longing after knowledge which is natural to humanity arose in their hearts, they betook themselves to the People of the previous Book, and sought information from them. These were the adherents of the Tourât (Old Testament) consisting of the Jews and such Christians as adopted their faith. But the adherents of the Tourât who lived amongst the Arabs were as rude as the Arabs themselves, and possessed on such subjects no other knowledge than that gained from tribes who professed to follow the Scriptures. Amongst the most important of these were the Himyarite (Christian) converts to Judaism. Although these, on coming over to Islam, adhered rigidly to Mahometan doctrine, yet, in all things not dependent on Moslem dogma, they held also to their old teaching, especially

[1] The connection between Arab philosophy and Christian literature is interestingly discussed in the essay on "Arab Peripateticism," in *Three Essays on Philosophical Subjects*, by T. Shedden, M.A. London, 1866.

to the stories concerning the origin of the world, and the former prophets, and the prophecies of future events and wars.—Sprenger, iii. p. cix.

The chief patron of Jewish commentators was Ibn Abbâs, son of the Prophet's uncle. Born while Mahomet and his kinsmen were shut up under the ban of the Coreish in the Hâshimite quarter of Mecca, he was yet a boy when the Prophet died. Powerful in make, he was clear in intellect, energetic, arrogant, but crafty and variable. Like his father Abbâs, he followed wind and tide; and, at first attached to the side of Aly, went over, on Aly's death, to the Omeyyad dynasty. In politics a cypher, he ruled with despotic power in matters spiritual.

Ibn Abbâs revised his own edition of the Coran with the aid of Zeid (editor of the recognised version), and collated it with the recensions of Ibn Masûd and others. He numbered its verses, its words, and even its letters. Profoundly versed not only in tradition, but in the poetry and dialects of Arabia, he found little trouble in mastering his difficulties by construing this word in its Himyarite, and that in its Ethiopic sense. Jewish legend he borrowed from Kab the Rabbin, a Himyarite of Jewish parentage, who was converted to Islam on the reconquest of Yemen under Abu Bekr, and afterwards settled at Medina. From him, and from another converted Jew named Wahb, also from Yemen, Jewish legend was thus copiously drawn, and became embodied in the stream of Mahometan tradition.

Ibn Abbâs himself was called the "Arab Rabbi." It is related that Mujâhid went three times over the Coran with him, dwelling upon each word. He appears to have held certain esoteric views which he communicated only to his most intimate friends, saying,—Were I to teach *all*, the people would stone me. His high social rank was not in those days inconsistent with his assumption of the office of teacher. He held public lectures on the Coran and, according to the custom of the time, was stormed by his auditors with questions and difficulties,—enigmas to them, but trifles to him. As we have seen, he left a mass of manuscript notes. Thus Ibn Abbâs acquired a prodigious influence in the development of theology: he is the father of exegesis, and his lectures form the mould in which all the Commentaries of the first four centuries were cast. The notes of his scholars grew into bundles, and these into books. Successive editors added fresh traditions professing to be derived through independent channels from Ibn Abbâs, interpolating at the same time other matter of their own. The six editions of his Commentary now extant, are thus full of variations, and even of contradictory interpretations; but they all undoubtedly contain (as Sprenger thinks) much matter that really proceeded from Ibn Abbâs himself

There are no other early Commentaries extant: but we know, by the quotations taken from them, that there formerly existed many such. Sprenger gives a list of thirty in the first two centuries. The most ancient grew out of the School collections; and while he thinks it possible that these may have preserved a greater number of early traditions than the *Sunna*, it is at the same time admitted that they were less critical and trustworthy. Tabari (*d.* 310) carefully sifted the labours of his predecessors, and preserved what he deemed to be serviceable. A large fragment of his work is in the Library of the Asiatic Society in Calcutta.

All the Commentaries are based on traditions exactly similar to those already described, setting forth the exposition of difficult passages as given by the early leaders of Islam. They contain also detailed narratives of those incidents in the Prophet's life which, as is supposed, gave occasion to special revelations, or are otherwise alluded to in the Coran; and in this lies their service to the Biographer of to-day. The later Commentaries contain nothing historical that is not borrowed from these earlier works. Special schools took up different branches of the subject. The Grammarians busied themselves with the text of the Coran long before Tabari; some wrote treatises on the rare expressions; others on the difficult phrases. Some illustrated the style; some the sense of the darker, and others the rhetoric of the more remarkable passages; and these grew up side by side with the historical exegesis. The labours of both classes have been made use of by Thalabi (*d.* 427), the best Commentator now available, and by Baghawi (*d.* 516), whose work has been lately lithographed at Bombay. By their time the exegesis had become dialectic, and that style has prevailed ever since. One of the most valuable collections is the Commentary compiled by Soyuty as late as the tenth century.

The following is Sprenger's estimate of the value of the Commentaries, as bearing on the biography of Mahomet:—

We are concerned here, not with the degree in which these writers illustrated the Coran, but with the accounts they contain of Mahomet's life. The traditions of this nature which they have preserved are so numerous and so detailed, that (excepting only the two points of chronology and the campaigns) it were an easier task to compile a life of Mahomet without the "Biographies," than without the "Commentaries." Their statements, further, are somewhat more trustworthy, for they were committed to writing at a much earlier period; and if their prejudices were deeper and more numerous, still they were of a different sort. They were also obliged to make mention of many incidents because of allusions to them in the Coran, which the Biographers pass over in silence. The Commentators, taken in conjunction with the Biographers, even where both are untrue, often enable us to pierce deeper into the real facts, or at least to detect untruthfulness. Moreover, although the Commentaries may have been always taken advantage of by the Biographers, it is not a sufficient reason for us to pass by the former, simply that the latter may have taken from them as much as served their own purpose (iii. p. cxx.).

The judgment of Sprenger is here, as elsewhere, tinged with prejudice against the Biographers. The Commentators in fact, as guides, are singularly unsafe. To illustrate allusions in the Coran they are ever ready with a story in point: but unfortunately there are almost always several different tales, all equally apposite to the same matter. The textual allusion, in fact, was often the father of the story. What was originally perhaps a mere conjecture of supposed events giving rise to an expression in the Coran, or a simple surmise in explanation of some passage, by degrees assumed the garb of fact. Thus the imaginary tradition and the facts which it professes to attest, often rest without doubt on no better authority than that of the verse or passage itself. Moreover, whatever really valuable traditional matter is to be found in the Commentaries, was made use of by the Biographers. We can hardly point to a single event in the life of the Prophet, which rests upon the independent evidence of the Commentators.

We come lastly to the GENEALOGIES; and this portion of the Essay appears to us by far the most curious and important contribution made to the early history of Arabia for many years. Dr. Sprenger has brought a close and philosophical analysis to bear on the copious materials amassed by him with great labour and erudition. The subject is somewhat recondite, and from its technical character not very easy to illustrate. But it has points of great interest, and we shall be pardoned if in seeking to place before the reader the results of Sprenger's researches, we are led into some detail.

At the outset, one is startled by finding an absolutely complete and accurate list of the warriors who followed Mahomet to the field of Bedr. We can tell off "the three hundred of Bedr" as exactly as, from its muster-roll, we could tell off three companies of H.M.'s army now proceeding to Abyssinia. Whence this absolute certainty in the midst of the otherwise dim and varying statements of tradition? The answer is plain. The heroes of Bedr were the nobility of Islam. They had cast in their lot with the Prophet when his fate was trembling in the balance, and this their first victory was the corner-stone of his claim to the temporal as well as the spiritual sceptre. Moreover, in the first days of the faith, the distinction was accompanied, as we shall see, with certain very substantial temporal benefits.

Another claim to the homage of the Moslem world was relationship to the Prophet. We need but look around us at the respect still paid to the Syud, infinitesimal as may be his share in Mahomet's blood, to understand the strength of the feeling cherished towards the near relatives of the Prophet. Each clan counted its dignity in proportion to the closeness of its connection with the Prophet's. The Coreish was the first tribe in the Peninsula, and its glory culminated in the immediate family of Mahomet.[1] Thus, relationship to the Prophet, and service

[1] It is one of the most marked distinctions between Islam and Christianity, that this feeling never had place in the latter. Apart from the homage paid to the Virgin (which rests on other grounds), relationship to the family of Jesus was never courted as conferring Christian nobility. The Christian knew Christ "no longer after the flesh." The Mahometans, however much

rendered to the cause before it became victorious, constituted the grand warrant in the early days of Islam to riches and honour.

The dues rendered by the Mahometan provinces, and the spoils of war, which streamed from all quarters to Medina, were distributed mainly on these two considerations. Shortly after the Prophet's death, when the tithes came in, Abu Bekr, with his wonted simplicity, called the faithful together, and divided the income equally amongst them all, men, women, and children. In the first year it yielded 9, and in the second year 20, dirhems to each. Under Omar the revenue increased enormously, and he established an Exchequer with a civil list (Dewân). The stipends were then arranged according to the above considerations. First came the Widows and immediate relations of Mahomet, to each of whom was assigned the annual allowance of 12,000 dirhems; the veterans of Bedr drew 5000; other converts who had thrown in their lot with Islam before that battle, 4000 each; their children, 2000;—and so on, by regular gradation, each was classified in proportion to the strength of claim. Indeed, Omar seems at one time to have conceived the idea of bestowing largesses upon the whole Arab nation, but the intention was never carried into effect. The fruits of Mahometan conquest outside the Peninsula were at the first enjoyed by Mecca and Medina alone; and so continued until the Holy cities were gradually superseded by other centres of power and influence. Thus the Dewân, or Civil list, of Omar, an official register accessible to the public, afforded the traditionist a sure guide to the names, and partially also to the descent, of all who held a place in the history of the first days of Islam.

The record of tribal distinctions was likewise preserved and fostered by the peculiar organisation of the army. There was no arbitrary constitution of battalions; each corps was formed of a tribe, or of two or more allied tribes. When a province was subdued, a portion of the victors with their families settled in it; but the greater part returned laden with booty to one of the great

they may have magnified the supernatural character of their Prophet, still continued to know him most emphatically "after the flesh." The distinction illustrates the radical difference between the two religions.

military stations, Cûfa, Bussora, Fostât, etc., where they waited for the next campaign. When thus cantoned, distinct quarters were assigned to each tribe, or corps of allied tribes; the military rolls were kept accordingly, every tribe going up as a separate body for its pay. The officers were paid at from six to nine thousand dirhems. Every boy born in these military quarters received from his birth 100 dirhems yearly, and two measures of wheat a day,—the allowance rising with age to 600 dirhems. Such was the constitution of that force which like wild-fire overran so many fair and powerful provinces. There were individual soldiers who received their pay separately,—belonging, as it would seem, to none of the Arab tribes; but these formed the exception. Such of the tribes as did not go into the field received no pay; but largesses were often made by the Caliphs to various tribes throughout the Peninsula. The system was long maintained; and we find it adduced as a reproach to the Caliph Walîd, near the end of the first century, that he had withheld their allowances from some *Junds* or tribal corps settled in the military stations.

Before the rise of Islam, tribal distinction was the sole nobility of Arabia. Each tribe vied with its neighbour; and the rivalry was not only for victory in the field, but for the laurel of the poet and orator, pre-eminence in hospitality and munificence,—for whatever, in fact, conferred, in the eyes of an Arab, glory and honour. It is true that a new and higher nobility, that of relationship to Mahomet and service to Islam, now sprang up, before which the pride of clan waned, and finally (excepting in the Peninsula itself) wholly disappeared. But for a time the military organisation above explained fostered the tribal spirit; and thus afforded the antiquarians of the day exact and ample materials to describe the races and clans of Arabia, and trace their ancient history.

Genealogies divide themselves into three classes, the *person*, the *family*, and the *tribe*. The love of genealogies amounts in the Mahometan to a passion. There are more genealogical trees among them than in the whole world beside. The taste survives to the present day; and even in India we find clans and families who trace, or pretend to trace, their descent to the early nobility of Islam. Sprenger adduces a curious example in the Moslems of Paniput. These are composed of four castes: the descendants of Abu Ayûb (the citizen whose guest the Prophet was on his first arrival at Medina); the descendants of Othmân; Affghans; and converted Rajpoots. The first two do not intermarry with the two last. They carefully maintain their genealogical trees, in which the pedigree is followed up step by step to the founders of the family in the very age of Mahomet; in later days the births and deaths are entered, and sometimes the marriages also, with the dates. The pedigree of the Othmânite clan is carefully kept in the custody of the Nawab, the head of the house, but Sprenger does not think it really above a hundred years old. For the last seventeen or eighteen generations, that is, up to the time of Ala-uddeen Shah, when the family first entered India, the details may be founded more or less on fact. Beyond that, the descent runs through kings of Herat, Sheraz, Kafaristan, Balkh, etc., and is pure fabrication. The same is the experience of Sprenger with all the other pedigrees he has met in India. "Life in the East," he says, "is all too insecure, and under too arbitrary a government, to look for archives extending over several centuries. In the deserts of Arabia such documents are altogether unknown; and it would be childish to imagine that the minute ramifications of any tribe could be retained in the mere memory for a long series of years."[1]

It seems probable that registers of lineage, like the Paniput ones, were known at a very early period, and that the practice of keeping them soon became common.[2] These would be first compiled by their respective families or partisans, for the more distinguished heroes connected with the rise of Islam; and thus it may be concluded that when, say in the second century, the

[1] It is a mistake to suppose that the Arabs keep any long pedigree of their blood horses. The certificate they give contains merely the name of the clan, it being presumed that the purity of the blood is notorious throughout the tribe (vol. iii. p. cxxvii.).

[2] Sprenger ingeniously proves this not only by direct evidence, but by such early variations of names as could only have arisen from mistaking the form of the *letters*, and would not therefore have occurred under *oral* transmission.—*Ibid.*

pedigree of such person is traced upwards (as it invariably is) to the time of Mahomet, or indeed two or three generations beyond it, the details are founded on records of this nature, and are generally trustworthy. When genealogical study became the fashion, prodigious pains and learning were expended on the work. A Peer might as well want his armorial bearings, as a professed descendant of one of the early Moslems his pedigree; and rather than have none, it had to be invented. The contemporaries of Mahomet known by name, number no fewer than 9000. By the end of the first century, the genealogy of each one, and also of every distinguished Arab before and after, was traced up to his family and tribe, and thus connected with a pedigree reaching to Adam! Such is Arab lineage.

Next in trustworthiness comes the Family tree, which is generally grounded more or less on fact, whereas the descent of tribes is based on mere symbol or theory. The family trees of an Urban population are, from their settled habits, much longer than those of the Nomad tribes. The pedigree elaborated with the greatest known care is that of the two Medina clans, the Aus and Khazraj, which is carried back with all its links and ramifications to a common ancestor thirteen generations distant. The genealogy of the Meccan families is traced up to Fihr Coreish, twelve generations; but Cossai, the fifth in the line from Mahomet, is the earliest of whom it can be said with any confidence, that he is an historical personage.[1]

[1] Sprenger indeed (though apparently admitting Cossai's historical reality) casts suspicion on the pedigree of the Abd Shams branch of the Coreishite tree,—a branch descended from a common ancestor only *three* removes from Mahomet; but his doubts seem without any good foundation. The case is this:—

According to the received genealogy, Hâshim, the great-grandfather of Mahomet, had three brothers: the descendants of Hâshim and of one of his brothers, were called the Hâshimite clan; those of the other two brothers were called the Abd-shamsite clan. The latter was strongly opposed to Mahomet, and from it sprang the Omeyyad dynasty, between which and the Prophet's immediate family there was long nursed a mortal rivalry and hatred. The Abd-shamsite branch (very naturally) was never admitted to equal pensionary privileges with the Hâshimite, notwithstanding that Othmân (who belonged to it) interceded for them. Hence Sprenger con-

It will thus be understood that the lower links of the family pedigrees are for the most part historical. The more distant are legendary, and consist of names assumed from the floating elements of popular tradition, or invented sometimes on grounds of probability, sometimes without any grounds at all, for the purpose of fitting in the family pedigree to the great tribal system of the Peninsula.

The family tree of Mahomet, embracing the Coreish and allied stocks, was naturally the first elaborated, and hence became the standard by which all other pedigrees were framed. The succession ascends through eleven generations from the Prophet to Fihr Coreish, the progenitor of the clan or family; and through eight generations more to Nizâr, the common ancestor of the tribe

cludes that they did not really stand in the same close relation to Mahomet as represented by tradition, but that this fictitious relationship was conceded with two objects,—first, to add prestige to Mahomet's own branch, the Hâshimite, by the establishment of a close connection between them and the "patrician," or leading clan of Abd Shams; and secondly, with the view of aggrandising the latter powerful family when its representative Othmân was Caliph, by placing their privileges on a par with the Hâshimite. Both reasons (besides their inherent improbability) are inadequate to account for the unanimity of tradition on the descent of Abd Shams and Hâshim from the same father. It is inconceivable that the relationship could have been invented in the way supposed, or that Othmân could have effected a change in the popular tradition so many years after Mahomet's death, without eliciting fierce declamation from his bitter antagonists, the adherents of Aly. It would certainly in after days have been paraded as a leading charge against the Omeyyads by the Hâshimites and Abassides, in whose cause it would have been a most effective argument. Yet not a whisper is on any side raised, casting doubt on the common descent of the four stocks from Abdmenâf. There were aged men alive when Mahomet reached power, to whom the facts must have been known at a time when all claims to relationship with his family would be closely canvassed; and in a society like that of Mecca, where the ties of blood were paramount, it is hardly possible to conceive the deception supposed by Sprenger gaining currency. The truth is, that the prominence assigned by the Coran (S. VIII., v. 42) to the relations of Mahomet, originated at a time when the Abd-shamsite branch was waging open war with Mahomet; that family was consequently on political grounds placed on a lower scale than the Hâshimite; and the difference was perpetuated in the practice of Mahomet himself, and in the civil list of Omar.

or combination of tribes acknowledging that name. The Beni Nizâr embraced many subordinate tribes, numbering, as Sprenger thinks, in the time of Mahomet, some five or six million souls, and connected mostly by no other tie than the common name. They spread over the whole of Northern Arabia and Mesopotamia: but the Beni Modhar, or branch to which Mahomet belonged, had their seat chiefly on the shore of the Red Sea. Descending the line, each progenitor's name represents a gradually diminishing affiliation of tribes. Thus the Beni *Nizâr* (tribe of Nizâr, the patriarch of the race) include the distant stocks of Bekr and Taghlib. The Beni *Modhar* (son of Nizâr) exclude these, while embracing the numerous groups sprung from Modhar through *Cays Aylân*,—which latter again are excluded from the branch next in descent bearing the appellation of Beni *Khindif*;—and so on till the circle is narrowed to the families descended from Fihr, that is, the "Coreish."

Each tribe had thus its central column of descent; and the more remote the progenitor, the more numerous the tribes ranging under his name. This central column was termed by traditionists, "The Genealogical Tree," *Amûd al nasab*: and with this stem, every clan of the race supposed to spring from the common patriarch was connected, by assigning its descent from some of the successive progenitors;—the common appellation of the group of sub-tribes thus affiliated together being generally assumed as the name of such progenitor. It became necessary, therefore, to provide that the number of links in the tree of a sub-tribe reaching up to the progenitor under whom it branched off from the main tribe, should correspond with the number of links in the parent stem. For example, as there are eighteen generations between Mahomet and Modhar, it follows that in the family tree of the Beni Suleim descended from Aylân son of Modhar, there must be seventeen links. These removes are termed *Cúdûd* (close relations) in the technical language of the genealogists; and as they were drawn out merely to square with a theory, so they were no doubt filled up generally in an arbitrary manner. If real names were not forthcoming for a gap, names were invented, and so the synchronism maintained.

It was a gigantic undertaking this work of the Genealogists. They not only traced the pedigree of every individual of note among the contemporaries of Mahomet and their followers to its family in some one of the Arab tribes, but they affiliated every tribe to its proper stem, and gave the name of every progenitor through whom step by step each tribe was connected with one or other of the great races which peopled the Peninsula. This vast genealogical web was woven up to the earliest epoch: but it is only the lower threads of it that we can count upon with certainty. The warp and woof of the ancient portion is almost entirely pure invention. Certain great ancestral names were current in Arabia as the patriarchs of the various affiliations of tribes, and constituted, we might say, the ethnological symbols of the nation. These were laid down as the ruling pattern. Upon it again was delineated the position of every tribe, in accordance with the popular tradition of descent, the received symbols of ancient ethnological division, or the mere fancy of the genealogist. The outline was enriched with sketches of battles, inter-tribal rivalries, or personal incident, grounded no doubt for the most part on legends current among the Arabs; some of them, perhaps, like the episode of Antar, adopted from the recitations of Bedouin rhapsodists, or based on the remains of ancient poets; but excepting for recent periods, all equally fabulous. The details are given with the greater freshness and confidence the farther the scene is shifted back into the depths of the past; for there imagination had the freest scope.[1]

The Bedouin nation exhibits a phase of society ever restless, ever changeful. A tribe would divide itself in search of pasture or in consequence of some dispute or other trivial cause, and the branches would wander far from each other, separated probably ever after, and forgetful of their common origin. The fortune of war sometimes exterminated a whole clan, or forced it into combinations which gave a new colour to the genealogical traditions. On the other hand, success in war, or a

[1] An article on the *Tribe Poets* of the Arabs, by Goldzihet, has just appeared in the *Asiatic Society's Journal*, illustrating the vast number of these poetic Deivans, April 1897, p. 325.

prosperous settlement, would attract fresh adherents; and loosely floating clans, thus coalescing with a larger tribe, would merge in it their individuality. Hence the surface of society was ever shifting, like the changing collocations of a kaleidoscope. When we remember that in Arabia there were no archives wherein the record of such changes could be preserved, it is vain to look for any trustworthy outlines of the more remote periods of Arabian history. Some great tribes may, no doubt, have maintained their individuality through many ages,—as the Mozeina and Suleim, for example, have done from the time of Mahomet to the present day: but it must also be remembered that Islam has introduced an element of fixity into the social system unknown before, and we must not estimate the restless chaotic state of ante-Mahometan Arabia by its subsequent history.

All then that we can look for in the elaborate and voluminous work of the Genealogists, is a picture of tribal distinctions as they existed in the time of Mahomet, with an approximate sketch of the great families to which each was affiliated. We may here and there catch a glimpse of the grand outlines of race reaching back to some antiquity, but further than this we cannot attach weight to the system. It was based on the mere theories of the Genealogists who, when fact was wanting, contrived, invented, fabricated, without stint or scruple, both the outlines and detail. The vast pile of Arab genealogy, beautiful and symmetrical as it is, melts away, like a fabric reared of snow, before the merciless criticism of Sprenger.

Scrupulous in harmonising the steps and "distances" in the various pedigrees, the Genealogists were incapable of weighing wider and more important considerations. The rate of natural increase was not observed, or was cast aside as irrelevant. Thus (an example cited by Sprenger) two tribes, numbering in the time of Mahomet perhaps 50,000 souls, are traced to progenitors who were cousins of Cossai,—*i.e.*, only five generations back! The theory is perfect; but the facts divergent.

Sprenger was for a time puzzled to find a reason which would account for these strange inconsistencies. His first hypothesis was, that the genealogical system was elaborated from the local tradition current among the tribes settled in and around Cûfa, and such like military stations; but the insignificant place assigned to the clans occupying the vicinity of those stations, made him abandon the idea. He then hit on what appears to be the correct theory. The genealogical system and all its details were elaborated at Medina from the Dewân, or salary and pension rolls of Omar, and from such tradition as was still alive on the spot; and hence the various clans inhabiting the vicinity of that city were brought out in strong relief. As the tribes near Mecca and Medina supplied their full contingents for the wars, the names of the individuals would be entered in detail and each tribe assigned a separate heading in the Dewân. In proportion to their distance from Medina, the contingents furnished by the several clans were fewer and smaller. Perhaps bodies of not more than a dozen or twenty men would be supplied by some of the remote southern tribes; several of these small sections would probably encamp together, and in the Dewân would be clubbed under one head. Thus, the importance and numbers of a tribe to the eye and pen of the Genealogist would be magnified by its closeness to Medina; while distance would cause the outline to shrink, and the detail to become obscure. Medina, in short, was the centre of the perspective. Thus the tribes near at hand had a much longer and more elaborate pedigree than those far off, because each clan had a far greater number of groups to account for, and in tracing these up to a common progenitor a corresponding number of steps must be allowed; on the other hand, where the groups were few, the rule of "distance" curtailed proportionately the pedigree. In accordance with this very scholarly theory, we find the family pedigree of Medina itself the longest, and that of Mecca the next. As these were the centres from whence the Genealogists took their survey, they were also the spiritual centres of the Peninsula. Tribes were ennobled as they had any connection or interest with the Prophet or with his home; and so, in this view also, the genealogical perspective would radiate from those Holy places, producing an exaggerated effect on what was near, and diminishing that which was far off.

The chief use of the Genealogists' labours to the Biographer is that, besides legends of ancient battles and exploits, they have treasured up contemporary notices of the various tribes, and especially of the events which brought them into contact with Mahomet. They carefully note, for example, the names of any early converts who visited him; the part taken by the family or tribe in the campaigns of the Prophet; treaties made, or privileges conceded, etc. There is, in particular, an entire section of Wâckidi's work devoted to the Deputations which, chiefly in the 9th year of the Hegira, visited Medina from all parts of the Peninsula to tender their allegiance to Mahomet. Every surviving scrap of a treaty or letter connected with the Prophet was sacredly treasured up by the parties whom it affected; these were all sought out by the Genealogists, and transcribed in connection with the tribes to which they relate. In this way the historian finds much light thrown on the progress of Islam throughout Arabia, and even obtains casual glimpses of Mahomet himself.

We have said nothing of the steps by which the Arabs endeavour to connect themselves with the patriarchs of the Old Testament. The grand division of the nation into two races, Northern and Southern, and the classification of tribes as proceeding from the one or from the other, is no doubt based on solid ground. The record of dynasties and leading events in Southern Arabia has a special claim on our attention, because we know that it was the custom there to inscribe public events on monuments, which must have been available to the collectors of tradition, although illegible to us now from the loss of the key to the Himyarite alphabet. But although this consideration may enable us to grope some little way farther back in Yemen than in the rest of Arabia, it still leaves the elaborate genealogies of patriarchal times a mere fiction of the Traditionists. These identify Cahtân, the mythical progenitor of the Southern tribes, at the distance of thirty-six generations, with Joktan of the Old Testament! And similarly the Northern tribes rejoice in having traced the links which connect their Prophet, and consequently the entire Northern race, with Ishmael and Abraham, the founders of the holy Kaaba. But Mahomet himself discountenanced such fictitious pedigrees. "Beyond Adnân," he said, "none but the Lord knoweth, and the genealogists lie";—a safe enough judgment, seeing that Adnân (grandfather of the Nizâr spoken of above) was at the distance of two-and-twenty generations. In point of fact, the whole of the patriarchal genealogies are an undisguised plagiarism from the Old Testament and the legends of rabbinical writers. They are based upon nothing native, not even upon Arab legend. All that is not derived from the Rabbins of Yemen and Syria is pure invention. Sprenger has clearly proved this; and the large Jewish element is admitted by Mahometan writers themselves.[1]

There is yet one remaining source from which we derive information regarding Mahomet and the early Arabs, namely, the writings of contemporary POETS. No doubt poems and fragments of poetry, earlier even than the age of Mahomet, were handed down for a time in greater or less purity. Tradition makes frequent mention of Poems, satirical, eulogistic, and elegiac, having direct reference to the Prophet; and these are constantly quoted both by Biographers and Genealogists. But a class of *littérateurs* sprang up whose art and pride it was to counterfeit the compositions of the older poets. By study and practice they acquired so close a perception of the style and language of each period and of the individual poets who flourished in it, that they could assign any line quoted at random to its proper author, and could even coin verses cast so delicately in the desired type that the most careful scrutiny of the scholar could not always detect the forgery. Thus later pieces often circulated in the name of early authors, whose poems were interpolated with foreign matter blending with the original too closely to be afterwards separated.[2]

[1] See Muir's *Mahomet*, vol. i. pp. lxx., cvii., and cxciii.

[2] This of course is quite distinct from the more innocent practice of the Biographers, who put speeches and sayings of their heroes sometimes into the shape of verse. The use of the direct form of address fostered the concoction of set speeches, like those of the Roman historians. Deception was not intended in either case. No one imagines that the speeches pretend to be in the exact words, but merely in a supposed likely form.

For this cause, though these ancient poems undoubtedly contain much that is authentic, little reliance can be reposed on them as historical evidence.

The life of the poet Hammâd Râwy, as given by Sprenger, shows how fashionable was this practice, and is also a fair illustration of the manners of the age. Taken prisoner as a child, he regained his freedom and joined himself to a band of robbers. Amongst their booty he one day chanced upon a collection of poems by a Companion of Mahomet. He was charmed, committed them to memory, abandoned robbery, and devoted himself to literature.

On his being asked by Walîd, the Caliph, why he was called *Râwy*,[1] he replied, "Because I know by heart the works of all the poets thou art acquainted with, or hast heard the names of; and those thou never heardest of I know better than the poem thou art best acquainted with is known by thee! Moreover, if a piece of poetry be recited, I will tell thee with certainty to what period it belongs." "By thy father, thou art a prodigy of learning! How many verses dost thou know by heart?" "A vast number! For every letter of the alphabet I could recite a hundred long Casîdas (idyls) rhyming with it. And besides poems since the rise of Islam, I know innumerable ancient fragments belonging to the days of heathendom." The Caliph commanded him to be presented with 100,000 dirhems.

"When Hishâm succeeded to the Caliphate," says Hammâd, "I kept to my house in Cûfa, because he had before shown enmity towards me. After a year I began to go out, and one Friday repaired to the Mosque for prayer. At the door I was met by two policemen with an order that the Governor desired to see me. Filled with apprehension, I begged permission to go first to my home, and bid my family a last farewell: but even this was not allowed me. I went trembling to the Governor, who showed me a despatch from the Caliph, desiring that I should be sent forthwith to the Court at Damascus. Richly supplied, and mounted on a swift dromedary, I reached Damascus in twelve days. Then, taken straightway to the palace, I entered a gorgeous hall, the

[1] *I.e.* Narrator of stories or traditions.

floor and walls inlaid with gold and marble. The Caliph, robed in purple, reclined on crimson pillows: the air was redolent of musk and amber, which lay before him on a golden chafing dish; occasionally he shook the dish, and filled the hall with the sweet incense. He accosted me kindly, and desired me to approach. I kissed his foot, and in doing so caught a glimpse of two slave girls of superlative beauty standing behind, their great ruby ear-rings glancing by their cheeks like fire. He asked after my welfare; a verse had occurred to him, and he had sent for me, he said, because he could not remember where it was to be found. I told him at once, and was able, moreover, to repeat the entire poem. He was delighted, and desired me to present my request. I asked that I might have one of the slave girls. He gave me both, and commanded that I should be placed in a lordly chamber, to which I at once repaired, and found attendants and everything I could wish in readiness. Likewise, he gave me a present of 100,000 dirhems."

There are circumstances related by Sprenger of this poet which show that at times he was little better than a drunken and debauched sot. On one occasion he was found in a shameful state when sent for by the Caliph Mansûr. But rapidly recovering himself, he recited an elegy with such pathos as to draw tears from the Caliph's eyes.

The Caliph Mehdie once held a gathering of learned men versed in poetry. To Hammâd he presented 20,000 dirhems, remarking that he composed good poetry, but that when he recited ancient poems he inserted many spurious verses. To another, called Mofaddhal, he gave 50,000 dirhems, because he recited ancient poetry with critical accuracy.

This Mofaddhal tells us that Hammâd exercised a most pernicious influence in giving currency to erroneous and altered versions of the ancients poets. Mere errors learned critics might correct; but this man was so thoroughly versed in the peculiar language of Arabic poetry, and knew the style and manner of each poet so closely, that he could compose whole poems in the spirit and language of some ancient bard, and then give them out as authentic. These became mixed up with the genuine remains, and as such were handed down; thus it was only the most practised critic who could discriminate between what was genuine and what was interpolated (vol. iii. p. clxxiv.).

It is easy to perceive that, under such circumstances, whatever illustration the habits and adventures of the early Moslem heroes may receive from the remains of contemporary Poets, can be of no certain service in contested points of history. As a matter of fact, one meets in their statements with frequent anachronisms and allusions to later events, which of themselves would suffice to shake our faith in them as a sure ground of historical evidence.[1]

The concluding pages of Sprenger's essay are devoted to general considerations of much interest. He traces an essential element of early Moslem literature to the proud supremacy of Islam; and illustrates the position by the analogy of the English in India. He says:—

One must live and labour in India to know what grand aspirations this feeling of supremacy gives birth to. The heroic defence of Lucknow, and the daring siege of Delhi in 1857, prove to what a pitch of greatness such influences lead. The pride of belonging to the dominant nation makes every man a hero; and, even in the domain of mind, produces, under such circumstances, the elements of greatness. In the days of Muâvia, the finest provinces of the world, yielding a revenue of forty millions sterling, were at the feet of the conquering race. All non-Moslems were their slaves. And it was this that moulded the heroic character of the Mahometan world.

Supremacy begat assurance. But notwithstanding the nobility of sentiment thus produced, the Moslem world never rose above the rank of the barbarian. One must not mistake ability in practical life, and the natural products of Fancy in the province of speculation and religion, for the cultivation of Reason. Resembling other people of the age, the Mahometans altogether failed in the faculty of Observation, and the inductive exercise of the Reason. Like children, Imagination had the sway over them, and the more the spiritual life wrought in them, the more phantasy obtained the mastery over sound reason: for, the overweening assurance with which they aspired to the highest regions of science was based neither on true knowledge nor on the cultivation of the understanding, and attained to no other result than the bold imagery of an unbridled imagination,—inventions and lies. Excepting momentary displays of nobility and self-abnegation, it entirely failed in imparting Humanity, and the sense of Truth and Right.

---

[1] See examples in Muir's *Mahomet*, vol. i. p. lxxxiv.

These views are of the highest importance, coming as they do from so philosophical a thinker as Sprenger; and they are founded on truth. But in estimating the causes of the results above described, Sprenger has not sufficiently adverted to the repressive influence of Islam itself, which placed shackles on the independence of human thought, stifled free inquiry, and imprisoned the intellect in the close dark cell of dogma and superstition.

Of the incredible mass of inventions and fabrications called into life by the stir and spiritual activity of the first sixty years of the Hegira, Sprenger considers that but a small proportion has survived, and this the portion most congenial with the Mahometan mind. The principle of natural selection, as it were, preserved the materials which suited the requirements, tastes, and prejudices of the people, and dropped the rest. Tradition, as we now have it, was, in other words, moulded by the people themselves.

"Thousands and thousands occupied themselves with handing "down traditions. In every Mosque they committed them to "memory, and rehearsed them in every social gathering. All such "knowledge was the common property of the nation; it was learned "by heart, and transmitted orally. It possessed therefore, in the "highest possible degree, the elements of life and plasticity. Bun-"sen has discovered the divinity of the Bible in its always having "been the people's book. If this criterion be decisive, then no "religion has better claim to be called the *vox Dei*, because none "is in so full a sense the *vox populi*. The creations of the period "we have been considering possess this character for hundreds of "millions of our fellow-men; for modern Islamism is as far removed "from the spirit in which the Coran was composed, as Catholicism "is from the spirit of the Gospel; and modern Islamism is grounded "upon tradition. But in tradition we find nothing but the Ideal, "Invention, Fancy. Historical facts, however they may have been "floating full of life among the people in the days of Ibn Abbâs and "the other founders of genealogy, were trodden under feet:—because "men wished to remove every barrier which stood in the way of "self-glorification. And, of the thousand inventions which every "day gave birth to, only those were recognised as true which most "flattered the religious and national pride" (vol. iii. p. clxxviii.).

There is a depth of truth and reality underlying these sentiments. But it is needful to guard them by two considerations. In the first place, however much the nation was inclined to hand down only those traditions which symbolised with the tendency to glorify Mahomet, and also glorify the reciters themselves, and to throw the rest away,—still there were, fortunately for history, causes at work which to a certain degree counteracted the process. For Mahometan society was, from the earliest period, riven into factions which opposed each other with a mortal strife, and consequently were not indisposed to perpetuate traditions which would aid their cause by depreciating their adversaries; and partizanship has fortunately thus secured for us a large amount of historical fact which would otherwise have sunk unnoticed. Moreover, in the Biographers themselves we are bound to acknowledge the honest endeavour to draw with faithfulness the lineaments of the Prophet's life, though naturally in exaggerated outlines as seen through the medium of a supernatural atmosphere.

As regards tradition being "the voice of the people," Bunsen would hardly have recognised the applicability of his dictum to a state of society in which the range of thought was sternly circumscribed, and its results dwarfed, by the pains and penalties of a system far more powerful than the Inquisition,—a system which proscribed the free exercise of thought and discussion as incompatible with the profession of Islam. The result is not the *vox populi* in any intelligible sense.

The plastic period, however, soon passed away, and left the material of tradition in a form which, though it might be worked up into any of the Theological systems, could not henceforward in its own substance be altered. This is well stated by Sprenger in his concluding paragraph:—

"The time of creative activity, the gestation era of Moslem "knowledge, passed away. Hajjâj choked the young life in its "own blood; and the Abbâside dynasty with kingly patriotism "sold the dearly-bought conquests of the nation, first to the "Persians, and then to Turkish slaves, with the view of procuring "an imaginary security for their throne. And thus there arose "for the spiritual life also a new period.[1] Already Wâckidi had "begun to work up into shape the mass of his traditionary stores, "and busy himself in the department of scholastic industry. In "the Schools one could as little affect now the material of tradition, "or alter its nature, as attempt to change the organism of the new-"born child. However arbitrary might be the invention of the "Mirâj (Mahomet's heavenly journey), and other fabrications of "the first century, they still formed in this way the positive element "and soul of religious, political, and social life. The Schools, as "always, confined their exertions to collecting, comparing, abbre-

[1] The political history (Sprenger adds in a note) developed itself in this wise: "First came the civil contests, which maintained the warlike spirit of the nation in its integrity, and the party leaders were forced to follow the people's will. In the end, that party gained the ascendancy which was the most unscrupulous, but the one which knew best how to administer the finances,—namely, the descendants of Abu Sofiân, the once arch-enemy of Islam. At the conclusion of the civil wars, the object of the rulers was to break the arrogance of the people. The grand instrument for that was Hajjâj. This man, from A.H. 75 to 95, ruled from Babylonia to Scind, and in that interval massacred 120,000 persons. Simultaneously, the court entered on a course of boundless extravagance with all it usual consequences.

"I have elsewhere (*Asiatic Society*, vol. xxv., p. cxxxiii.) shown that this oppression and extravagance precipitated the new direction which the Moslem mind was under any circumstances destined to take. Already before the end of the first century, the ascetic turn and the theosophy inseparable there-from, a combination styled among the Arabs *Sûfeism*, had arisen. This made rapid strides; and in the end of the third century was already itself the subject of learned works. As might have been anticipated, the Moslem world has carried this system to the utmost extreme. Their Sûfies outstrip in every point of view both the Indian *Jogies* and our own Monks. The asceticism of the Sûfies is more systematic, their pantheistic teaching deeper and more consistent, and their vices more enormous, than those of any other people. Spinoza and Schelling are left far behind by Ibn Araby. But we must not be deceived by appearances. It requires small advancement to found a deep metaphysical system. Captain Latter was once telling me of the Burmese literature and theosophy, when I expressed my astonishment at the latter. He remarked:—'The same is found in all rude nations; for the supernaturalist has no need of learning; dreams suffice for him'" (p. xxix.).

No one is better qualified than Sprenger himself to trace the history of Mahometan philosophy, and especially its Sûfieism. It would be a subject worthy of his pen.

"viating, systematising, and commentating. The material was "altogether divine; and any unprejudiced historical inquiry, any "simple and natural interpretation of the Coran, any free judgment "on tradition or its origin, was condemned as apostasy. The only "task that remained was to work up, in scholastic form, the "existing material: and in this way was developed a literature "of boundless dimensions, which yet at bottom possessed nothing "real. The whole spiritual activity of the Mahometans, from the "time of the Prophet to the present day, is a dream: but it is a "dream in which a large portion of the human race have lived; "and it has all the interest which things relating to mankind "always possess for man" (vol. iii. p. clxxx.).

It is strange that a subject surrounded, as we might imagine, with so many attractions for the Oriental student, as that of the early records of Islam, should be almost unknown in India. For the English, it may be said that they have in this country small leisure from the busy work of life, to turn aside to the task; and for the Hindoo it would prove hardly a congenial subject. But to educated and thoughtful Moslems, as involving the first beginnings and the development of what they hold to be most sacred and precious, one might have expected the study to be fraught with the deepest interest. The sword of Omar no longer checks freedom of inquiry; the right of private judgment and of discussion is here in India as free as the air we breathe; and yet their mind would seem still dwarfed and scared by the apparition of that sword. The honest and enlightened Moslem ought not to shrink from a domain of inquiry, opening up a long vista of history and literature, which he naturally looks up to with veneration, and portions of which he may justly regard with pride. The Christian missionary, too, might draw many a polished shaft from the same armoury. In our seats of learning, a branch of study so closely affecting an important section of the human race, and India in particular, might find a fitting place. And upon the learned men who preside at those Institutions devolves the responsibility of rendering that study popular in our Indian empire.

THE INDIAN LITURGY

From the "Calcutta Review," 1850

1. *Origines Liturgicæ; or, Antiquities of the English Ritual, and a Dissertation on Primitive Liturgies.* By the Rev. William Palmer, M.A. of Worcester College, Oxford. 2 vols. London, 1845.

2. *Origines Ecclesiasticæ; or, The Antiquities of the Christian Church.* By the Rev. Joseph Bingham, M.A., formerly Fellow of University College, Oxford; and afterwards Rector, etc. 9 vols. London, 1844. Books XIII., XIV., XV., relating to Divine Worship in the ancient Church.

3. *The Syrian Churches: their Early History, Liturgies, and Literature, etc.* By J. W. Etheridge. London, 1846.

4. *Duáe Amím kí Kitáb, aur Sákriminton kí Tartíb, aur Kalísiya kí Dusrí Rasm aur Dastúron kí England aur Ireland kí muttahid Kalísiyá ke taríque ke mutábiq. Aqád-i-Dín ke Sáth.* Agra. Yatîmon ke Chhápe kháne men chhápí gai. 1847. [The Book of Common Prayer, and Administration of the Sacraments, and other Rites and Ceremonies of the Church, according to the use of the United Church of England and Ireland. With the Articles of Religion. Agra. Printed at the Orphan Press, 1847.]

WHATEVER comes into constant and familiar contact with man, and yet commands his respect or veneration, must of necessity exercise a wide and a deep influence upon him. Nor is this effect confined to the leading features of such an agency; it attaches also to its minor and even accidental details. Thus, legendary stories connected with the people's faith, and ritual formulæ wrought up into religious practice (as in the case of the Hindoos and Mohammedans), strike their counterpart upon the national mind. Thus, too, a system of jurisprudence will gradually impart something of its colour and character to a people long under its action. And the minute and unessential points, the adventitious custom and ceremony, or the chance cast of phraseology, will not be without even their corresponding effect. The stamp will impress not only its leading figures, but also its finest tracery, and faithfully perpetuate even flaws and defects.

The principle might be followed out into an endless detail of illustration. National poetry, such as the myths of Homer and Hesiod, no doubt imparted many broad, as well as delicate and intangible, traits to the Grecian character. The sculpture, painting, and architecture of Greece and Rome, as they grew out of, so unquestionably have reacted in a thousand ways upon the habits and mind of the people. The labours of Jerome still influence the character of Europe. "The rich and picturesque Latin of the Vulgate," where "the Orientalism of the Scripture is blended with such curious felicity with the idiom of the Latin," has had a manifest effect upon the language, and upon the thought, of the West. "It has, no doubt, powerfully influenced the religious style, not merely of the later Latin writers, but of those of the modern languages, of which Latin is the parent."[1] The English Bible has proved an agent no less deep and wide in its results upon the British tongue and mind; and every day tends only to strengthen its hold, and spread more widely the ramifications of its influence. The subject is one which presses with solemn responsibility on the translators of the Scriptures into the languages of India.

But it is to another department of religious literature that we mean at present to apply these considerations. The assimilative action upon the mind is probably as great in the daily, or weekly, services of the Church, as in any other department; indeed, greater perhaps, since the constant use of liturgies must, in proportion to its frequency, deepen and perpetuate the

[1] Milman's *Christianity*, bk. iv. ch. iii. vol. iii. p. 465.

lineaments of thought and language proper to themselves. We doubt not that the Missal and the Prayer-Book in their own field may vie with the Vulgate and the English Bible, in the depth and peculiarity of the features they have stamped.

In this view, the version of public service which the Episcopal Church shall give to the native Churches of India, assumes a deeply serious aspect. The form of liturgy, and the language in which it is clothed, will have a large share in influencing the character of that part of the community, nay of India itself. Constantly recurring,—repeated more frequently than the Bible itself,—every ceremony, every prayer, each individual word, will exercise an important effect, always present, steadily extending, and ever reproducing itself as a fresh agent of good or evil. It is, then, a matter of great interest that each form and every word should be weighed with care; that no ground be given for false impressions; and that all the associations and ideas resulting even incidentally from the version, should be in a right direction. The national mind will form itself around the type which we place before it, and take impression of the deformities as well as of the beauties of that type.

Labouring under this strong conviction of the importance of Vernacular liturgies for India, we have taken up the Urdoo translation of the Book of Common Prayer, noticed at the head of this article. But, before passing its merits under review, we purpose to consider generally the adaptation of the Anglican liturgy to the Native Churches of India; that is to say, how far a close translation, as the present professes to be, is suited to the position and requirements of the Native community. In this periodical, the use, or the absence, of a set liturgy is of course an open question; and we propose to consider it at present, simply as it affects those who have already decided in the affirmative.

Now it is perfectly evident that there are certain grand features of human nature and of Christian life, which are the same under every clime and in every age. Fallen nature requires the same confession of guilt from the American, the Russian, and the Hindoo, from Augustine and Justin Martyr, as from the Christian worshipper of Great Britain. And the same may be said of the expression of faith, hope, love, thankfulness, and all such topics. In these particulars, there exists no distinction of time and place: so long as they are offered by mortal man, the subject-matter of address to God must come under the same categories. In so far, then, as these are concerned, it would appear that no exception may be taken to the transference of approved forms of worship from any time and from any nation, to any other age or people.

But, admitting that this argument holds good with reference to devotional forms of the nature just specified, still a large portion of religious services must (if at all commensurate with the necessities of the worshipping body) have reference to their *special* circumstances. And it is evident that, as such circumstances are accidental, liable to vary in different times, countries, and societies, and not essential elements or adjuncts of Christian life and doctrine, so should the forms of public devotion be brought to bear upon them, vary accordingly. Now such accidental elements are, surely, often of too great importance, and frequently occupy too large a share of Christian life, to be passed over *sub silentio* in the public prayers. One or two illustrations of what is meant may assist likewise in bringing out the necessities of the Indian Church.

Our first illustration shall be taken from that department which, in general, least affects the character of prayer, viz., the phenomena of nature; and among these we select (perhaps in this land the most important) the setting in of the rains. Now, if this be found deeply to call forth the affections of the people, their fear, hope, and gratitude, it is not only the duty of the Church to raise these affections heavenwards, but it is her surest course in order to win her way into the hearts of the nation. Throughout a great part of India, life is so directly and manifestly dependent on the periodical rains, that, if the Heavens even for a short period delay their vivifying flood, a season of intense suspense is excited, and anxious aspiration to the Lord of all animates, as with one breath, the whole body of the people. The public feeling should surely, at such times, be inwrought into the language of public prayer; and, "Give us this day our daily bread" should be amplified, so as to suit and come up with the overwhelming exigencies of that critical period.[1] And here, too, are valuable opportunities for the expression of Faith in the Ruler of the natural world, and of Dependence upon Him in whose hand our breath so absolutely is. And when the long-expected rain does at length descend, how does the heart leap for joy, and what a season for the offerings of Gratitude! Foreigners as we are, does not the overflowing of thankfulness upon such occasions add a new flood of life even to our devotions? How intensely then might such feelings be called forth in the Hindoo's breast, whose sustenance, home, and very existence, depend upon the gracious providence! And does not the bursting life, the new creation of salient energy covering the late expanse of torrid dust, the smile of grateful nature instantaneously clad in a new vesture of verdant freshness, speak in living terms the language of religion and devotion, which might well find an echo in our prayers? How manifest the hand of the Almighty! How patent His goodness! How striking the type

[1] In the ancient Liturgy of St. Mark, there are prayers for the waters of the river Nile to be raised to their just measure.—Palmer, vol. ii. p. 86. The rise of the river in Egypt, analogous with the rains of India, thus formed the subject of *special* prayer in that land. So Tertullian: "Quoniam tamen Dominus, prospector humanarum necessitatum, seorsum post traditam orandi disciplinam (i.e. orationem Dominicam), 'Petite,' inquit, 'et accipietis'; et sunt quae petantur pro circumstantia cujusque, praemissâ legitimâ et ordinariâ oratione quasi fundamento; accidentium jus est desideriorum; jus est superstruendi extrinsecus petitiones," etc.—De Orat. C. IX. And no doubt the Church, as well as the private Oratory, should make provision in prayer for such necessitous contingencies, as may lie out of the beaten track, and yet form subject-matter of devotional aspiration to the people at large.

[I have been much struck with the ancient *Liturgy of the Nile*, as given in a recent number of the Asiatic Society's *Journal*. It is used at the period of the river's rise; and the prayers, responses, and appropriate lessons (as Ps. lxv.) show what use can be made of times and seasons, as touching the nation's heart, and giving us a lesson for India. The article, by the Rev. G. Margalivich, is well worth reading. Art. XV., *Journal Asiatic Society*, October, 1896.]

of the Resurrection from the dead! These ideas are germane to the human mind, wherever such phenomena appear: and the Prophet of Islam well knew how to turn them to account.[1] Are *we* to give no vent to such aspirations and feelings, or at best to put them off with Collects for "such moderate rain and showers," as may suit the slowly developing energies of an English spring, but only mock the rapid and gigantic agencies of heaven that usher in the Indian year? Ah, that faith, that dependence, that gratitude, those living witnesses of the nature and goodness of God,[2] have a latent habitation even in the idolatrous Hindoo's heart. They are chords of Nature's own; and at the inspiring seasons of anxious longing for the early and the latter rain, or of grateful joy at its reception, if swept by the skilful hand of the servant of the God of Nature, even the Heathen's heart will respond to the touch.

Our second illustration shall be from the moral and spiritual phenomena which surround our native Churches. Themselves patches of verdure but lately reclaimed from the vast wilderness, —tiny oases encircled by burning and interminable deserts,— they have a deep and a portentous interest in the neighbouring tracts, which are ever threatening to swallow them up and restore the wilderness again to its howling uniformity. Shall there, then, be no adaptation to this state of things, beyond the literal adoption of a liturgy which has grown up in a smiling country, with no howling wastes and wilderness to spoil its verdure? The Churches of India are planted in the midst of Heathens and Mohammedans: they are as drops in an ocean of idolaters and professed opponents of the Christ. A very large section, therefore, of their hopes and fears, their joys and sorrows, their

[1] Some of the most beautiful illustrations of the Resurrection, for instance, are derived by Mohammed from this source: "It is God, who sendeth the winds, and raiseth the clouds, and We drive the same into a lifeless country; and thereby quicken the earth, after it hath been dead. So shall the resurrection from the dead be."—Coran, Sura xxxv. 9. Comp. also S. vi. 100, xxv. 49, xxx. 24, xliii. 11.

[2] "Nevertheless he left Himself not without witness, in that He did good, and gave rain from heaven, and fruitful seasons, filling our hearts with food and gladness."—Acts xiv. 17.

duties and responsibilities, in fine of every department of the Christian life, both as individuals and as Churches, must have a direct reference to this isolated position, and to the masses which close them in on every side. In England there are no idolaters or Mohammedans, and but a scantling of professed blasphemers; and therefore the liturgy of England has little or no reference to such peculiar circumstances. Now the question arises, Is such a liturgy as this to be, without any adaptation whatever, imposed upon the Indian Churches? Is the only reference which their public devotions shall have to this subject of highest interest and daily concern, to consist in the passing allusion in the opening of the prayer "for all sorts and conditions of men," or to the still more passing and general allusion in the Litany, and to the Collect used once every year "for all Jews, Turks, infidels and heretics?"[1] If so, one of the widest and most important requirements of the native Church, affecting her internal trials and her external duties;—one in which, perhaps more than in any other, does she need to be constant and earnest in her common and united supplication, in which, more than in any other, should she feel her weakness and seek for strength, is altogether excluded from her public devotions!

The subject might have been followed out to much greater length, but we rest satisfied with these two simple illustrations. Omissions of equal importance, certainly many of perhaps less pressing moment, might have been pointed out; while certain portions of the service might have been shown to be inapplicable to the present state of the native Churches, or their use at least injudicious. Some of these may be incidentally brought forward in the course of this article. Meanwhile it is necessary to inquire how far it is possible and expedient to alter and adapt the Liturgy to the use of the Indian Church. While not insensible to the delicacy and difficulty of the subject thus set before us, nothing short of

[1] See the Collects for Good Friday, or Parasceve, in the Romish ritual. The use of such prayers, on the ecclesiastically appointed anniversary of the crucifixion, seems to be connected with the prayer for "mercy, even to the perfidious Jews," who crucified our Lord. By association of ideas, Pagans, heretics, Turks, and infidels are also commended to mercy.

the settled conviction of its paramount importance would have compelled us to enter upon it.

To what standard, then, shall we appeal, in order to arrive at a fair and just conclusion? The Churches of Europe have long existed among a population, in name at least entirely Christian; and the Syrian and other Eastern Churches have been for ages too devoid of life to serve for examples to us. But the state of the Church in the primitive age closely resembled that of our Indian Churches, in being encompassed by heathen opposition. This antagonism gradually died away, till, in the fifth and sixth centuries, Christianity had, at least in outward appearance, assimilated the entire mass of the Empire to herself. Now, if we can show that, even in the fifth century, an important part of the prayers of the Church was still directed to those who were not within the pale of the "Faithful," we shall have made out a strong case for a similar concession to the Indian Churches, whose present position so much more urgently demands it.

We shall produce, then, passages from Augustine to show that, in this century, heathens and unbelievers were still prayed for by the Church. In opposing the Pelagian heresy, and combating the doctrine that salvation is the result of free-will, and not the work of God's grace, Augustine brings home to his opponent the prayers of the Church in which the grace of God was implored on behalf of infidels, inquirers, and heathen nations.[1] He appeals to his antagonist, whether he would not himself respond Amen to the call of the priest, exhorting the people to pray to God, or else himself praying "ut incredulas gentes ad fidem suam venire compellat." Now, to warrant repeated notices couched in such language, it is manifest that there must have been very special and frequent petitions of the kind alluded

[1] Quando audis sacerdotem Dei ad altare exhortantem populum Dei orare pro incredulis, ut eos Deus convertat ad fidem; et pro catechumenis, ut eis desiderium regenerationis inspiret. Again, Numquid, ubi audieris sacerdotem Dei ad ejus altare populum hortantem ad Deum orandum, vel ipsum clarâ voce orantem, ut incredulas gentes ad fidem suam venire compellat, non respondebis, Amen?—*Epist. ad Vitalem.*

Augustine was made Bishop of Hippo, A.D. 395, and lived and wrote until A.D. 430.

to, and commonly used *ad altare*, *i.e.* as a part of the liturgical, or Communion, service. If such was the case when the Roman world was nominally Christianised, we may safely conclude that similar petitions occupied even a more prominent position when it was professedly heathen.

That the Ante-communion service of the third, fourth, and succeeding centuries contained prayers for inquirers and others without the Church, is clear from every account remaining to us, and indeed from the very constitution of the service of that period. The prevailing order of service was founded upon the classification of the people (which is traced to the third century) into the "Faithful," and the "Catechumens." The "Mystical liturgy," or Sacramental service, was exclusively reserved for the Faithful; that part of the worship (the εὐχαὶ πιστῶν) was common to the Faithful alone, and might not be heard, much less shared in, by any unbaptized adherent of Christianity. The Lord's Prayer was confined to this part of the service; and was termed *par excellence* εὐχὴ πιστῶν,—The prayer of the Faithful. The use of it was permitted to no unbaptized person.[1] So careful and thorough was the exclusion of intruders, that, in the third

[1] There appears, however, to be no ground for holding that the prayer itself was *concealed* from the uninitiated, as Palmer would seem to imagine (Orig. Lit. vol. i. p. 14). We can see no ground in his references for thinking so. Indeed, how could the prayer have been suppressed when it existed in the Bible, which *all* were encouraged to read in the Vernacular? (Bingham's *Antiq.*, bk. x. ch. i. s. 7); and they could not but see its prominent insertion on divine authority there. Besides, it was openly referred to, and specifically quoted in the sermons and writings of the early Christians, *e.g.*, of Tertullian, Cyprian, Chrysostom, Augustine; and these were common to believers and uninitiated.

Its *use* was certainly restricted to the "Faithful"; and it was introduced only in *their* service, every particular of which was surrounded by a curtain of mysterious secrecy. But this is quite another matter. The prayer was well known; though its position, and accompaniments in the "tremendous mystery," were not divulged.

The catechumen was not taught this prayer till on the eve of baptism, under the impression that it was wrong to encourage him, while yet unregenerate, to make use of petitions suitable only for the regenerate children of God.

and fourth centuries, the Sacramental liturgy was as secret from the uninitiated vulgar, as the Masonic institute in our own day, from those without.[1]

But, though excluded from the prayers of the Faithful, the Catechumens and others were not uncared for. A separate and previous service was held on their account, termed εὐχαὶ κατηχουμένων, *missa Catechumenorum*—the service of the unbaptized. This comprised the entire worship as it preceded the "Mystical liturgy," or Sacramental service; it was intended for the edification of all; and to it heathens, heretics, and candidates for baptism, had equal and indiscriminate access.[2] Its order consisted of the singing or repetition of Psalms, the reading of the Scriptures, the sermon, and prayers. There are clear notices that, in the fourth century, the latter embraced a prayer for the Energumens, "or possessed," a prayer for the Catechumens, and one for the Penitents. The penitents were parties who had been baptized, but, having relapsed into sin, were excluded from the Communion, although sometimes the higher ranks were permitted to be present at its celebration. With this exception, each class quitted the assembly on the conclusion of the prayer appropriated to itself. Chrysostom says that the prayers were common betwixt the priest and the

[1] But we have good authority for holding that such secrecy did not originate long before the third century. Bingham (x. 5, s. 3), writing on the subject, says, "the first beginning of it seems to have been about the time of Tertullian, for he is the first writer who makes any mention of it." And the quotation from Tertullian refers only to the exclusion of heretics and heathens from the sacred celebration, not to the prohibition of divulging what was then practised.

[2] Bingham (bk. xiii. ch. i. s. 3) quotes a rule of the Fourth Council of Carthage, interdicting the Bishop from prohibiting any one to enter the Church and hear the Word of God, whether Gentile, heretic, or Jew, until the service of the Catechumens was ended. And it is evident from other Canons, and from the sermons of Chrysostom, that the privilege of general access was freely acted upon, and was regarded by the ministers as a valuable opportunity for attracting outsiders to the faith. The Council of Laodicea, indeed, forbids heretics to enter the house of God; but the authority is singular. It was probably a *local* rule, or may possibly have applied only to the Sacramental service.

people;[1] he gives specimens of the petitions for the Catechumens, and likewise of the Deacons' prayer, containing supplications which they were encouraged to put up for themselves.

Both the *penitents* and *catechumens* embraced large classes of men; practically, in fact, all who were not heathen or faithful. Of the penitents, for instance, there were two divisions; the hearers, who departed with the catechumens, and had probably neither the desire nor suitableness of character for further fellowship; and the kneelers, who were nearer restoration to the privileges of the faithful, and stayed to receive the prayers of the Church and the Bishop's benediction.[2] So among the "catechumens" there were both the simple inquirers or parties interested in Christianity, and also the "competentes," or candidates ready for baptism; and for each, as occasion required, separate prayers were put up.

Now it has been already shown that the heathen were specially prayed for; so that, in the fourth and fifth centuries, the prayers of the Church unquestionably had a particular and direct reference to all classes of men according to their spiritual requirements. It is not indeed affirmed that the arrangement or classification of the prayers then prevalent was perfect, or worthy of entire imitation: on the contrary, the operative effect of baptism entered banefully into the system. But what we do say is, that the Church intended to provide special prayers for each class suited to their state, and actually did so in conformity with the views then prevalent. Such was the case without controversy at the period selected for our analogy, when the sceptres of Kings and the thrones of Bishops had already intermeddled with the purity of Christian discipline: and, the higher up the stream we ascend, the greater must have been the distinction between the Faithful, the inquirers and the unbelievers; and the more distinct

[1] *Καὶ ἐν ταῖς εὐχαῖς δὲ πολὺ τὸν λαὸν ἴδοι τις ἂν συνεισφεροντα, καὶ ὑπὲρ των ἐνεργουμενων, ὑπερ των ἐν μετανοια, κοιναὶ καὶ παρὰ τοῦ ἱερέως καὶ παρ' αὐτῶν γίνονται εὐχαι, καὶ παντες μιάν λέγουσιν εὐχην, εὐχην την ἐλεου γέμουσαν.* —Tom. IX. Hom. XVIII.

[2] The penitents are sometimes divided into four classes,—*flentes*, *audientes*, *genu-flectentes*, and *consistentes*. This division is evidently borrowed from that of the catechumens, into *audientes*, *genu-flectentes*, and *competentes*.

the provision of the devotional services suitable for each, had we the materials for tracing it.

It is evident, then, that to satisfy those who take the primitive Church as their guide or model (and we know of no other period in the annals of the Church which can at all furnish an analogy suited to our position in India), the Church services should have respect, directly and prominently, to each main division of men (spiritually considered) within and without her pale.

Let us now see how far the liturgy of the Church of England fulfils these conditions with respect to the Native community. The penitential discipline has ceased, and with it the prayers appropriated to Penitents; there is now no service for the Catechumens, neither is there any part of the Common Prayer which has any special reference whatever to Inquirers, or Candidates for baptism. And it has been already shown that the petitions for the Heathen, or unbelievers, are but perfunctory and allusive.

The entire English Prayers are emphatically εὐχαὶ πιστῶν, the worship of Believers. The service is throughout strictly adapted to the people of God. The whole body of the aspirants, it is taken for granted, are regenerate, or at the least seriously professing Christians. In this respect there is betwixt it and the Communion service no difference. The latter, from the inspiring nature of its symbolical ceremony, is characterised by a more intense devotion, and by a depth of feeling suited to the sublimity of the occasion. But both are composed alike of such aspirations as true Christians alone can offer. Particular petitions may have a more general character; but the whole drift of the service leaves no doubt of this. The confession betokens sincere repentance; the absolution, though couched in approvedly general terms, holds forth the assurance of pardon: the Te Deum is the triumphant profession of a Christian's faith and adoration: and the Creed[1] is an explicit declaration of belief. Every essential

[1] The repetition of creeds in the liturgy, was not introduced till the sixth century (Bingham, vol. v. p. 140). They were never repeated in the early Church (except immediately before baptism), either in the communion or ante-communion services.

It is to be noted that the forms alluded to above (excepting the absolution) are "to be said of the *whole* congregation."

grace of the fully-developed Christian character is here presupposed and brought into play. There is, in fact, in the English Church, no Ante-communion service in the sense in which that term was understood in the early Church; and were a disciple of Chrysostom suddenly to appear in our Assemblies, the most decisive test to him, of what we have advanced, would be the repeated use of the Lord's Prayer. "How can anyone," he would exclaim, "say *Our Father*, but a regenerate and real Christian, an adopted *child* of God?"[1]

The liturgy of our Church is thus a service for an avowedly Christian community. It has no reference whatever to such bodies as the Hindoo and Moslem communities amongst whom in this land we dwell. And yet these we are seeking to win. It is the grand object of our Missions to attract the Gentiles to the light of the gospel.[2] And still when, as curious visitors or

[1] However unreasonable thus to confine the Lord's Prayer, or to deduce such strict application from the term "Our Father," yet no doubt there is a depth of serious and instructive meaning in its limitation by the early Church to real Christians. The Lord's Prayer is, in truth, the most absolute and unlimited expression of Christian faith and resolution. For instance, "Thy will be done," can only in sincerity be said, when it is the *intention* or *desire* of the speaker's heart to do that will, as well as to see it done by others.

So also, as has been well remarked by Chrysostom, the petition, "Forgive us our trespasses, as we forgive," etc., is a solemn denunciation upon himself by the suppliant who sends it forth from an unforgiving heart: *φοβερὸν γάρ ἐστι τὸ λεγόμενον* ("Αφες ἡμιν, κ.τ.λ.), *καὶ σχεδὸν εἰπεῖν, τοιοῦτο πρὸς τὸν Θεὸν βοᾳ, ὁ τοῦτο λέγων,* 'Αφῆκα, Δέσποτα, ἄφες . . . *εἰ ἐκράτησα κράτησον, εἰ μὴ ἔλυσα τῷ πλησίον, μηδὲ σύ λύσης τὰ ἐμὰ ἁμαρτήματα. ἐν ᾧ μετρω ἐμέτρησα, ἀντιμετρηθήτω μοι.*—Tom. V. Hom. in Pæn. Chrysostom pressed these opinions so strongly, that some were for omitting the qualifying clause in their repetition; but this he did not approve of.

[2] That Hindoos, Mohammedans, and unbaptized inquirers do frequently, from curiosity, or more hopeful causes, resort to our churches, is notorious. To quote from the first Missionary report we happen to take up, Mr. Menge, of Goruckpore, writes as follows: "I have, for the last few months, observed with pleasure, that several Zemindars, Brahmins, and others, have been attending my Hindustani service in the Station Church on a Sunday; and my Pundit, who, six years ago, would not come near the Mission compound, has regularly for more than a twelvemonth gone to my Sunday afternoon service, and taken off his turban without my saying a word to him on the subject.—*Report of the Church Missionary Society* for 1849, p. 76.

serious inquirers, they do come to our churches, we make no provision for them in the devotional services. There is no single reference to them in our public prayers. We neither pray for them, nor invite them to join in praying for themselves. Now here is a great and a palpable want, a serious blank, without controversy, in our liturgy for the wants of India.

Surely some alterations, some adaptations, additions or modifications, are absolutely required. How, then, are these to be made?

The spirit of the Church of England is professedly favourable to necessary changes. We learn this from the preface to the Prayer-Book: "It hath been the wisdom of the Church of England, ever since the first compiling of the public liturgy, to keep the mean between the two extremes, of too much stiffness in refusing, and of too much easiness in admitting, any variation from it;—and it is but reasonable that, upon weighty and important considerations, according to the various exigency of times and occasions, such changes and alterations should be made therein as, to those that are in place of authority, should from time to time seem either necessary or expedient."

Recognition of the propriety of change upon necessary occasions is thus in strict conformity with the principles of our Church, and with the practice of the fourth and fifth centuries. The several Bishops had then free authority to alter their forms of prayer at pleasure; though a general uniformity of substratum was preserved.[1] The earliest restriction, indeed, which we find to have been put upon this authority, is found in the Canons of the third Council of Carthage (of which Augustine was a member), which simply prescribe that, "before any one uses new prayers, they be first examined by the more learned brethren."[2] Such being the practice of those earlier

[1] The authorities on this point are clear, and need only be referred to. Bingham, *Orig. Eccles.*, bk. ii. ch. vi. s. 2, and bk. xiii. ch. v. s. 1; Palmer, *Orig. Liturg.* Introd. vol. i. p. 10.

[2] "Et quicunque sibi preces aliunde describit, non eis utatur, nisi prius eas cum instructioribus fratribus contulerit."—*Con. Carthag.* iii. ch. 23; Bingham, xiii. 5, s. 7. So in the African code (c. iii.), it is appointed "that such prayers as had been approved by the synod (τὰς κεκυρωμένας

days, and such the slow advance of uniformity, we may easily understand that the still earlier stages of the Church's history would even more decidedly favour the facility of effecting needed alterations.

Our "provincial Bishops," then, under sanction of the Metropolitan, should, according to the authorities just quoted, make such changes in the Indian liturgy as may appear indispensable. This opens up the interesting subject of the appointment of Bishops expressly for Native churches. It is evident that the Metropolitan of India, and other Presidency Bishops, are never likely to be suited either by habit or education for such a task. They are little versed in the vernacular languages, and have no intimate acquaintance with the prejudices and views of their Native flocks. But subordinate Bishops, possessing the requisite qualifications, might be selected; and if it were thought injudicious or unwise to accord the title of Bishop, the new prelates might, after the German style, be termed Superintendents. The exigencies of the Native churches, so rapidly increasing in India, will soon demand, according to the Episcopal system, such superintendence, whether European or Native; for, even apart from their want of Native experience, our present Bishops have no leisure, from the vast and important duties connected with their European labours, to apply themselves, with the necessary concentration of purpose, to this subject.[1]

ἐν τῇ συνόδῳ ἱκεσίας), should be used; and that none, which opposed the faith, should be introduced, ἀλλ' αἵτινες δήποτε ἀπὸ τῶν συνετωτέρων, συνηχθησαν, λεχθήσονται. Upon these passages Bingham remarks: "This seems to be the first beginning of that custom, which afterwards prevailed all over the Church, that all provincial Bishops should use the same form of prayer, that was established in the Churches of their Metropolitan" (vol. iv. p. 263).

[1] There is, of course, in these remarks not the most distant notion of depreciating our excellent Metropolitan. It is surely no affront to his truly Episcopal virtues and accomplishments, to say that he has by no means either the early or acquired associations absolutely necessary for the work now proposed. It is next to impossible that he, or indeed that any party under the present system appointed to the post, should be so qualified. And the same remark, with a similar deprecatory caution, applies equally

There is another method in which the want of adaptation we have been considering may in some degree be met, and which in actual practice is often resorted to; that is, the use of unfixed or extempore prayer. Very frequently much of the deficiency in Native congregations is in point of fact supplied by such prayers, before or after the sermon. But though this habit is partially supported by the practice of our good Metropolitan himself, and by some of his worthiest clergy even in their English ministrations, we are not sure whether some Churchmen might not yet denounce it as uncanonical and dangerous.

But surely even these should have little reason to find fault with a custom practised by some of their own choicest models in the fourth and fifth centuries. Thus Bingham, after showing that "extempore discourses were frequent among the ancients," and explaining the terms employed by Chrysostom and Augustine, relative to the Divine assistance to be looked for upon such occasions,—adds :—"And, upon this account, it was usual for the preacher many times to usher in his discourse with a short prayer for such Divine assistance, and also to move the people to pray for him."[1] Several such unliturgical prayers are quoted by the same author, as occurring not only at the beginning, but during the course and at the end, of the sermons of Ambrose, Origen,

to the good Bishop of Madras, and to the learned and Venerable Archdeacon of Calcutta. A Native of the country would of course surpass all others in a close knowledge of the habits and requirements of the Native churches. But where, in a Native, are we as yet to find the rare conjunction of qualities which would warrant us to place in his hands the Episcopal crook? where that learning, devotion, humility, judgment? Closely connected with this subject, and indeed with the whole drift of the article, is the degree of independence ultimately contemplated for the Indian Episcopal Churches. Are they to be a mere appendage of the Church of England? Is the centralisation of Rome to be copied by Britain, in the case of her colonial Churches? or is there to be any, and what, degree of independence? The agitation of the question may be premature; but it is of the last importance for their ecclesiastical rulers to have sound principles in view regarding it. They should not, even at this early stage, compromise such principles by any injudicious intolerance, or by giving precedent to the dangerous theory, that *uniformity in details is essential.*

[1] Bk. xiv. ch. iv. s. 13.

and Augustine. The latter especially, always closed his sermon by a prayer,[1] which he varied "as the matter of his sermon required." After quoting a piece from Augustine,[2] Bingham observes :—

I have related this passage at length, because it shows us . . . what sort of prayers those were, which they commonly made before sermon, viz. not the common prayers of the Church (as some mistake, who measure all usages of the ancient Church by the customs of the present) ; but these short prayers for the assistance and conduct of the Spirit, to direct both them and the people in speaking and hearing (vol. iv. p. 561).

Now, could any possible harm or disorder ensue, if such occasions were improved for supplying the deficiencies in our public prayers already pointed out? Why should not the addition of unliturgical prayers be openly permitted at the discretion of the minister, after the due performance of the fixed service? To answer this important question,—and that upon grounds which should carry weight with those who now advocate the exclusive use of forms,—let us inquire into the early use of liturgies, and the original authority for them: the subject is large, yet its importance forbids us from passing it by. In one respect the subject is at first sight unpromising. Opinion is generally extreme on either side. Thus one writer holds that the ancient

[1] Commencing, "Conversi ad Dominum."

[2] The passage alluded to is so excellent and relevant, that we introduce it here entire :—"The Christian orator should pray both for himself, and others, before he begins to teach ; that he may be able to speak those things that are holy, just and good ; and that his auditors may hear him with understanding, with willingness, and with an obedient heart. To this end, before he looses his tongue to speak, he should lift up his thirsting soul to God, that he may be able to discharge what he has imbibed, and pour forth to others that wherewith he has filled himself: and this the rather, both because we and all our words are in the hand of God, who teaches us both what to speak, and after what manner to speak." He also quotes Luke xii. 11 and 12 :—"Take ye no thought how or what ye shall speak," etc., with the same application.—*De Doctrina Christiana*, iv. 51.

How often we find what are virtually prayers, quietly introduced in their preaching by clergymen who would not otherwise dream of using an unliturgical prayer, recorded or extempore, either at the beginning or close of their discourses.

Jews, our Saviour, His Apostles, and the primitive Christians, never joined in any other than pre-composed set forms; it being impossible to conceive that if the joint use of extempore prayers had been ever practised by the Apostles and first Christians, it could so soon have been laid aside. He, therefore, concludes that the joint use of pre-composed set forms was fixed by the Apostles in all the Churches they planted, and that, by the special Providence of God, it has been preserved as remarkably as the christian Sacraments themselves.[1]

And here is a specimen of the contrary view:—" No such thing " as a prescribed form of prayer appears to have been known in " the Christian Church for several hundred years after Christ." Again: " We think it perfectly evident that no forms of prayer, " no prescribed liturgies, were used in the apostolical age of the " Church. . . . Would not all this be manifestly absurd, if " public prayer had been by a prescribed liturgy in Basil's days? " The truth is, it is evident that extempore or free prayer was " generally used in the primitive Church, and continued to be " used until orthodoxy and piety declined, and the grace, as well as " the gift, of prayer greatly diminished. Then ministers began to " seek the best aid they could procure. The Church, however,

[1] Wheatly's *Rational Illustration of the Book of Common Prayer*, pp. 16–18. There is a rare instance of this writer's *rational* illustration, at page 10 of his work, where he holds with regard to the prayer reported in Acts iv. 24, etc. ("When they heard that they lifted up their voice to God with one accord, and said"), that "they all joined together with audible voices, which they could not possibly have done, unless the prayer they used was a *pre-composed set form*"; in favour of which view he argues at some length. But surely the whole circumstances related in this chapter give the prayer so unpremeditated and extempore a character, that we could hardly have conceived it possible to have imagined it a pre-composed form. Wheatly refuses the idea that one spoke, and the "rest joined mentally with him," which is the natural explanation; and which we find borne out by the Homilies of the English Church. Witness the Ninth Homily of the second book, where, referring to this passage, it is said, "And no doubt of it, they did not all speak with several voice, but some one of them spake in the name of them all, and the rest, giving diligent ear to his words, consented thereunto; and therefore it is said that *they lifted up their voice together*."

"at large even then, provided no liturgies." And after quoting from Augustine, the writer adds,—"Surely this could never "have happened, if the Church had been accustomed at that "time to the use of prescribed liturgies. In short, the very first "document in the form of a Prayer-Book of which we read, is a "*libellus officialis*, mentioned in the proceedings of the Council "of Toledo, in the year 633 after Christ: and that was evidently "rather a 'Directory for the worship of God,' than a complete "liturgy."

Now, such extreme views are not infrequent on either side. The liturgist appeals to immemorial practice, and the proprieties of public worship, for the exclusive use of a prescribed form; and puts down any approach to unfixed or "extempore" prayer, as an odious departure from ecclesiastical discipline. The anti-liturgist, again, exclaims that public prayer, moulded in any set form of words, is unscriptural, condemns its formal spirit and prayerless tendency, and sometimes holds it upon these grounds to be unlawful. Where either view is so rigorously held, it is vain to hope for any favour to the *via media*, which we have recommended. But both parties will bend in some measure to the authority and practice of the primitive Church; and, with this view, we propose to inquire what evidence there is of the use of liturgies in the earliest ages of Christianity, and how and when they became prevalent.

This subject has been discussed by an author already alluded to. Bingham devotes three chapters of his learned work expressly to its consideration. Invaluable upon whatever matter he treats for the vast mass of authorities brought to bear upon it, he is neither philosophical, nor over-critical; and his renderings sometimes want that uniform exactness, which enables the reader implicitly to rely on the impression produced by their perusal. His verdict, too, is not always strictly in accordance with the evidence; and from doubtful, and sometimes irrelevant testimony, he occasionally deduces confident, and even triumphant, conclusions. Confining ourselves to his general theory, we find it to be thus stated, that at the first,—

"Prayers, immediately dictated by the Spirit, made up a part of the ordinary service. . . . When the extraordinary Spirit of Prophecy ceased, then the rulers of the Church supplied the want by proper forms of their own composition, according to Christian prudence and discretion. And this seems to have been the true original of liturgies, or stated forms of divine service."

Such supposed forms he considers "every Bishop had at first the privilege and power to compose and order," under the independent authority which the Bishops then severally possessed. And "this privilege to frame their own liturgies," he thinks they retained for several ages. It is sufficient upon this to remark, that the only instances he adduces in proof, are of date long subsequent to the primitive age, and throw no light whatever upon the *first rise* of stated forms of prayer.

To account for the subsequent uniformity of the various liturgies, which each Bishop had thus originally to frame for himself, Bingham states that,—

"In after ages, Bishops agreed by consent to conform their liturgy to the model of the Metropolitical Church of the Province to which they belonged. And when the Roman Empire began to be cantonised, and divided into different kingdoms, then came in the use of national liturgies, whose use was commensurate to the bounds and limits of their respective nations and kingdoms" (bk. xiii. 5, sec. 2).

But the several Councils to which he refers in proof of this assertion belong to the sixth century.[1] In fact, he admits that the rudiments of this discipline were *first* laid in the French Churches; for in the Council of Agde, a canon was made about the year 506, "that one and the same order should be equally observed in all Churches of the Province, in all parts of divine service." But we shall immediately see that a very considerable uniformity prevailed in the fourth century; and for this, Bingham accounts just as little as he does for the first rise of liturgies.

There is another treatise, however, of a more philosophical character, in which this subject is handled in a really scientific and conclusive manner, namely, the "Dissertation on Primitive Liturgies" prefixed by the Rev. William Palmer to his *Antiquities of the English Ritual.* The plan here followed is eminently

[1] Agde, A.D. 506; Gironde, 517; Braga, 573.

simple and original. It is that of ascending from present liturgies and known facts up the stream of time, and noticing every allusion met with, in analytic and backward progress, with reference to the country and ecclesiastical jurisdiction of the writer. Bingham commences at the primitive age with an assumed position, which he brings regularly down with him. Palmer assumes nothing but what is known, and therefore proceeds along his argument with sure and certain step.

At the outset, he rejects the assumption of an original and common type,—

"It seems to have been assumed by the learned, that there was originally some apostolic form of liturgy in the Christian Church, to which all the monuments of ancient liturgies, and the notices which the Fathers supply, might be reduced. Were this hypothesis supported by facts, it would be very valuable. But the truth is, there are several different forms of liturgy now in existence which, as far as we can perceive, have been different from each other from the most remote period. And with regard to the propriety of the Apostles instituting one liturgy throughout the world, it may be observed, that it is quite sufficient to suppose that all liturgies originally agreed in containing everything that was necessary for the due celebration of the Eucharist; but that they adopted exactly the same order, or received everywhere the same rites, is a supposition equally unnecessary and groundless" (vol. i., Introd. p. 6).

Instead, therefore, of "attempting to reduce all the liturgies and notices of the Fathers to one common original, he has rather sought for the original by a reference to acknowledged facts." Beginning with existing monuments, he traces them backwards. Thus, taking the liturgy of a country, he inquires whether there be any trace of a different form having existed before it; and upon the liturgy which, *primâ facie*, is found to be the prescriptive rite, he brings to bear all the notices of public worship found in the Fathers *of that country*, or its immediate neighbourhood. It will be easily perceived, that a species of co-incidental proof may thus be obtained, at once conclusive and unexpected. In now attempting to place before the reader an illustration of this line of argument, it must be premised that the term *liturgy* is employed by Palmer "in the restricted sense it generally bears in the writings of the ancients, viz., as denoting *the service used in the celebration of the Eucharist.*" In other words, it means the sacramental ritual, to the exclusion of all ante-communion prayers and acts of worship. The catechumenical service is assumed to have been performed, and the catechumens and others dismissed, before its commencement. Further, the name, even in this sense, has an uncertain meaning: as applied to later times it signifies an *embodied and recorded composition*; but in the earlier ages, where conjecture takes the place of evidence, it means simply *the order of the parts, and main substance, or tendency, of the chief prayers.*[1]

The "liturgy of the Patriarchate of Antioch" is selected for illustration, because the steps are far more complete, and the early authorities for it incomparably more numerous and detailed, than any other. Judæa, Mesopotamia, Syria, and part of Asia Minor, were included in this Patriarchate. A ritual called "the liturgy of St. James" prevails throughout this tract at the present day, as well among the Monophysites as the Orthodox;[2] that of the former being in Syriac, of the latter in Greek. These existing monuments being compared together, that of the Orthodox Church is found slightly to vary in having admitted several rites and anthems peculiar to the Constantinopolitan Church; and this is exactly in accordance with what we should *à priori* expect, from the relative position of the two Churches. There are, besides, other prayers, etc., peculiar to the Orthodox liturgy, supposed to have been introduced by the Orthodox patriarch of Jerusalem. These alterations in the original rite all occurred before the tenth century, because they are found as they now stand, in an ancient MS. at least of that date; and they are subsequent to the fifth century, as we shall presently see.

[1] Thus Palmer: "The liturgy may be old, though many *Missæ* may be modern; nay, all the prayers now existing in the Missal may be modern, and yet the liturgy be most ancient. The number and order of the parts is that which gives us the characters of the liturgy" (sec. 10, Introd. p. 168). So a *form of liturgy, meaning its main order and general substance,* is often spoken of, as ascending to a primitive age when no liturgies existed in a recorded form.

[2] That is, the Jacobites or Eutychians, and the Melchites; among the latter, however, the commanding influence of the Greek, or Constantinopolitan, Church has introduced its own liturgy; and the liturgy of St. James is now read only on the anniversary of that Apostle.

Making allowances for these and other minor differences, it is astonishing how closely the Monophysite and Orthodox texts, thus extant and in actual use, agree together.[1] The following is the collation which, to show the force of the argument, is given nearly entire from Palmer:—

"After the kiss of peace, these liturgies begin the *Anaphora*[2] with the benediction, 'The love of God . . . be with you all.' Then follow the address, *Sursum Corda*, etc.,[3] and a preface of a thanksgiving; then the hymn *Tersanctus*,[4] followed by a continuation of the thanksgiving; then a commemoration of our Saviour's deeds and words at the Last Supper; a verbal oblation; and a prayer for the Holy Ghost to sanctify the elements into the Sacraments of Christ's body and blood. Whoever compares these parts of the Orthodox and Monophysite liturgies together, will be surprised at their minute agreement in sentiment and expression, when he considers the centuries that have elapsed since the separation of the Orthodox and the Monophysites. After this, the solemn prayers for all estates of men, and for all things, succeed. The order of these prayers is a little different in the two liturgies, but their substance and the words of the petitions generally agree. . . . The difference, as to expressions, is chiefly caused by a greater fulness and variety of epithet in one, than in the other. After the prayers and commemorations follow a salutation, and a bidding prayer by the Deacon:[5] then a collect

[1] The Monophysite text for the main body of the liturgy is "perfectly ascertained, not only by means of MSS. of various ages, but by ancient commentaries, which all accord with it" (Introd. p. 21).

[2] The Oriental name for the "Mystical Liturgy," or Communion Ritual.

[3] After "Lift up your hearts" follows the invariable response—"we lift them up," etc.; after which "Let us give thanks," with its "it is meet so to do."

[4] This response, "Holy, holy, holy," by the whole body of the Faithful at an appropriate break in the thanksgiving, distinguishes all the early liturgies. It was always prefaced in the thanksgiving by a reference to the cherubim, and seraphim, and myriads of heavenly intelligences, in company with whom the Faithful upon earth join in song. The allusions to this practice are very common, and very early, among Christian writers.—*Vide* Etheridge's *Syrian Churches*, pp. 203 and 227; and Bingham, vol. v. p. 63.

[5] "Peace be with you," and the invariable response—"and with thy spirit."

introductory to the Lord's Prayer; then the Lord's Prayer and a benediction. After this comes the form of address τα ἁγια τοις ἁγιοις," followed by the people's confession of the unity of the Holy Trinity; then the bread is broken with some rites, which are not probably of any primitive antiquity, and communion takes place. After which come a prayer of thanksgiving, and a benediction of the people. The Orthodox liturgy gives these last forms at greater length than the Monophysite"[1] (vol. i., Introd. s. 1, pp. 27–29).

Such being the conformity between the existing liturgies, in present and actual use by two distinct and opposed Churches, it is next proved by various testimony reaching back to the seventh century, that the liturgy thus common to both, has from that early period been dominated by the Liturgy of St. James.

Now the Monophysites derive their origin from Eutyches, whose errors were condemned by the Council of Chalcedon, A.D. 451: and ever since, a complete separation has obtained betwixt them and the Orthodox. Each regards the other as heretical, and shuns the slightest communion with or acknowledgment of the other, as an ecclesiastical body. Whatever is common to both now must therefore, by strong presumption, have been equally common before the middle of the fifth century.

The "order, substance, and expressions" of both liturgies having thus been proved to be throughout "almost exactly the same," it is impossible to refuse assigning them a common origin earlier than the separation of the two bodies, or to deny "that they furnish sufficient means for ascertaining all the substance, and many of the expressions, which were used in the solemn *Anaphora* of the Patriarchates of Antioch and Jerusalem, before the Council of Chalcedon, A.D. 451." The common *title*, too, we may infer, is older than that Council; and this Apostolic

[1] The force of this coincidence of order, substance, and generally of expression, will be fully appreciated by comparing this description with the translation of "St. James's Liturgy," in Etheridge's *Syrian Churches*, pp. 203–227.

appellation warrants us in inferring, not only that one and the same liturgy lay at the point of divergence, but that such common liturgy was "considered even at that time to be very ancient, and therefore must really have been long used in the Church."

Now commences the last step. The scattered and incidental notices of early writers who lived in the vicinity are brought to bear upon the identity of the ancient service of the Church with that now in use, both as to order and substance.

Theodoret, Bishop of Cyprus, early in the fifth century, quotes the benediction, and adds—"This is the beginning of the mystical liturgy in all Churches."

Jerome specifies an expression still extant in the liturgy, as daily repeated by the priests.[1] He also quotes the Lord's Prayer, as every day recited in the (Commemorative) sacrifice.

Chrysostom makes frequent reference to the service and dismissal of the catechumens; after which he refers to a prayer of the Faithful, and the kiss of peace. "He mentions the benediction; the address 'Sursum Corda,' etc.; the call to thanksgiving, and the usual response 'it is just and right,' etc.; the solemn Thanksgiving, which he describes in such terms as leave no doubt of its identity with that of the Monophysite and Orthodox liturgies of St. James: the hymn *Tersanctus*." The commemorative words of our Saviour are also hinted at, and the invocation of the Holy Spirit is distinctly referred to.[2] "He speaks plainly of the general prayers, which follow. . . . He mentions the use of the Lord's Prayer, the form τὰ ἅγια τοῖς ἁγίοις, the breaking of bread, and the Communion" (pp. 30-34).

Still earlier, *Ephrem Syrus*, of Odessa, though he speaks mystically on account of the secrecy of the liturgy, yet "plainly refers to the order of the solemn prayer used in the consecration of the Eucharist. He mentions the oblation; then the prayer of deprecation and repentance to God; then the invocation of the Holy Spirit to sanctify the gifts; then the prayer of the priest for all things; then the Communion. He plainly refers to the thanksgiving, and the hymn *Tersanctus*.

Cyril, Bishop of Jerusalem, about the middle of the fourth century, gives a detailed account of the service, "with a minuteness which is most satisfactory, and which establishes in a remarkable manner, the antiquity of

---

[1] Sacerdotum quotidie ora concelebrant, ὁ μόνος ἀναμάρτητος, quod in lingua nostra dicitur, "qui solus est sine peccato."—Lib. ii. *adv. Pelag.*

[2] A paucity of reference to this part of the service is attributed to the secrecy with which it was kept from the world. And the reason is valid throughout the fourth century at least.

St. James's liturgy." An outline of his description will be found in the annexed Schedule of liturgies.

The same may be said of the complete "Clementine Liturgy," given in the 8th Book of the *Apostolical Constitutions*,[1] the order of which will also appear from the Schedule.

The process is now complete.[2] The "liturgy of St. James," in its main features, has been traced up to the Sacramental service in common and already time-honoured use in the middle of the fourth century. The order of service, the general tendency of the several prayers and suffrages, many of the identical expressions with their context, as repeated in that early age throughout Syria, correspond in inimitable coincidence and accuracy with the present liturgy. No reasonable man can withhold the conclusion, that in the main they are part of an originally one and the same ritual.

The subject cannot be pursued further in detail. We shall confine ourselves now to general results.

Following out in each case the above process, Palmer classifies all liturgies of which we have any remains or notices, into four great Families, the differences between which are ascribed to

[1] The *Apostolical Constitutions* are quoted by Epiphanius, Bishop of Salamis, A.D. 368: but it is improbable that the work then existed in its present state; and the 8th Book, which contains the liturgy, may not have been written till the fifth century.—*Vide* ch. lxxxv. of Lardner's *Credibility of Gospel History*. The liturgy, given in the *Constitutions*, bears the name of Clement of Rome; but it coincides with the substance and order of the Oriental, not of the Roman, liturgy. Palmer thinks that it "ought not to be regarded as an authentic copy of the liturgy of any Church. . . . In its order, substance, and many of its expressions, it is identical with that of St. James; but the author has evidently permitted his learning and devotion to enrich the common formularies with numerous ideas full of piety and beauty." It was apparently one of the attempts, in those days common, of improving the liturgies, which had lately begun to assume a recorded form. Palmer argues for the antiquity of this liturgy from the absence of the Lord's Prayer, which was evidently used universally in the fourth century. The circumstance is strange, but does not appear to prove any antiquity: since this prayer, from its Divine institution, must be presumed to have entered into the composition of the very earliest recorded liturgies.

[2] Palmer attempts to carry up the proof a step higher—viz., by *Justin Martyr*—to the second century. But the notices of Christian service given by that writer, are only such generalities as we might expect in any service founded on our Lord's institution, at a time when the verbal detail had not yet been fixed or recorded.

variety in the primitive type as set up by the Apostles themselves, or by others in the Apostolical age.

I. The Oriental Liturgy. Under this head come the liturgies of Antioch, Cæsarea, and Constantinople. The first we have considered at large. The second bears the name of Basil, Bishop of Cæsarea, in Capadocia, who composed it in the latter part of the fourth century; and the third (now used in the Greek Church) differs from Basil's liturgy only in "a greater fulness of idea in one than in the other, but in nothing else."

The liturgy of Basil exists in three texts—Greek, Syriac and Coptic. The latter is used by the Monophysites of Egypt, and is considered to be of antiquity beyond the Council of Chalcedon. There are hardly any early notices of this liturgy beyond the historical fact that Basil was its author. Palmer considers it to be of great importance:—"In one respect this liturgy must be considered as the most valuable that we possess. We can trace back the words and expressions to about the year 370 or 380. This is not the case with any other liturgy. The expressions of all other liturgies we cannot certainly trace, *in general*, beyond the fifth century" (sec. 2, p. 67).

The order of the *Armenian* liturgy corresponds exactly with that of Basil. It is supposed to have been derived from Cæsarea by Gregory the Illuminator, who founded most of the Armenian Churches in the beginning of the fourth century. This supposition (it can be called nothing more) affords, according to Palmer, "a very strong presumption that the order and substance of Basil's liturgy prevailed in the exarchate of Cæsarea long before his time" (Appendix, p. 191).

II. The Alexandrian Liturgy. The Coptic liturgy of (the Alexandrian) Cyril used by the Monophysites, is considered to be the ancient rite of Alexandria. It coincides in a remarkable manner with "the liturgy of the Ethiopians," and with the Greek Orthodox "liturgy of St. Mark." These three differ from all other liturgies, in the position of the prayers for all estates.[1] Very minute and satisfactory allusions to the order, and expressions occurring in it, are quoted from Isidore, Cyril Alexandrinus, Athanasius, Dionysius, and Origen.

III. The Roman Liturgy is traced by some dubious notices up to the time of Gregory Vigilius and Gelasius.[2] Leo the Great (A.D. 451) is said to have added "to the Canon certain words"; and it is therefore considered to be older than his time. There exists in the authentic writings of the primitive ages no collateral notices whatever of the liturgy of Rome. The "Ambrosian Liturgy" of Milan is supposed to have been an early offshoot from the Roman, and retains the original position of the Lord's Prayer, which was altered by Gregory.[1] There are some slight allusions to this

---

[1] *Vide* Schedule. [2] Viz., to the years 600, 538, and 492 A.D.

ritual in the works of Ambrose. The Roman rite is distinguished by the absence of any invocation, and by the position of the kiss of peace at the *close* of the service.

The *liturgy of Africa*, of which no remains have been left from the ravages of the Moslems, is classed by Palmer with the Roman because, differing from all others, it agrees with it in placing the kiss of peace at the conclusion of the Eucharist. It, however, fraternises with the Oriental form, in having an invocation of the Holy Spirit. Many incidental notices, sufficient to give a clear outline of this liturgy, are gleaned from the African Fathers, viz., Fulgentius, Augustine, Optatus, Cyprian, and Tertullian.

IV. The GALLICAN LITURGY appears to have been distinguished by the position of the prayer for the living and departed Saints, which here *preceded* the opening kiss of peace. It seems also doubtful whether it contained any prayer for the catechumens, or any prefatory prayer of the Faithful; in place of these, the Deacon, probably in the form of a litany, made prayers for the people, which were summed up by the priest. The *liturgy of Spain* is thought to have corresponded with, and been derived from the practice of France.

By a train of somewhat fine-drawn reasoning, the Gallican is traced to a supposed liturgy of Ephesus. "If this be so," adds Palmer, "we may feel almost certain that the Gallican liturgy was derived from a period of Apostolical antiquity." There is no early authority or reasonable proof to support this assumption.

It is conjectured that the early liturgy of Britain resembled the Gallican. But in the fifth century the Roman ritual gained prevalence in Ireland; and, in the sixth or seventh century, the Sacramentary of Gregory was introduced into Britain also.

Now, the main conclusions thus briefly sketched may be at once accepted. The result is this, that a fixed order of sacramentary service is traced back to the fourth century, with four grand variations, as then prevailing in as many different quarters of the Roman Empire. The lesson will be best learned by an examination of the accompanying Schedule, prepared chiefly from the details presented in Palmer's book. The English ritual is added to facilitate comparison. The Nestorian liturgy, which Palmer passes slightingly over,[1] is also inserted.

[1] *Vide* Appendix to vol. i. p. 194. A translation of the entire Nestorian liturgy is given by Etheridge in his *Syrian Churches*, p. 221. From the Schedule it will be observed that the Nestorian differs from other liturgies in placing the prayer for all men between the thanksgiving and invocation. Renandot thinks that this is the rite which was current in Mesopotamia, before the rise of Nestorianism. But Palmer discards this opinion, because

Comparative Schedule of Ancient and Modern Liturgies.

I.—Oriental Liturgy.							II.—Alexandrian Liturgy, as extant.	III.—Roman Liturgy.		IV.—Gallican Liturgy.		
Liturgy of St. James, as extant.	**Liturgy of Basil, Constantinopolitan.**	**Armenian Liturgy, as extant.**	**"Clementine Liturgy," from the Apostolical Constitutions.**	**Cyril's Description of the Liturgy at Jerusalem.**	**Chrysostom's Notices of the Sacramental Liturgy.**	**Nestorian Liturgy, as extant.**		**Ancient Roman Liturgy.**	**African Liturgy, from Notices of African Fathers.**	**Ancient Liturgy of Gaul.**	**Spanish or Mozarabic Liturgy.**	**Modern English Liturgy.**
Prayers of the Faithful.	Three prayers of the Faithful.	Scripture, etc.	Lessons.	Washing of hands by Priest.	Sermon, etc	Scripture.	Dismissal of unbaptized.	Anthem.	Anthem.	Gospel.	Collect.	General prayer, for all estates, with mention of departed Saints.
Salutation, and Kiss of Peace.	Kiss of Peace.	Dismissal of catechumens.	Sermon.	Kiss of Peace.	Prayers for energumens, catechumens, and penitents.	Prayers.	Prayers of Faithful.	Collect.	Scripture.	Deacon's prayer for people.	Scripture, etc.	Address.
Benediction.	*Benediction.*	Kiss of Peace.	Prayers of Catechumens, penitents, etc.	*Sursum Corda, etc.*	Dismissal of these.	Dismissal of unbaptized.	Salutation and Kiss of Peace.	Scripture.	Sermon.	Dismissal of unbaptized.	Dismissal of catechumens.	Confession.
Sursum Corda, etc.	*Sursum Corda, etc.*	*Benediction.*	Prayer of the Faithful.	Thanksgiving, with Tersanctus.	Prayer of the Faithful.	Prayers.	*Sursum Corda, etc.*	Sermon.	Dismissal of unbaptized.	Address.	Address.	Absolution.
Thanksgiving. Tersanctus. Contin. of thanksgiving.	Thanksgiving. Tersanctus. Contin. of thanksgiving.	*Sursum Corda, etc.*	Kiss of Peace.	*Invocation of Holy Ghost.*	Salutation and Kiss of Peace.	Verbal oblation.	Thanksgiving; prayer for all estates, and commemoration of dead; thanksgiving resumed with Tersanctus.	Dismissal of catechumens.	Washing of hands.	*Invocation of blessing* (not early).	Prayer commending oblation to God.	*Sursum Corda, etc.*
Words of Institution.	Words of Institution.	Thanksgiving. Tersanctus. Contin. of thanksgiving.	Ablution of hands.	Prayers for all men and things, and commemoration of dead.	*Benediction.*	Salutation and Kiss of Peace.	Words of Institution.	Silent prayers.	*Sursum Corda, etc.*	Commemoration of departed and living Saints.	Commemoration of living and dead.	Thanksgiving, with Tersanctus.
Verbal Oblation.	Verbal Oblation.	Words of Institution.	*Benediction.*	Lord's Prayer.	*Sursum Corda, etc.*	*Benediction.*	Prayer of deprecation.	*Sursum Corda, etc.*	Thanksgiving. Tersanctus.	Kiss of Peace, and collect for peace.	Collect, and Kiss of Peace.	Prayer of Consecration, with Words of Institution, and Fraction.
Invocation of Holy Ghost.	*Invocation of Holy Ghost.*	Oblation of elements.	*Sursum Corda, etc.*	The Holy to the Holy, response of divine unity.	Thanksgiving, with Tersanctus.	*Sursum Corda, etc.*	*Invocation of Holy Ghost.*	Thanksgiving. Tersanctus.	Verbal Oblation.	*Sursum Corda, etc.*	*Sursum Corda, etc.*	Communion.
Prayers for all estates, and commemoration of living and dead.	Prayers for all men and things.	*Invocation of Holy Ghost.*	Thanksgiving. Tersanctus. Contin. of thanksgiving.	Communion (with Ps. *Gustate et videte*, etc.)[1]	Words of Institution (perhaps).	Thanksgiving. Tersanctus.	Fraction.	General prayers for the living.	Commemoration of the living.	Thanksgiving. Tersanctus. Contin. of thanksgiving.	Thanksgiving. Tersanctus. Contin. of thanksgiving.	Lord's Prayer.
Bidding prayer by Deacon.	Lord's Prayer.	Prayers for all men and things.	Words of Institution.	Thanksgiving.	Invocation (alluded to).	Contin. of thanksgiving; Prayers for all estates, and commemoration of departed.	Lord's Prayer.	Prayer that the oblation might be blessed.	*Invocation of Holy Ghost.*	Words of Institution (verbal oblation and *invocation* sometimes).	Petition for sanctification of the elements.	Hymn.
Lord's Prayer.	Benediction.	Lord's Prayer.	Verbal Oblation.		General prayer and commemoration of living and dead.	*Invocation of Holy Ghost.*	Benediction.	Words of Institution.	Mention of Christ's passion and death.	Fraction.	Words of Institution.	Benediction.
τὰ ἅγια τοῖς ἁγίοις. The Holy to the Holy, and response of unity.	Fraction of the bread.	Benediction.	*Invocation of Holy Ghost.*		Lord's Prayer.	General prayer for peace.	The Holy to the Holy.	Verbal oblation.	Commemoration of departed Saints.	Lord's Prayer.	*Invocation of Holy Ghost.*	
Fraction of the bread.	The Holy to the Holy.	The Holy to the Holy.	Prayers for all men and things.		The Holy to the Holy.	Fraction.	Communion.	Commemoration of departed Saints.	Fraction.	Prayers.	Fraction.	
Communion.	Communion.	Fraction.	Benediction.		Fraction.	Benediction.	Thanksgiving.	Fraction.	Benediction.	Benediction.	Lord's Prayer.	
Prayer of thanksgiving.	Thanksgiving.	Communion.	The Holy to the Holy, and response of unity.		Communion.	Lord's Prayer.		Lord's Prayer.[1]	Lord's Prayer.	Communion (with Anthem).	Blessing.	
Blessing.		Thanksgiving.	Communion.		(The *order* is in some cases *assumed*; the notices being casual and dispersed.)	The Holy to the Holy, and response of unity.		Kiss of Peace.	Salutation and Kiss of Peace.	Thanksgiving.	Communion (with Ps. *Gustate et videte*, etc.)	
			Thanksgiving.			Communion.		Communion.	Communion (with Anthem).		Thanksgiving.	
			Benediction.			Thanksgiving.		Prayer.	Thanksgiving.			
						Benediction.						

Cyril: [1] (*Jerome* states this practice to have been customary in Palestine.)

Ancient Roman: [1] (Since the time of Gregory, the *Lord's Prayer* has been put before the *Fraction*. The Milan Liturgy retains the old practice; it omits the [illegible] oblation; in other respects its order resembles the Roman rite.)

Sursum Corda, "Lift up your hearts," always with the reply—"We lift them up," etc.; and generally also with the addition—"Let us give thanks," and "it is just and right so to do."
The Salutation, "*Peace be with you*," with the reply, "*and with thy spirit*," generally preceded the Kiss of Peace. It also occurred in many places (Chrysostom mentions six or seven) in the earliest Oriental service.
The Words of institution generally embraced also a recital of our Saviour's acts and words at the moment.
The *Tersanctus* is the Seraphical hymn, "Holy, holy, holy."

But the evidence on which these conclusions are founded, does not go back beyond the middle of the fourth century. As you ascend higher, the incidental notices of acts and expressions belonging to the ritual, such as we find in Chrysostom or Cyril, become fewer, and at length altogether cease. There is no longer any kind of detail; allusion and description merge into the purely general. In a footnote are thrown together all the references we can find, having any bearing on the use of forms of prayer prior to the time of Cyril of Jerusalem; and it will be observed that they give no evidence whatever of the general use of any ritual in a recorded form; and hence the presumption that, had any such existed, the terms in which it was expressed would have been suitably mentioned as occasion offered.[1]

Ephrem Syrus, "who lived at Edessa, the very centre of Apostolical preaching," in the passage already quoted, speaks of the general prayer, as *following* the invocation of the Holy Ghost. But his expressions are very general. He notices prayers (pro servis orat Dominum, etc.) as *preceding* the invocation, which might answer to the Nestorian petitions, considered by Palmer out of place: and the prayer after the invocation is also spoken of, in such general terms (orationem *pro cunctis* faciente), as might apply to the prayer for the peace of the whole world, the Church, empire, etc., and the departed, which actually follows the invocation. This last-mentioned prayer agrees with the commencement of the general prayers referred to by Cyril, much more closely than does the "liturgy of St. James." The position of this prayer, moreover, might not have been essential; it might have been customary either before or after the invocation.

It will be observed from the Schedule that this liturgy possesses much in common with the Monophysite and Orthodox liturgies; it also coincides in some remarkable particulars with the Alexandrian liturgy; but with the Churches practising these rites, the Nestorians have, from the fifth century, held no communion. How could they then, upon Mr. Palmer's own oft-repeated grounds, have derived such common material from Churches whose fellowship they abjured? The Nestorian Church is, besides, as ancient and as venerable as the Monophysite or Orthodox, and has been more independent, and at some periods more extensive. She was at one time a burning and shining example of missionary zeal to the Church at large. And we cannot help assigning a position to her liturgy as honourable and ancient, as to that of the Monophysites.

[1] (1) *Athanasius* has few allusions to forms: he mentions the symphony of the people's united voice (implying some sort of stated prayer): their saying "Amen," and their praying for the Emperor. He speaks

Supposing, then, that in the first ages of the Church there was no embodiment of prayer in a written form, how and whence did the liturgies arise which were recorded with much general uniformity throughout the Christian world, before the close of the fourth century? Palmer holds that the concurrent uniformity of several such liturgies, as traced thus up to the fourth century, warrants us in ascribing the source of their order and substance to the most primitive antiquity; as, for instance, in the Alexandrian liturgy, "to the instructions and appointment of the blessed Evangelist Mark." Thus in his Introduction:—

"The liberty, which every Christian Church plainly had and exercised in the way of improving its formularies, confirms the antiquity of the four great liturgies; for where this liberty existed, it could scarcely have been anything but reverence for the Apostolic source, from which the original liturgies were derived, that prevented an infinite variety of formularies, and preserved the substantial uniformity which we find to have prevailed in

---

of the oblation (προσφορά) being offered in the absence of the catechumens.

(2) *Cornelius*, Bishop of Rome (A.D. 250), as quoted by Eusebius, refers to the *Amen*, pronounced by the communicant on receiving the bread.

(3) *Dionysius* of Alexandria (A.D. 250), similarly quoted, objects to baptizing a man, after he had long been a communicant, "heard the thanksgiving, and added aloud his *Amen*, stood by the table, and stretched out his hands to receive the sacred food."

(4) *Cyprian* (250) says that "before prayer the priest prepared the minds of the brethren by the prefatory "*Sursum Corda*," to which the people replied, "*Hebemus ad Dominum*," etc.

He mentions the commemoration of the living and the dead; and he notices the recitation of our Saviour's sacramental words at the communion. —*Epist. ad Cæcil.*

(5) *Firmilian* of Cæsarea, in a letter to Cyprian, speaks of a woman, who administered the sacraments, and consecrated the bread "invocatione non contemptibili," and pretended "Eucharistiam facere, et Sacrificium Domino, non sine sacramento solitae predicationis, offerre." The prayers, here alluded to, were evidently fixed as to their main character and tendency, and the juncture at which they were offered up; but whether they were fixed and recorded, as to *verbal* expression, is uncertain; the epithet given to the invocation argues rather for its being unfixed.

(6) *Origen* mentions the kiss of peace, as founded on Rom. xvi. 16, etc.; the Eucharistal thanksgiving, and the sanctifying effect of that and prayer upon the elements; he also "appears to quote from the prayers" (π ολλά κ

vast districts of the primitive Church" (p. 8). Again, with respect to the different branches of the Oriental family, "The uniformity between these liturgies, as extant in the fourth or fifth century, is such as bespeaks a common origin. Their diversity is such as to prove the *remoteness* of the period at which they originated. To what remote period can we refer, as exhibiting a perfect general uniformity of liturgy, except to the Apostolic age?" (s. 3, p. 81).

ἐν ταῖς εὐχαῖς λέγομεν, Θεὲ παντόκρατορ, τὴν μερίδα ἡμῖν μετα των προφητῶν δὸς. κ.τ.λ.); and something of the kind is still found in the African liturgy. How far we are to understand that the forms alluded to were fixed, and uniformly and widely adopted, it is difficult to say.

(7) *Clemens Alexandrinus*, early in the third century, speaks of the "congregation, prostrate at their prayers, having as it were a common voice, and one opinion." Unless this be metaphorical, prayers, fixed to some extent at least, are implied.

(8) *Tertullian* mentions the kiss of peace "after prayer had with the brethren"; alludes to the use of the "Tersanctus"; the response "Amen," and ἀπ' αἰῶνος εἰς αἰῶνας. He states also that the emperors and public officers were remembered in their prayers, and adds, "denique sine monitore, quia de pectore, oremus."

(9) *Irenæus*, in the end of the second century, says that the earthly bread after receiving τὴν ἐπικλησιν τὸν Θεοῦ, is no longer common bread, but the Eucharist; and refers to the expression εἰς τοὺς αἰῶνας τῶν αἰώνων, as said at the Eucharist, or thanksgiving, probably at its usual termination.

(10) *Justin Martyr*, in the middle of the second century, specifies prayers common to the assembled Church (κοινας εὐχὰς) after baptism; describes the assemblies on Sunday; the reading of the Apostles and prophets; the president's sermon founded thereon; and finally ἔπειτα ἀνιστάμεθα κοινῇ πάντες, καὶ εὐχας πέμπομεν. The sacramental service is thus narrated: "Having ceased from prayer, they kiss each other: then bread and the cup are brought to the president of the brethren; and he, receiving them, offers praise and glory to the Father of all through the name of the Son and the Holy Spirit: a thanksgiving for these benefits is made at great length (επι πολυ); which, as well as the prayers, being ended, all the people say "*Amen*." He repeats this, without any addition: καὶ ὡς προεφημεν, πανσαμενων ἡμῶν της εὐχῆς, ἄρτος προσφέρεται. . . . καὶ ὁ προεστὼς εὐχὰς ὁμοίως καὶ εὐχαριστιάς ὅση δύναμις αὐτῷ ἀναπεμπει, καὶ ὁ λαὸς ἐπευφημει, λὲγων το 'Αμην. He also speaks of the food being blessed, δι εὐχῆς λόγου, which Palmer refers to the words of our Lord (vol. i. p. 42).

(11) *Pliny* (A.D. 107) speaks of the Christians singing a hymn alternately to Christ as God, which is quoted by Bingham, as bearing on the subject; but hymnody is perfectly consonant with the use of unfixed prayers. We have already mentioned Bingham's references to *Lucian* and *Ignatius* as untenable.

Nevertheless he repeatedly holds[1] that "the primitive liturgies were not committed to writing at first, but to memory" (pp. 9, 121); and he is only "*strongly inclined* to think that St. James's liturgy was already committed to writing in the time of Cyril, or before the middle of the fourth century." The Apostolical element, then, of whatever nature, was originally committed to memory, and by *memory alone* was perpetuated. Palmer nowhere tells us what he thinks was the nature or extent of that Apostolical authority or liturgical institution, which maintained itself so long essentially intact in the memory of the Church, and with such rare tenacity of its proper and original dress, that when, after the lapse of centuries, it began generally to be recorded, the result was everywhere such extraordinary uniformity. Such faithfulness might in vain be expected from the treacherous memory of man.

In what, then, does this supposed Apostolical element consist? It will be observed that Palmer's expressions on this point are vague, and capable of the most elastic interpretation. They carefully exclude particulars; and it may be possible to construe them as referring simply to the general order and procedure followed in the sacramental service. The equivocal sense of the term *liturgy*, already noticed, helps towards this supposition. And in this view, there would no doubt be a large substratum of solid truth in Palmer's theory. The liturgies composed by Basil, by Hilary, and by Cyril of Alexandria, would hardly have taken their place so quietly and generally, had they not been in accordance, either with a previously recorded liturgy, or with the groundwork of a service in current and established use.[2] Such groundwork, again, being in so many places common, argues that something common must be traced up to a convergent point,—if not to the Apostolical era. Supposing, then, this common material to have been confined to the general order or plan of procedure in the sacramental worship, let us see whether there were any causes at work pre-

[1] The same view is held by Bingham and Renaudot.—*Vide* Bingham, bk. xiii. ch. 5, s. 3.

[2] Thus Basil informs us that "the customs of divine service, which he had appointed, were consonant and agreeable to all the Churches of God."

paring the Church, in whole and in its several parts, spontaneously to adopt such a uniformity of expression as we find prevalent in the fourth century. The following appear important considerations of this nature.

First, then, from whatever source derived, strange and awful ideas regarding the sacramental rites began to spring up in the third century, if not earlier. The ceremony, irrespective of the faith of the recipient, possessed a mysterious efficacy. Baptism took the lead in this illusion; the *rite itself*, the "pool of regeneration," was early talked of as wiping away sin, and a correspondingly early importance was attached to the verbal ritual accompanying it.[1] The Eucharist followed with willing steps: an unearthly virtue entered the elements; they became (metaphorically at first) the body of the Lord; and the commemorative act passed into a sacrifice offered up for the assembly, and for the whole Church. It became a most "dread," "awful," "tremendous mystery."[2] But what imparted this heavenly character to the elements and oblation? Evidently it was the consecrating prayer of the priest. No wonder, then, that a mysterious virtue began to attach to the *words* themselves, and a deep anxiety to

[1] We accordingly find that the formulæ of Baptism were fixed long before those of the Eucharist. Thus Firmilian mentions that the woman who administered the sacraments, "baptizarat multos, usitata et legitima verba interrogationis usurpans, ut nil discrepare ab ecclesiastica regula viderentur." Much stress is also laid on the rite having thus been performed "ad imaginem veritatis" (Epist. LXXV. Cyprian's *Works*). Bingham adduces many early notices of the baptismal formulæ from Tertullian and others.

[2] Φρικωδεστατα μυστηρια. "Most dread-inspiring rites." The contrast has been well drawn between these "terrible and astounding mysteries," and the simple "kindly soothing and gentle practice" of the early Church, by Isaac Taylor, in his *Ancient Christianity*, p. 537; although he appears to fall back too exclusively on the celibate institution as its cause.

See this subject, and its collaterals, well brought out in "Chrysostom; a Sketch," in No. II. of Kitto's *Journal of Sacred Literature*. Transubstantiation was not a formal doctrine of the Church in the fourth century, but the uneasy dread with which the *sacrifice* and *oblation* began then to be looked upon, led to the most equivocal expressions on the subject. Thus, as Jeremy Taylor remarks, Chrysostom's authority has been quoted on both sides.—*Works*, vol. x. p. 84.

pervade both priest and people, lest the efficacy of the sacrament should be impaired, or entirely lost, by the use of an illegitimate or informal ritual. Bishops of sanctity and learning would be looked to as the safest guides. Words used by such men might be adopted without any apprehension of a deficiency that would vitiate the saving virtue. It was security even to err in company with a Cyprian or a Gregory Thaumaturgus.[1] The consecrating forms employed by such men, would thus be imitated or reduced to writing, and come universally into use.[2] The *framework* of the sacramental liturgy already existed in the simple institution of Christ as followed by the Apostles; and within the various parts of this framework the forms now beginning to be introduced would materially be interwoven, forming thus a complete recorded liturgy.

Next, the federal bond which united the early Church, and the constant communication kept up betwixt its various quarters,

[1] The forms of Gregory Thaumaturgus were long closely observed in the Church of Neo-Cæsarea. Basil, speaking of the admiration in which he was held, says "for which reason they have not taken up any custom, word, or mystical rite, beside what they received from him. Insomuch that Church appears *defective* in many respects, because they have nothing but what is *ancient*: for they who have succeeded him in the government of the Churches, would admit none of those things that have been since invented, but have kept entirely to the first institutions, as derived from him."—*Vide* Lardner's *Cred.*, vol. vii. p. 621. This illustrates the manner in which the liturgy grew up. Basil's endeavour to introduce his own antiphonal mode of singing at Cæsarea, shows that they had admitted the use of *litanies*, since the time of Gregory.

[2] The following from Basil illustrates this position :—Τὰ *τῆς ἐπικλήσεως ῥήματα, ἐπι τῇ ἀναδείξει τοῦ ἄρτου τῆς εὐχαριστίας καὶ τοῦ ποτηρίου τῆς εὐλογίας, τίς τῶν ἁγίων ἐγγράφως ἡμῖν καταλέλοιπεν· οὐ γὰρ δὴ τούτοις ἀρκούμεθα ὧν ὁ Ἀπόστολος ἢ τὸ Εὐαγγελιον ἐπεμνήσθη, ἀλλὰ καὶ ἐπιλεγομεν ἕτερα, ὡς μεγάλην ἔχομτα πρὸε τὸ μυστήριον τὴν ἰσχὺν, ἐκ τῆς ἀγράφου διδασκαλίας παραλαβόντες.* —*De Spiritu Sancto*, c. 27. This seems to prove that there were, even in Basil's time, no *written* prayers of Apostolical authority. The only documents, even in that late age believed to be of primitive times, were the narratives of "the Gospel and the Apostle" (Paul). Besides the commemorative words and directions there recorded, they added, "before and after, other things, *as having great efficacy towards the mystery*, taking them from the *unwritten teaching.*"

would produce an interchange and diffusion of the sacramental forms, when they came to be recorded. One cannot read the early Fathers, without seeing that there was a constant tendency to oneness of detail throughout the Church. Cyprian's correspondence will illustrate not merely this spirit, but the mode also in which such correspondence was itself an efficient agent in producing uniformity.

The Councils of the third and fourth centuries tended directly to the same result. Witness the apparently annual synods of the third century;[1] the Council at Carthage (A.D. 256) regarding the baptism of heretics; that of Rome (251) against Novatian;[2] and the assembly at Antioch (269), to which bishops, presbyters, and deacons hurried from all directions to convict Paul, "the defiler of Christ's flock."[3] Such gatherings would tend, not merely by the communion and sympathy excited among the orthodox party, indirectly to uniformity of sentiment and of rite, but directly by the decisions then passed. Every heresy, real or supposed, and every Council denouncing such heresy, narrowed by degrees the sphere of private judgment; and the safest mode of avoiding the suspicion, or the reality, of unsound doctrine, would be to adopt the practice of some approved orthodox leader, and make use of forms of devotion sanctioned by his authority. The life-long struggle and truly heroic tenacity of Athanasius, for the finest-drawn points of orthodoxy, had perhaps as much effect as anything else in setting the type of liturgical forms.[4]

[1] Compare Firmilian, Bishop in Cappadocia, writing to Cyprian, Bishop of Carthage: "Necessario apud nos fit, ut per singulos annos seniores et praepositi in unum conveniamus, ad disponenda ea, quae curae nostrae commissa sunt, ut, siqua graviora sunt, communi consilio dirigantur."

[2] At which sixty bishops and a greater number of presbyters and deacons were present, besides the district assemblies.—Eusebius, *Eccl. Hist.*, vi. 43.

[3] Eusebius, after enumerating the chief bishops from various countries present at this Council, says that "the vast number of others, both presbyters and deacons, one could hardly number.—*Idem.* vii. 28.

[4] The influence of Councils upon forms is well exemplified by the immediate introduction throughout Christendom of the Nicean Creed as an expression of belief at baptism.—*Vide* Bingham, vol. iv. p. 226; Bk. xiii. 5, s. 7. An analogous influence was no doubt immediately exercised by

Monasticism helped much to embody and assimilate the various forms of prayer. The spirit of the institution, as graphically described by the author of "Ancient Christianity," required the continual excitement of an ever-recurring service, which thus provided matter for the unwholesome vacuity in the minds of multitudes of men and women taken from the natural employment of public and domestic life. The daily and nightly prayers would necessarily settle down into a recorded form. The fraternities of monks and virgins, scattered over various countries, must have co-operated in giving a uniformity of character and detail to the services in whose introduction they had themselves been instrumental.[1]

Lastly, the imperial establishment of Christianity supplied the place of an Œcumenical authority.[2] The Emperor summoned,

this Council on the sacramental liturgy also, though the Creed was not introduced into it for some time after.

[1] This may be illustrated from Palmer's account of the liturgy of Cæsarea: "To account for the introduction of this liturgy into Egypt is not difficult. Basil was no doubt particularly famous in Egypt, for being the great founder of the Monastic institute in Pontus and the neighbouring provinces, the Monastic rule, whether of Macherites, or Cœnobites, prevailed sooner and more extensively in Egypt, than perhaps anywhere else. And it was here, and in Syria, that Basil learnt the discipline, which on his return he established in Pontus. It is not wonderful, therefore, that his liturgy should have been gladly received in Egypt" (sec. 2, p. 62).

[2] It does not seem probable that liturgies were introduced in Constantine's reign: but to the diligent peruser of his life, it will be evident how readily the new element must have acted in formalising religion. He gave a form of prayer to be used by his *heathen* soldiery.—Euseb., *Life of Const.*, iv. c. 19 and 20. He called himself "a Bishop ordained by God, to overlook whatever externally related to the Church."—*Idem.* c. 24. The meetings of heretics were suppressed by him both in public and private;—involving an inquisition into their doctrine and form of worship.—*Idem.* iii. 65. He enacted that Sunday should be the special day for prayer.—*Idem.* iv. 18. He arrayed his Palace like a Church; and himself read the Scriptures, and offered up the regular prayers, *εὐχὰς ἐνθέσμους*.—*Idem.* 17. What sort of prayers those were, that an unbaptized person, like Constantine, could offer up (on the liturgical system), does not appear. The last-mentioned is almost the only expression regarding him which might refer to fixed prayers, and even that is very general. In the 36th chapter of the 4th book is a letter from Constantine, commissioning Eusebius to procure fifty copies of the

and presided over, the general Councils of the Church. And the centralising and formalising influence, thus produced, must powerfully have contributed to stereotype, if not originate, general and uniform services of religion.

Now, if these reasons be regarded as sufficient to account for the prevalent uniformity of liturgies springing up in the fourth, or even the third century, then the silence of previous writers on the subject may be accepted as a presumption that there did not exist any fixed and recorded liturgies at an earlier period.

Etheridge, in his *Syrian Churches*, gives a brief summary of reasons for "concluding that the practice of reading prayers from a MS. form was unknown in the Christian Church for the first three hundred years." In the persecutions under Diocletian, the books of worship, used in the Churches, were demanded under pain of cruelties and torture: we read of the Scriptures, sacramental vessels, etc., being delivered up: but there occurs no allusion whatever to manuscript services.[1] Again, there is the use of expressions, such as ὅση δυναμις[2] with reference to the eucharistal prayer and thanksgiving, "which evidently betokens an extempore effort, and precludes the idea of a defined and limited document."[3]

sacred Scriptures for the increasing number of Churches in Constantinople, "the provision and use of which you know to be most needful for the instruction of the Church." He gives detailed instructions as to their preparation ; but he does not allude to any other sort of book, or formulary, as required for the Churches.

[1] This argument is stated at length by Bingham. Speaking of its conclusiveness against the existence of images in the age of Diocletian, or the beginning of the fourth century, he adds, "And I think that the argument will hold as well against having their liturgies compiled into books and volumes, since it is scarce possible that such things, in difficult times, should have wholly escaped the notice and fury of their enemies" (bk. xiii. 5, s. 3). This, considering Bingham's views, is an important concession.

[2] Justin Martyr. The expression of Tertullian, "sine monitore, quia de pectore," is not so conclusive ; but he elsewhere states that there was no written law (scripturam nullam invenies) for the modes of solemnising the Sacramental rites.—*De corona.*

[3] We need hardly allude to the absence of forms in the Acts and Epistles. In the chapter that most bears on the subject (1 Cor. xiv.), the only requisite is that the prayer be not only "with the spirit," but in the

Had the several Apostles left forms of prayer which, preserved by memory or writing, became the types of the four great liturgies, we should unquestionably have found them referred to specially, as the production of their inspired authors, or bearing their names. The testimony of Palmer is, however, clear against such a supposition. He says:—

"In my opinion, this appellation of St. Mark's liturgy began about the end of the fourth, or beginning of the fifth century, after Basil had composed his liturgy, which appears to have been the first liturgy that bore the name of any man. Other Churches then gave their liturgies the names of their founders. And so the Alexandrians and Egyptians gave theirs the name of 'St. Mark,' and they of Jerusalem and Antioch called theirs 'St. James's'" (sec. 4, p. 93).

Moreover, before the middle of the fourth century, no doctrine or expression of a liturgy is quoted by any writer in proof or illustration of what they have in hand.[1] But mark, the moment we come to the acknowledged age of liturgical forms, we meet with a profusion of references to their substance, their teaching, and their words. Augustine makes repeated quotations, as we have seen, against the Pelagian heresy; Jerome also with the same object; Chrysostom's works abound with such references; and subsequent Councils support their positions by open citations

common tongue, and intelligible to the unlearned. It is not indeed impossible that such customary forms, as "for ever and ever, Amen," at the close of the thanksgiving; *Amen*, at the reception of the elements; *sursum corda*, and *peace be with you*, with their responses, may have been of Apostolical usage, and so perpetuated in the Church. But this is mere supposition; and, even if admitted, it would not follow that they had been laid down, or imposed, by the Apostles. Indeed, if one reflects on the tendency of the human mind to seize upon accidental ceremonies or forms, and turn them into talismans of saving virtue, the unceremonial simplicity of the New Testament cannot be sufficiently admired. When even those simplest of simple rites, Baptism and the Lord's Supper, have suffered so wonderful a transubstantiation, what would not the fate have been of even the merest scraps of any formulary proceeding from the Apostles?

[1] The expressions of Cyprian and Origen, formerly quoted, can hardly be viewed as exceptions; and if they were, would prove little. Forms might have been *beginning* in their times.

of liturgical authority. Now, of the Fathers previous to the era specified, we have remains of all descriptions, epistolary, didactic, allegorical, hortative, exegetical, commentatory, historical; nay, there is a discussion in Cyprian as to the mode of celebrating the Lord's Supper itself, and yet no quotation from, or reference to a liturgical service. Surely then there is good reason to conclude, that there was no prescribed form of words in current and general use before the fourth century.[1]

In conclusion, it must also be borne in mind that, even in the fourth and fifth centuries, the liturgical quotations and allusions refer almost exclusively to the *Sacramental* liturgy. But this was not the only service in early times.[2] Justin Martyr speaks of the prayers having ceased before the Communion service began; and it is evident that there were other occasions of public devotion besides. It is most probable that

[1] A further proof, that there were no ancient liturgies prescribed by the Church, occurs in Euseb., *Eccl. Hist.* bk. v. ch. 28, where a late author is quoted as combating the argument that Unitarian doctrines were held by the Apostles, and were introduced by Victor in the beginning of the third century. He does so, by appealing to the Scriptures, to writers more ancient than Victor, and to "the psalms and hymns written by the brethren from the beginning, which celebrate Christ the Word of God, by asserting his Divinity." Had there existed any liturgy in prescriptive use, it is hardly conceivable that it would not have been appealed to before any other human authority.

[2] Chrysostom, and the author of the *Apostolical Constitutions*, are the only authorities that give detailed references to the expressions of the catechumenical service. The "small number of collects," appearing in the early liturgies, seemed to Bingham so unfit to take up the space of time reasonably allotted to public service, that he concludes much of it was occupied in the "silent prayers" (διὰ σιωπῆς). One such mental prayer is expressly directed by the Council of Laodicea.

A circumstance full of meaning is related by Palmer regarding the Roman liturgy. At a particular point of the service, the priest said "Oremus," and the whole Church prayed in silence. "This custom of secret prayer became obsolete at Rome from no form being appointed for the purpose." In the sister liturgy of Milan, however, a collect was provided, which still continues. At Rome we have still the "Oremus," but no prayer. It is an affecting relic of secret and warm devotion now departed (vol. i. pp. 122 and 129).

An instance of silent prayer will be found in the office of "ordination of priests" in the English service.

these remained unrecorded and unfixed long after the Sacramental liturgy had assumed a prescribed, and even recorded, shape.

From this long digression we return to the Indian liturgy, and place our case upon the example of the early Church. By all means let our Native Christians have the Anglican liturgy adapted to them. But to its regular and canonical use, add likewise the primitive and Apostolical practice of unfixed and unrecorded prayers; for, without these, her liturgy cannot meet the varied wants and changing character of the Churches of Hindostan. Let permission, then, be freely accorded, and the custom encouraged.

If this proposition be negatived, then the only remaining alternative is, as formerly explained, to adapt, alter, and add to the recorded liturgy, much more largely than would otherwise be required. The catechumens and inquirers of the various classes that attend our services, must be prayed for, and encouraged to pray for themselves. And the "incredulous nations" must be extensively introduced into our petitions, both as subjects of intercession, and in connection with the reflex influence they exercise upon the state and prospects of the Church itself. All this we have shown to be imperatively required: and regarding all this, the English liturgy presents a vacant blank.

Throughout this article, we have expressed ourselves freely regarding the liturgy of our Church. We now seek to guard such expressions by a deliberate record of our love and veneration for the English ritual. England owes to it a deep and weighty debt of gratitude. It has proved the bulwark of religious life and doctrine in the British isles.

So much space has already been occupied, that our notice of the Urdoo work placed at the head of this article, must be brief and rapid. It is a complete translation of the English Prayer-Book, embracing, with a few exceptions,[1] the whole

[1] The exceptions are, the services for use at sea, the *Gunpowder Treason, Charles the Martyr*, and the *Restoration of the Royal Family*. The addition of the ecclesiastical tables (above 40 pages) has much swelled the book, and added to its expense. The greater part of them was quite unnecessary *for*

services of the Church, ordinary and occasional, with the Articles. It has been printed separately in the Roman and Persian character.[1]

We have before us another Urdoo translation, embracing all that the present work does, except the service on the anniversary of the Queen's accession. It was printed in 1829, at Calcutta, "for the Prayer-Book and Homily Society." It is a literal rendering of the Prayer-Book, and in the main executed with ability. It abounds, however, with high and difficult words, and would, in many parts, be unintelligible to the ordinary frequenters of our Churches.

The translation of 1829 has apparently formed the groundwork of the present; and it has been so far improved upon, that the great mass of the learned and rare words have been vernacularised, and brought down to the comprehension of common hearers. Much skill and knowledge of native idiom have been brought to bear upon this task. The natural language of everyday life has often been applied with great happiness to the expression of what was before conveyed in a learned and recondite style. Nevertheless there still exist in the present work many rare and learned terms, which might, without much difficulty, have been replaced by more common words.

the present. The perplexed calculations regarding the *golden numbers* and the *dominical letter* (ahdí haraf, aur zehbí adád) were especially needless. It has a curious effect to read so much about the *Vigils*, *Fasts*, and *Days of Abstinence*. "I adwal *Bedárion* aur *Rozon* aur *Riázat* ke dinon kí sál bhar ke liye." Considering the terms employed, and especially the associations connected with the words *roza* and *riázat*, it is unfortunate that so much has been said about them, in the present unfixed and unenlightened state of our Native Christians. By and by they will find out that we mean no harm by them; but at present they may either do damage by creating wrong impressions, or possibly lead to the exclamation—"Ye observe days and months and times and years; I am afraid of you."

[1] The chief author of this translation is, we believe, the Rev. Mr. Smith, an excellent and talented missionary of the English Church at Benares. The opinion and advice of other missionaries were taken regarding it. The missionaries at Agra (no mean judges on such a question) were not favourable to its publication, without important alterations, which were not adopted.

But the great demerit of this work arises from the attempt to make it a *literal* translation. It is more servile to the letter of the original than the rendering of 1829, and just in proportion to this servility is the real spirit and idea of the English version injured or lost.

It is, in truth, one of the most illusory of conceits to fancy that, by verbal transference, a correct counterpart is obtained of the idea and spirit of a passage. A translation may be etymologically perfect, and yet no more give the force of the original, than the awkward dancing of a bear represents the graceful pirouettes of the ballet. The reason is obvious. Words and phrases gather around them an idiosyncrasy of their own, often quite independent of their grammatical derivation. The peculiar meaning and associations connected with them are the birth of place and circumstance, of national temperament, and the progress of civilisation. A word or phrase, which has grown up in Indian society, may thus have acquired a totally different colour, and convey an utterly diverse meaning, from that which it represents in the English lexicon and grammar: and so likewise with words in construction, and the interminable diversities of relative meaning, caused by the reflex influence of one word upon another. Each bears the stamp of its own nationality; and thus ideas, conveyed from one language to another by a simply grammatical transfer of words and sentences, are liable to differ entirely from the original. There may be a verbal counterpart, and yet no approximation to an ideal counterpart. To transfer the spirit and mind of a passage is an incomparably harder task. It requires an "intimacy with native processes of thought." The idea of the original, thoroughly grasped, must first be thrown into the mental cast and habitude of the people for whom the translation is intended, and then into their language. An accomplished author, himself accustomed to translation, well remarks that this intimacy with the working of the native mind "is the most essential requisite" in translation. He says :—

"For where languages, like Urdoo and English, are the product of a civilisation differing in history, tendency, character and development, it is obvious that even the most simple and elementary ideas, having been obtained through different channels, and having clothed themselves in forms altogether foreign the one to the other, can only be fully realised to the mind by reference to the sources whence they are derived. But any one, who has mixed with the people, and has informed himself of their social state, of which the vulgar tongue is the index and the exposition, and who knows the inlets by which truth can best insinuate itself into their minds, will not find any great difficulty in presenting to them a strange idea in its most significant shape, and in determining how the meaning in each sentence can best be expressed, so as not to run counter to the general current of their experience. Should there be no other alternative than to introduce an innovation, it will be easy for him to consider what novel mode of expression—what parallel metaphor—can be devised consistently with the scope and genius of the language, and with least violation of idiomatic propriety." [1]

We are far, indeed, from saying that, in the work before us, there is no attempt at the adaptation here so excellently explained; or that the attempt has not often been successful where it was possible to assimilate the English and the Indian composition, and preserve the idea also. But there are innumerable cases in which this was not possible, and in which the translation must be pronounced, as a transfer of meaning, entirely defective.

The close adhesion to English words and idiom has, besides these tangible defects, given a stiff, foreign and repulsive air to the whole work. It is not calculated to win its way among the Native communities by coming amongst them in a naturalised and attractive dress, and must therefore share the dislike with which everything foreign and strange is viewed by the society on whom it is imposed. Some of the quotations made below may illustrate this position: [2] but the impression we refer to, it is not possible to bring out in a brief space. It is a pervading colour which affects the whole stream, though perhaps hardly perceptible in a few detached passages. This general repulsiveness destroys the effect of the happy renderings before commended. The lustre of the gem is lost in the rudeness of the setting.

[1] Letter of Sir H. M. Elliot to the Government of India, prefixed to a "Specimen translation of the Penal Code. Calcutta, 1848. For private circulation."

[2] [Being in the Urdoo language, these are here omitted.]

No doubt the necessity of a literal version was forced upon the translator, either by the strictness of his own views, or the mandate of his ecclesiastical superiors, — which, we do not know. For our own part, we cannot perceive any reason whatever for enforcing such excessive closeness in the translation of a liturgy, at the cost of greatly impairing its usefulness. With the inspired Scriptures, it must ever be, for obvious reasons, a deeply important object to cling, with as close tenacity as possible, to an undeviating etymological transfer; though even there a too strict adherence will defeat its own purpose, and injure the translation as a *transfer of ideas*.[1] But with an uninspired production, the great object of which is to hold up a standard of Christian thought and faith as the guide of public devotion coming in contact with many points of social life, surely it is the most unnecessary and mistaken strait-lacedness, by insisting upon a verbal translation, to impair its efficiency, and injure its suitableness for accomplishing the very objects designed by its introduction. We contend for a more common-sense and liberal course than this. We plead for the translator, that he be allowed a wide field for adapting the sense and spirit of the liturgy to native apprehension, and that a sufficient licence be given him for "considering what novel modes of expression, what parallel metaphors, can be devised," to make the liturgy "consistent with the scope and genius of the language," and the mind of India.

. . . .

[There follow two or three pages of the kind of Urdoo phrases objected to, which it is not necessary to repeat here.]

. . . .

The Collects are in general translated with care; but many parts of the baptismal and sacramental services are done in an inferior style. The Articles are rendered with less ability than any other part of the book; so badly, indeed, as to be in some places, we fear, scarcely intelligible.

The prayers for the Queen and Royal Family ought un-

[1] [How sadly the disregard of this principle has injured the Revised Version of the New Testament.]

questionably to be remodelled. Whoever has attended a Native service, needs not to be told that they are altogether unsuited to the knowledge and ideas of the Hindoo congregation. In place of these, and the prayer for the Parliament, etc., a new prayer, or series of prayers, suited to the notions and positions of the Native community, might with great propriety be substituted.

The "Form of prayer with thanksgiving for the 20th of June, being the day on which Her Majesty began her happy reign," and which has been verbatim translated into Urdoo, appears to be remarkably ill adapted to the Natives of this country. A service, embracing all the references to Her Excellent Majesty which her Indian subjects are capable of appreciating, might with much benefit be constructed out of it; and advantage might be taken to introduce suitable notices of the blessings gained to India by the British accession, thanksgiving for the benefits of peaçe, justice, and the light of the Gospel therefrom accruing, and prayers for their continuance. A service in behalf of the Supreme Authority in the State, thus modelled upon the conceptions and feelings of the people, would reach their hearts, and be offered up with a fervency never attainable by a foreign production, possessing so few points of contact with the Native mind as this does.

But we have more than occupied our allotted space. We conclude by again repeating that the liturgy will never gain the affections of the people, till it be thoroughly adapted to their circumstances,—their modes of thought as well as modes of speech. Let the subject-matter and its treatment be that which affects Native life and exigencies. Let that be the paramount consideration, and forbear to introduce anything foreign in its reference, or inappropriate to the Indian mind, simply because it is found in the English liturgy.

The importance of the object demands that it be not trifled with, nor the task carelessly slurred over. It calls for the best abilities and the highest talents in the ecclesiastical body. It is plain that those who have authority in the Episcopal Church, should take early and vigorous measures for securing to their Native flocks that which these have a right to expect and to demand—A LITURGY SUITED TO THE WANTS OF THIS OUR GREAT DEPENDENCY.

FIFTH ARTICLE

THE PSALTER

ITS LARGER AND DISCRETIONARY USE DESIRABLE

A.D. 1887

The Psalms have been the refuge of the soul, the voice of the Church, the song of the saint, in all generations. They are still the same, as well in privacy of the still chamber as in public ministrations of the great congregation. From the treasury of the Psalter, be his outward state or inward frame what they may, the child of God is ever borrowing words that do give shape and substance to flitting thought, life to the soul, and fire to heavenward aspiration.

Here is stored up Divine food, rich and abundant, for every time and place. Something for the morning dawn, something for the busy day, and something for the dark watches of the night; something for the sick and solitary closet, something also for the thronging crowd. The backsliding, the penitent, the weak and afflicted, the doubting and the tempted; the soul dwelling in darkness, desolate, disowned by man, or dreading to be forsaken by the Almighty; and not less, the Saint on fire with godly zeal, hungering and thirsting after the living God, borne upwards on wings of love and joy,—each may find in the Psalms words framed, as it were, to suit his very case. And as in personal, domestic, and social life, so also in a nation's history, whether in peace or warfare, whether the year be crowned with goodness or the staff of bread be broken, in the day of wealth and prosperity, as well as in the night of calamity and pestilence; in short, at every turn of public life the people's voice of sorrow or of joy will ascend, as it can no otherwise ascend, in the Psalmist's very words. And, what is much to be observed, while Psalms abound with cries of anguish as well as with the "tenderest appeals to God's compassionate love that ever trembled on human lips,"[1] there is yet nothing weak or morbid, nothing extravagant or strained (as we too often see in our modern hymnody) throughout the Psalter: all is true and real, manly, simple, noble, and well-nerved. There are also in the Psalms of David revelations of the glory and attributes of the Almighty amongst the most instructive and sublime in the whole Bible. So well, indeed, have the sweet Singers of Israel been guided, both in probing the reins and "making manifest the secrets of the heart"[2] of man, and in the unveiling of Divine truth, that this alone were sure evidence of inspiration. Where else, indeed, than in the Psalms can we find that which is so keen "a discerner of the thoughts and intents of the heart," and answers better the description of the Word of God, as "quick and powerful, and sharper than any two-edged sword, piercing even to the dividing asunder of soul and spirit, and of the joints and marrow"?[3]

True, we have not here fully revealed to us, as in the Gospel, the fatherhood of God, the good tidings of mercy to all mankind, or the virtue of forgiveness of injuries; for "the law was given by Moses, but grace and truth came by Jesus Christ." Still in every page we cannot but see that it is the same God of love shining in the Royal songster's heart as, in later ages, shone in the believer's heart, "to give the light of the knowledge of the glory of God in the face of Jesus Christ."[4] A remarkable feature in the Psalms is also this, that although the future life, as a distinct conception, lay almost concealed from the Poet's eye, and there are but the barest allusions to it, yet whensoever our hearts ascend heavenwards, it is still most frequently the sweet Singer of Israel that gives us substance and material for our hopes and aspirations. What sentiment, for example, in reference to the future state, is more frequently on the Christian's lips than this—

[1] Perowne, vol. i. p. 247. [2] 1 Cor. xiv. 25.
[3] Heb. iv. 12. [4] 2 Cor. iv. 6.

"Thou shalt guide me with thy counsel,
And afterward receive me to glory.
Whom have I in heaven but thee?
And there is none upon earth that I desire beside thee.
My flesh and my heart faileth:
But God is the strength of my heart, and my portion for ever."[1]

Another very noticeable thing is this, that although the knowledge of sin could not have been in the mind of the ancient Jew as it was fully brought to light by the teaching, example, and passion of our Lord, yet the first words that rise on the Christian's lips, oppressed by the burden and crying for pardon, are still the Psalmist's words.[2] And so the believer finds in these Psalms expression for his thoughts, be they dark or bright, joyful or tearful, doubting or trusting, for time or for eternity, as he finds it nowhere else. His cries and lamentations are all written for him in the book, and so are also the very words that give substance to thought when "his mouth is filled with laughter, and his tongue with singing."[3]

Such being the case, it is no wonder that the Christian world has made the Psalms in all ages its organ of expression for the devotions of the closet, the family, as well as for the services of the sanctuary. We find notices of their use, as such, in apostolic times, when "psalms and hymns" evidently formed a material part of the ordinary worship.[4] The earliest Christian services were to some extent founded upon those in the Synagogue and the Temple; and we know that in both of these, certain fixed Psalms were prescribed for the several days of the week, as well as suitable selections proper for the various festivals. Thus a similar practice would be continued naturally in Christian congregations. The hymn sung by the little company

[1] Ps. lxxiii. 24-26.

[2] Commenting on Ps. xviii. 20-30, Perowne, after denying the imputation of self-righteousness, adds—"Some allowance, too, must perhaps be made for the fact that under the Old Covenant the knowledge of sin was more superficial than it is under the New." And yet it is in David's words, more perhaps than in any other, that the Christian makes his confession of sin.

[3] Ps. cxxvi. 2.

[4] 1 Cor. xiv. 26; Ephes. v. 19; Col. iii. 16.

at the Last Supper was in all probability a part of the Hillel used according to custom at the eating of the Passover.[1]

In the earliest age, the Christians no doubt continued to follow the Jewish example in the services which they held by day, or rather by night. Psalms may also have formed to some extent an adjunct to the office of the Lord's Supper, after the example of the original institution. Proper Psalms, probably from the custom of the Synagogue, or otherwise chosen as suitable for the occasion, were apparently used for certain times and seasons, as the Fifty-first for the night, and the Sixty-third for the morning service; otherwise, it may be supposed that the selection of Psalms for ordinary worship was more or less at the discretion of the minister. But gradually, in course of time, the Psalms gained a pre-eminent position of their own;[2] and the Church, going beyond the practice of the Jews, adopted for liturgical use the whole body of the Psalter. At what period their serial repetition or chanting from beginning to end, within specified limits of time, was introduced, is uncertain and obscure. Some authorities see indications of the practice in Basil's writings, as having prevailed in the fourth century; but the evidence is hardly conclusive. There is no doubt, however, that the custom of reciting in continuous sequence the entire book is of great antiquity. It prevailed early, as we find it still to prevail, in the ordinary services (as distinct from the Eucharistic services) of all the ancient Churches. In the Greek community, for instance, the entire Psalter is sung through once in every

[1] Ps. cxiii.-cxviii.; Matt. xxvi. 30; Mark xiv. 26. For the Jewish use of the Psalms, see *Temple Service* by John Lightfoot, London (no date): at p. 59 will be found the proper Psalms for each day. "These were the Psalms sung ordinarily throughout the year; but at some certain days there were other Psalms and songs used, as the Song of Moses on Sabbaths; Ps. lxxxi. on the first day of the year; proper Psalms for each day at the Feast of Tabernacles." There was no serial repetition of the Psalms among the Jews of old, nor is there at the present day; indeed, a considerable portion of the Psalter was never intended for liturgical use at all. The Psalms are only read as a whole by the Jews as they stand in their place in the Old Testament, gone through once in the year.

[2] Toto orbe cantantur.—*Aug. Conf.* ix. 4. See also Freeman's *Principles of Divine Service*, vol. i. p. 62.

week, and at certain seasons twice; in some monastic institutions *every day.*[1]

But while the serial recitation of the Psalter multiplied exceedingly throughout the world, the more ancient and edifying custom of appointing proper Psalms and selections of Psalms for days and seasons grew still more rapidly apace.[2] It took deep root and was widely practised in all the ancient churches, and thus the provision of special Psalmody, to be used more or less discretionally in substitution for the daily portion, tended in some degree to displace the serial use. Some of these selections of proper Psalms, or portions of the Psalter, are of great antiquity, as the fifteen Psalms (cxx.–cxxxiv.) repeated in the Greek Church every evening during the fifteen weeks preceding Christmas, and in the Western Churches during Lent. The enormous growth of festivals, saints' days, etc., in all the Catholic Churches (other than our own) has in this way led to the appointment of fixed Psalms appropriate for the occasion, and in practice superseded to a considerable extent the daily serial recitation. All this, and also the Western liberty of substituting certain devotional passages for the Ferial offices of Thursday and Saturday (when the

[1] We read of the whole Psalter being committed to memory; and in some Churches that the ability to repeat it by heart was one of the conditions of ordination (see some curious anecdotes about this in Smith's *Dictionary*, "Psalmody without Book," vol. ii. p. 1747). One remembers, in the island of Arran, coming across a bed-ridden Highlander who was going steadily through his daily recitation of the entire Psalter from memory: about the forenoon he had reached the middle of the Psalms (Scotch version).

[2] Smith's *Dictionary of Christian Antiquities*, vol. ii. p. 1749. In early times Psalms appear to have been sung at the Lord's Supper. Thus in the Coptic Church a Psalm was sung during the distribution; and "Caelestinus (422 A.D.) is said to have directed that Psalms of David should be sung before the sacrifice" (Smith's *Dictionary*, vol. ii. pp. 1021, 1032). Again, "Psalm xxii., as we learn from Augustine, was sung in the North African congregations at the Easter celebration of the Lord's Supper. More than fourteen centuries have passed since the Vandals drowned those songs in blood; but a stranger who happens to look in upon a Scottish congregation on a Communion Sabbath will be likely enough to find the Psalm turned to the same holy and solemn use" (Binnie, quoted by Perowne, *in loco*).

Psalms for the day are unusually long) has led to the frequent omission of large portions of the daily Psalms. While, therefore, the service of these churches is enriched, to a degree unknown with us, by selected Psalmody of the kind described (as well as by the introduction of other songs and hymns occurring throughout the Bible), the habit has at the same time materially interfered with the constant and unvaried repetition of the whole Psalter in serial order.

There is also practised in other churches the *antiphonal* mode, unknown amongst us;—that is, the intercalary response of some sentence, taken either from the Psalm itself or otherwise (sometimes a verse from the New Testament), bearing on the Psalm, and to some extent guiding its interpretation. The ancient habit, still followed in some of the Eastern Churches, was for this antiphonal response to be intercalated between each verse of the Psalm; but ordinarily it is now recited only at the close of a Psalm or division of Psalms (*kathismata* and *staseis*). The antiphon, varied thus according to the occasion and subject in hand, must, no doubt, often bring out with clearness the doctrinal application of the several Psalms to the season or special occasion on which they are used. Neale, indeed, thinks the guide thus afforded to be so effective, that he compares it to the helm of a ship.[1] Whatever the help from this ancillary organ may be, it is wholly wanting with us.

Coming now to the use of the Psalms in the Church of England, we observe that, with rare exception, it is a serial repetition pure and simple. When the ancient English Office was remodelled for us at the Reformation, the whole growth of festival and other special services was, so far as Psalmody is concerned, almost entirely cut down, and the daily recitation in serial course alone

[1] Thus on Good Friday, the Gregorian antiphon for the 22nd Psalm is, "They parted my garments among them," etc. For the song of Isaiah (xxvi.) the antiphon is, "Thine anger is turned away, and Thou comfortedst me" (Isa. xii.). "Let us completely change the antiphon," says Neale, "and observe how the signification will be altered. I never thus notice the way in which the Psalm, so to speak, obeys its antiphon, without calling to mind that verse, 'Behold the ships'" (Jas. iii. 4).—Neale, i. p. 53. He profusely illustrates this subject, pp. 34–58 *et passim*.

retained. We have proper Psalms, indeed, for Christmas, Ash Wednesday, Good Friday, Easter, Ascension Day, and Whit Sunday; but that is only six out of the three hundred and sixty-five days, making practically no variation in the daily use.[1] And so it has come to pass that the Church of England and the Episcopal bodies in Scotland and Ireland are the only liturgical communions in the world in which the use of the Psalter is confined to an almost exclusively serial repetition.

We say the churches of Great Britain and Ireland, for the *Protestant Episcopal Church in the United States of America* has provided an alternative series of Psalms for use in its ordinary services. It is now over a hundred years ago when the American Church, partly to avoid the vindictive psalms (against the recitation of which a strong feeling prevailed), and also to secure greater variety, made this selection. In their Book of Common Prayer, the list is placed before "The Psalter or Psalms of David," and is headed, "SELECTIONS OF PSALMS, to be used instead of the Psalms for the day, at the discretion of the Minister." They consist (besides the Selections for "Holy days," sixteen) of ten series, each containing several Psalms or parts of Psalms.[2] It is thus in the power of the Minister to give greater variety, richness, and appropriateness, to the portions for the day, as well as to avoid the recitation of any imprecatory passages. But these selections, in comparison with what can be done in the same direction, are scant and meagre. They might have been greatly multiplied and expanded with the utmost benefit. And the adoption freely into their number of such songs as abound in Isaiah and throughout the Bible, according to the example of other Churches, would have imparted an unimaginable fulness, freshness, and breadth to the thoughts and aspirations of the congregation.

[1] There are also the four fixed Psalms used as Canticles in the morning and evening services. We take no account of the Proper Psalms for special services, as for Burial, Marriage, Visitation of the Sick, etc., as these do not affect the *daily* use.

[2] The tables will be found at the close of this article. The omissions are such "vindictive" passages as Ps. cxxxix., from ver. 19, "Surely Thou wilt slay the wicked," to ver. 22, "I hate them with perfect hatred, I count them mine enemies," the last two verses being retained.

Looking beyond our Episcopal churches, it may be germane to the subject to add that the Presbyterians take the lead, one might say, of all other bodies of Christians, in their love for the Psalms, and attachment to their constant use. The "Psalms of David in Metre," rugged and ungainly as the version is, and abounding in barbarisms, still maintains its place in the affections and service of the Scotch, generally, however, in portions of but four or five verses at a time. The chanting of psalms from the prose version begins also occasionally to find a place in some of the Presbyterian Churches. Serial or continuous recitation in any form would be foreign to the free and unliturgical habits of the Scotch; but there is no body in the world among whom the Psalms are more assiduously sung, both in public assemblies and at private worship. Indeed, some branches of the Presbyterian Church go to the strange extreme of holding unlawful, in the psalmody of the congregation, any hymns or human compositions but the Psalms alone. Even the "Paraphrases," or passages of Scripture freely rendered into verse as hymns, are excluded. And this (which finds its parallel curiously enough in the early Church) occurs, not in Scotland only, but amongst the Presbyterians in America and other parts of the world.[1]

The Nonconformist Churches in England, it is sad to say, have gone quite to the extreme in the opposite direction. They make little use of the Psalms at all, excepting to read them as they do other parts of the Bible. Occasionally a Psalm is chanted, or it may be sung as an Anthem. But the great body of their psalmody is taken from bulky Hymn-books, the contents of which, beautiful in some parts, do not always compare advantageously with the

[1] *The Psalms*, by Dr. Carl B. Moll. Edinburgh: J. & G. Clark. 1874. See p. 40 of the valuable Introduction to this work. Binnie is there quoted as saying: "The Psalms retain to this day something of their ancient prominence in the Genevan and French Churches. In Holland a numerous party in the Reformed Church scruple, like the primitive African Church, to employ in public worship any hymns but those of the Psalter, and it is well known that the same scruple is somewhat extensively prevalent in Scotland and the United States of America." For the prohibition in the early Church, *vide ibidem*, p. 36; and Hotham's article "Psalmody" in Smith's *Dictionary*, p. 1743.

Psalms of David, whether in substance and poetic life, or as organs of worship representing at once the needs of humanity and the resources of Divine help.[1]

It thus appears, speaking broadly, that our own Episcopal Churches stand almost alone in the exclusively serial repetition of the Psalter, month by month, for their daily service, without any attempt whatever to vary and adapt the rich material stored therein, according to the circumstance of times and seasons. No discretion is given, as in every other Church is given, to make any change whatever by alternative selection, or to depart in the least from the beaten order. The Psalms of the six days for which proper Psalms are appointed probably strike and impress the congregation from their appropriateness, as the Psalmody on no other occasion does. But with this small exception, whatever the season or the burden of the hour, it is still the same invariable round. And so is, too often, fostered the tendency towards a mechanical repetition. How seldom again are the Psalms explained from the pulpit, either exegetically or historically, and yet how much of the point of their lesson and spirit depends thereon![2]

Looking now to all these considerations, and to the practice of other Churches, the question occurs whether some freer and more intelligible use might not be made by our Church of the rich and varied materials stored up in the Psalter. Freeman, who will be listened to with respect as an unprejudiced authority, says,—

It is chiefly in the amount of her Psalmody that our present Offices contrast unfavourably with those of the West, and yet more with the Eastern. This,

---

[1] This supersession of the Psalms, often in many respects by very inferior matter, is ascribed by Binnie to the influence of Watts. He says: "In the course of last century the use of Watts' Adaptations of the Psalms led the way to a general introduction of modern hymns among the English Nonconformists, to the exclusion of the Bible Psalmody; and a similar change took place in the greater part of the American Churches." In Germany one never hears the Psalms sung in the Lutheran Churches, but only the Hymnal.

[2] Take *ex. gr.* the Second Psalm. The words, "Kiss the Son" are probably repeated by nine out of ten worshippers without any distinct sense of what is intended.

in itself to be earnestly regretted, could it be avoided, is a result of the brevity of the Offices themselves.[1]

Again, after noticing the revision in the middle of the sixteenth century of the older forms of PRIVATE DEVOTION, by which the Prayers, Lessons, etc., in the Morning and Evening Offices were interspersed with selected Psalms, he adds,—

Nor can I forbear to remark that, if any revision of our Morning Office were undertaken, on the principle of enriching it, with the least possible amount of disturbance or increase of complexity, from the older forms, the Office which we have just reviewed would suggest one effective method of accomplishing the object. The weak points of our present Office, so to speak—those in which it fails to render with as much *fulness* as could be desired the mind of the older forms—are, (1) the small amount quantitatively of Psalmody, and (2) the absence of any expression, by means of *selected* Psalms, of Laud and Prime ideas. The expression of these is thrown upon other features, as Canticles (or Psalms used as Canticles), Collects, Petitions, etc. Now, by introducing immediately after the Te Deum, or Benedicite, a small group of Lauds or Prime Psalms exactly as is done in the Private Office before us, the defect would be in a measure remedied.[2]

Then, after suggesting several Psalms that might be suitably selected for different parts of the service,—

But the great purpose answered would be the increased fulness of expression hereby given to the Lauds or Prime ideas.[3]

Again, speaking of the service of Praise in our Morning and Evening Offices, he says,—

The *want* which can scarcely fail to be felt here, is that of a greater body and abundance of Psalmody.

And then he proceeds to dilate on the bearing of certain descriptions of Psalms that might be selected for the various times of the day.[4]

Again he says,—

It is only when looking back to the multitudinous and unstinted Praise of the Apostolic times—the vast volume of Psalms, Hymns, and Canticles, . . . it is only then that, notwithstanding compensations involved in our Lessons and Prayers system, I confess to feeling our measure of Psalmody and similar features somewhat scanty and unsatisfying.[5]

---

[1] *Principles of Divine Service*, by the Rev. Philip Freeman, M.A. Oxford and London: Parker, 1855. Vol. i. p. 156.

[2] *Ibid.* p. 299. [3] *Ibid.* p. 299. [4] *Ibid.* p. 332. [5] *Ibid.* p. 391.

Then, adverting to the risks and dangers that might arise in making any such changes in the services of our Church, he writes,—

Still it is frankly to be conceded, that if the present needs of the Church so require—if any serious loss is being suffered for want of alteration, or some great gain is even probably to be achieved by it—no reasons of antiquity or association, no theoretical excellence of structure, ought to avail against it. With such objects in view, even some degree of risk may reasonably be run. But it may confidently be asked, Has any such case been made out for the changes or additions advocated?[1]

This question he answers, though somewhat hesitatingly, in the negative, partly because the ordinary Office can already be amplified and enriched by "the free use of Hymns," and partly because the enterprise would be a "great and hazardous" one. But there surely would be little risk or hazard in the attempt to give the wanting elasticity and breadth to the Psalmody of our Church by a well-devised selection of Psalms that might be used at discretion alternatively with the serial portion for the day. Why should the Church of England not follow in this respect the example of her American sister, an example that would involve no disturbance of the existing Offices, nor any points of doctrine or questions of ritual? But if the needed richness and variety are to be attained, the American programme must be vastly enlarged and adapted to our various wants. Moreover, our Church should surely, as all other Churches do, adopt into frequent use as part of her collection, some of the other Prayers and Songs of worship, penitence, and praise, scattered throughout the Bible. Why, for example, have we dropped out of our Service altogether that beautiful hymn the Twelfth of Isaiah, or the Third of Habakkuk?[2] It is nothing short of lamentable that these and many other Divine and noble songs, so eminently fitted for devotional use, should never be thus employed

[1] *Principles of Divine Service*, vol. i. p. 392.

[2] These are used weekly in the Lauds service of the Western Church, and they are also in use in the Oriental Churches. Other such beautiful hymns or songs are Isaiah xxv., xxvi., xxxv., xxxviii., etc.; Jeremiah xxxi.; Jonah ii.; two Songs of Moses, the Song of Hannah, etc. The Twelfth of Isaiah is, we might say, the pearl of the Old Testament, and one marvels greatly at its disuse.

as other Churches do employ them, but read only in course perhaps once only in the year.

A further advantage which it would be difficult to overestimate arising out of such enlargement is, that it would present an altogether unobjectionable alternative to the obligatory use of the vindictive and minatory Psalms in our congregational worship. These we read with reverence as part of God's holy Word. But it is one thing to read them so, and quite another thing to use them as devotional songs, expressive in some measure of the subjective language of our own hearts;—to adopt their language, in fact, more or less as our own. Could we have something else substituted for them, it would be to many (to many more than perhaps we think) a sensible relief.

This matter of the vindictive character of some of the Psalms is surrounded with difficulties. Few of the various theories set forth to explain their bearing, or reconcile them with the Christian rule of the forgiveness of injuries, are of a satisfactory kind. For example, it has been argued that the Jewish dispensation, not recognising the doctrine of future rewards and punishments, was based on the notion of a final adjustment in the present life; so that under it the saint was justified in longing to see the balance of retribution struck against his enemies—an utterly untenable doctrine, and one moreover which, even if true, would not justify the Christian worshipper in appropriating the language as expressive of his own feelings.[1] Equally unfounded is the theory that the imprecatory passages must be taken in a prophetic sense, the verb being equally capable of a future as of an optative construction.[2] Still less acceptable to the judgment are the mystical interpretations so profusely and fantastically assigned to the Psalms by early Christian writers,—meanings which,

[1] Papers by Joseph Hammond in the *Expositor*, vol. iv. p. 236.

[2] Bishop Seabury, the first American bishop, went so far as to prepare and publish a Psalter in which the *Imperative* of the imprecatory passages is replaced by the *Future* tense in ninety-seven places, asserting on the authority of Horne that the Hebrew is equally capable of either interpretation. The subject was occupying much attention in America at the time the revision of the Prayer-Book was carried out, and the alternative selection introduced (1789).

instead of edifying, can hardly fail of provoking a smile at the puerility of most of their conceptions.[1]

The subject is treated with much delicacy and discretion by Perowne:—

The real source of difficulty lies in our not observing and bearing in mind the essential difference between the Old Testament and the New. The older dispensation was in every sense a sterner one than the new. The spirit of Elias, though not an evil spirit, was not the spirit of Christ (Luke ix. 55). "The Son of man came not to destroy men's lives, but to save them." And through Him his disciples are made partakers of the same spirit. But this was not the spirit of the older economy. The Jewish nation had been trained in a sterner school. . . . It is conceivable how even a righteous man under it, feeling it to be his bounden duty to root out evil wherever he saw it, and identifying, as he did, his own enemies with the enemies of Jehovah, might use language which appears to us unnecessarily vindictive.[2]

Again, having noticed certain denunciations in the New Testament that have been held by some as parallel with the minatory passages in the Old, Perowne adds,—

But even these expressions are very different from the varied, deliberate, carefully constructed, detailed anathemas of the Psalms. . . . But after all, whatever may be said of particular passages, the general tone which runs through the two Covenants is unquestionably different.

Then, after adducing certain palliatives in behalf of the Jewish writers—as their zeal for God's house, ignorance of judgment in the world to come, and impatience for God's righteousness to be manifested in this, he concludes,—

They longed to see that righteousness manifested. It could be manifested, they thought, only in the evident exaltation of the righteous, and the evident destruction of the wicked here. Hence, with their eye always fixed

---

[1] For example, take Ps. cxxxvii. 9, "Happy shall he be that taketh and dasheth thy little ones against the stones." Neale, *in loco*, adopts the explanation of Theodoret. Babylon is the *Flesh*. "The *happy* one is he who subdues the flesh with fasting and austerities, and who takes the *children* of the flesh, the first motions of evil thoughts, while they are still new and weak, and dashes them against the Rock, which is Christ (1 Cor. x. 4), who hath said of Himself, 'Whosoever shall fall on this *Stone*,'" etc. (Matt. xxi. 44). Neale and Littledale's *Commentary*, vol. iv. p. 302.

[2] Perowne, vol. i. p. 315.

on temporal recompense, they could even work and pray for the destruction of the ungodly. The awful things of the world to come were to a great extent hid from their eyes. Could they have seen these, then surely their prayer would have been, not "Let the angel of the Lord persecute them"; but rather, with Him who hung on the cross, "Father, forgive them, for they know not what they do."[1]

Referring elsewhere to what he had thus written, he adds,—

I have there endeavoured to show that, whilst we need not suppose that the indignation which burns so hotly is other than a righteous indignation, yet that we are to regard it as permitted under the Old Testament rather than justifiable under the New. . . . How clearly our Lord Himself teaches us, that his spirit and the spirit of Elijah are not the same! Yet surely no prophet of the Old Testament occupies a higher place as an inspired messenger of God than the prophet Elijah. Our Lord does not condemn the prophet for his righteous zeal; He does not forbid the manifestation of a like zeal on the part of his disciples. As in the Sermon on the Mount He substitutes the moral principle for the legal enactment, so here He substitutes the spirit of gentleness, meekness, endurance of wrongs for the spirit of fiery though righteous indignation. The Old Testament is not contrary to the New, but it is inferior to it.[2]

And so again he says further,—

An uninstructed fastidiousness, it is well known, has made many persons recoil from reading these Psalms at all. Many have found their lips falter when they have been called to join in using them in the congregation, and have either uttered them with bated breath and doubting heart, or have interpreted them in a sense widely at variance with the letter.[3]

In point of fact, the passages in question are too often recited or chanted with a forgetful indifference to the dire tenor of the words; or they occasion the "recoil" so well described above; or, more probably still, there may be a mental process going on all the while in the heart of the worshipper, unconsciously perhaps, reconciling the maledictions to his judgment as the fruit of a lower dispensation. In every reflecting mind there is probably the insensible contrast made of such vindictive prayers with the Christian axiom to "heap coals of fire on the head" of our enemies. Compare, for example, the maledictions in the 69th Psalm with our Saviour's inculcation, uttered in immediate and pronounced contrast to the Mosaical precepts:—"But I say unto

[1] Perowne, vol. i. p. 316. [2] *Ibid.* p. 64. [3] *Ibid.* p. 315.

you, Love your enemies, bless them that curse you, do good to them that hate you, and pray for them that despitefully use you, and persecute you."[1] And, "If ye forgive not men their trespasses, neither will your Father forgive your trespasses."[2] And so we have the following conclusion by Perowne as to the use proper to be made by us of the imprecatory passages. While admitting the lessons they are designed to teach, he nevertheless says,—

Surely then we are justified in saying that the imprecations in the Psalms, though springing from a righteous zeal for the glory of God, and not from any mere thirst of personal revenge, still are not such as a Christian can lawfully, in their natural sense, use now.[3]

Now, looking gravely at these serious difficulties—looking also to the practice of all other Churches which avail themselves of a sensibly fuller and richer resort to the Psalms of David, and admit a certain latitude and variety in the discretionary use of the materials they so freely offer, instead of the bare and unvaried daily repetition of the same month by month,—would it not be a worthy and a fruitful undertaking to follow the example of the sister Church across the Atlantic, on even a greatly wider and extended scale, and provide for use in our congregations alternative series from the Psalms and other Divine songs throughout the Bible? This might surely be done without in the least degree disturbing otherwise the liturgy of the Church, or tampering with any of its doctrines, or with the ritual of its beautiful and endeared service. To multitudes it would afford relief, and for all vastly increase the means of edification.

Looking to the services of Native churches in other lands,

[1] Matt. v. 44. [2] *Ibid.* vi. 15.

[3] Perowne, vol. i. p. 65. Delitzsch takes, on the whole, a similar view. "The Psalms are the purest and most faithful mirror of Old Testament piety." In the mind of David, the future of Israel is bound up with his own fortunes; and his wrath kindles at his enemies, "in connection with the history of redemption. It is, therefore, holy fire; but as Jesus Himself asserts in Luke ix. 55, the spirit of the New Testament is in this respect, nevertheless, a different spirit from that of the Old." Delitzsch's *Biblical Commentary*. Hodder & Stoughton, 1887. Vol. i. p. 501. See also p. 502 on Ps. xxxv., where the curses are viewed as prophetical: "And it is only in this sense that the Christian can use them in prayer," that is, with a mental reservation.

as India and Africa, a very special advantage would be gained by adopting a system which, while it gave greater variety and freedom of choice, would avoid the constant repetition of minatory passages far less likely to be properly understood by the Churches there even than among ourselves.

From the Appendix it will be seen that within the last twenty years, the Conventions of Canterbury and York have brought the subject of *Selections of Proper Psalms for Certain Days*, before the Queen; and we believe a similar desire exists on the part of the Scotch Episcopal Church. No doubt difficulties have been found in the way; but these can hardly be insuperable. Why, then, should not our Convocation and Church Congresses address themselves to such a worthy task?

APPENDIX

In the American *Book of Common Prayer*, we find the following instruction regarding the Order of Psalmody :—

"The Minister shall, on the days for which they are appointed, use the Proper psalms. . . . But *note*, that on other days, instead of reading from the Psalter as divided for daily morning and evening prayer, he may read one of the selections set out by the Church."

Then follows "A Table of Proper Psalms on Certain Days,"—being sixteen in number, as follows :—

First Sunday in Advent.	Morning. 8, 50	Evening. 96, 97	Easter-even.	Morning. 4, 16, 17	Evening. 30, 31
Christmas-day.	19, 45, 85	89, 110, 132	Easter-day.	2, 57, 111	113, 114, 118
Circumcision.	40, 90	65, 103	Ascension-day.	8, 15, 21	24, 47, 108
Epiphany.	46, 47, 48	72, 117, 135	Whitsunday.	48, 68	104, 145
Purification.	20, 86, 87	84, 113, 134	Trinity Sunday.	29, 33	93, 97, 150
Ash-Wednesday.	6, 32, 38	102, 130, 143	Transfiguration.	27, 61, 93	84, 99, 133
Annunciation.	89	131, 132, 138	St. Michael's.	91, 103	34, 148
Good Friday.	22, 40, 54	69, 88	All Saints' Day.	1, 15, 146	112, 121, 149

After this we have the

TABLE OF SELECTIONS OF PSALMS.

	Psalms.		Psalms.
FIRST.	1, 15, 91	ELEVENTH.	80, 81
SECOND.	4, 31 to v. 7, 91, 134	TWELFTH.	84, 122, 134
THIRD.	19, 24, 103	THIRTEENTH.	85, 93, 97
FOURTH.	23, 34, 65	FOURTEENTH.	102
FIFTH.	26, 43, 141	FIFTEENTH.	107
SIXTH.	32, 130, 121	SIXTEENTH.	118
SEVENTH.	37	SEVENTEENTH.	123, 124, 125
EIGHTH.	51, 42	EIGHTEENTH.	139, 145
NINTH.	72, 96	NINETEENTH.	147
TENTH.	77	TWENTIETH.	148, 149, 150

At the proper places, both in the Morning and Evening service, there is the following instruction:—"Then shall follow a portion of the Psalms, as they are appointed, or one of the Selections of Psalms." The 51st Psalm is also to be read on Ash-Wednesday, and indiscriminately throughout Lent.

Selections proposed by

CONVENTIONS OF CANTERBURY AND YORK.

It is interesting to note that the Conventions of Canterbury and York, in "Reports presented to Her Majesty the Queen in the year 1879," recommended the following selections of special Psalms:—

PROPER PSALMS FOR CERTAIN DAYS.

	MATINS.	EVENSONG.
Advent Sunday.	8, 50	96, 97
Circumcision.	8, 40, 90	92, 103
Epiphany.	46, 47, 67	72, 117, 135
Purification.	20, 48, 84	87, 93, 134, 138
Annunciation.	89	113, 131, 132
Thursday before Easter.	23, 26, 42, 43	141, 142, 143
Easter Even.	4, 16, 17	31, 49
Trinity Sunday.	29, 33, 46	93, 97, 99
St. Michael and All Angels.	34, 91	103, 148
All Saints.	1, 33, 34	146, 147, 149

INDEX

LOTZE'S MICROCOSMUS.

Microcosmus: Concerning Man and His Relation to the World. By HERMANN LOTZE. Translated from the German. Cheaper Edition, in Two Volumes, 8vo (1450 pp.), price 24s.

Messrs. Clark have pleasure in announcing this Cheaper Edition of Lotze's 'Microcosmus,' which the 'Athenæum' refers to as 'the greatest philosophic work produced in Germany by the generation just past.' It is issued in two handsome 8vo volumes (1450 pp.), and is in every way complete.

N.B.—A few copies of the 36s. Edition, printed on thicker paper, may still be had.

'The English public have now before them the greatest philosophic work produced in Germany by the generation just past. The translation comes at an opportune time, for the circumstances of English thought, just at the present moment, are peculiarly those with which Lotze attempted to deal when he wrote his "Microcosmus," a quarter of a century ago. . . . Few philosophic books of the century are so attractive both in style and matter.'—*Athenæum.*

'These are indeed two masterly volumes, vigorous in intellectual power, and translated with rare ability. . . . This work will doubtless find a place on the shelves of all the foremost thinkers and students of modern times.'—*Evangelical Magazine.*

Kant, Lotze, and Ritschl. A Critical Examination. By LEONHARD STÄHLIN, Bayreuth. Translated by Principal SIMON, D.D., Bradford. In demy 8vo, price 9s.

'This learned work goes to the very root of the philosophical and metaphysical speculations of recent years.'—*Ecclesiastical Gazette.*

Elements of Logic as a Science of Propositions. By E. E. CONSTANCE JONES, Lecturer in Moral Sciences, Girton College, Cambridge; Joint-Translator and Editor of Lotze's *Microcosmus.* In demy 8vo, price 7s. 6d.

'We must congratulate Girton College upon the forward movement of which the publication of this work is one of the first steps.'—*Cambridge Review.*

The Philosophical Basis of Theism: An Examination of the Personality of Man, to ascertain his Capacity to Know and Serve God, and the Validity of the Principles underlying the Defence of Theism. By Prof. S. HARRIS, D.D., LL.D. In ex. 8vo, price 12s.

'Full of suggestive thought, and of real assistance in unfolding to the mind the true account and justification of its religious knowledge.'—*Spectator.*

The Self-Revelation of God. By Professor SAMUEL HARRIS, D.D., LL.D., Yale College. In extra 8vo, price 12s.

'In "The Philosophical Basis of Theism" Dr. Harris laid the foundation, in the present work he raises the superstructure, and in both he has done good service to philosophy and theology. His is a mind full of knowledge, and rich in ripe reflection on the methods and results won in the past, and on the problems of the present hour.' —*Spectator.*

Modern Pantheism. Essay on Religious Philosophy. Translated from the French of M. EMILE SAISSET. Two Vols. 8vo, price 10s. 6d.

BY PRINCIPAL A. CAVE, D.D.

An Introduction to Theology: Its Principles, Its Branches, Its Results, and Its Literature. By ALFRED CAVE, B.A., D.D., Principal of Hackney College, London. Second Edition, largely rewritten, and the Bibliographical Lists carefully revised to date. In demy 8vo, price 12s.

'The best original work on the subject in the English language.'—PHILIP SCHAFF. D.D., LL.D.

'Its arrangement is perfect, its learning accurate and extensive, and its practical hints invaluable.'—*Christian World.*

'A marvel of industry, and simply invaluable to theologians.'—*Clergyman's Magazine.*

The Scriptural Doctrine of Sacrifice and Atonement. By ALFRED CAVE, D.D., Principal of Hackney College, London. In demy 8vo, New Edition, revised throughout, price 10s. 6d.

'Every page in this edition has been carefully revised in the light of the latest relative researches. The literary references have also been brought down to date. . . . In the New Testament section there is considerable variation. Upon the Doctrine of the Atonement especially, conclusions upon which affect so materially the presentation of Christian truth, the author's views have been steadily ripening, as he believes, during the thought of years. Consequently more than half of the New Testament portion has been rewritten.'—*Extract from the Preface.*

'Let readers judge—is this not now the best systematic study of the Atonement in the English language?'—*Expository Times.*

BY PRINCIPAL D. W. SIMON, D.D.

The Redemption of Man: Discussions Bearing on the Atonement. By Principal D. W. SIMON, D.D., Bradford. In demy 8vo, price 10s. 6d.

Principal FAIRBAIRN, Mansfield College, writes:—'I wish to say how stimulating and helpful I have found your book. Its criticism is constructive as well as incisive, while its point of view is elevated and commanding. It made me feel quite vividly how superficial most of the recent discussions on the Atonement have been.'

'Its learning, ample although that be, is its least merit: it has the far higher and rarer qualities of freshness of view and deep ethical insight. I hope it will find the general and cordial reception it so well deserves.'—Professor R. FLINT, D.D.

The Bible an Outgrowth of Theocratic Life. By Principal D. W. SIMON, D.D., Bradford. In crown 8vo, price 4s. 6d.

'This book will well repay perusal. It contains a great deal of learning as well as ingenuity, and the style is clear.'—*Guardian.*

'Dr. Simon's little book is worthy of the most careful attention.'—*Baptist.*

'Dr. JOHN BROWN, of Bedford, writes:—'I feel sure that such of your readers as may make acquaintance with it, will be as grateful for its valuable help as I have been myself.'

Delivery and Development of Christian Doctrine. By ROBERT RAINY, D.D., Principal, and Professor of Divinity and Church History, New College, Edinburgh. Price 10s. 6d.

'We gladly acknowledge the high excellence and the extensive learning which these lectures display. They are able to the last degree, and the author has, in an unusual measure, the power of acute and brilliant generalisation.'—*Literary Churchman.*

'The subject is treated with a comprehensive grasp, keen logical power, clear analysis and learning, and in devout spirit.'—*Evangelical Magazine.*

History of the Christian Philosophy of Religion, from the Reformation to Kant. By BERNHARD PÜNJER. Translated from the German by Professor W. HASTIE, D.D. With a Preface by Professor FLINT, D.D., LL.D. In demy 8vo, price 16s.

'The merits of Pünjer's history are not difficult to discover; on the contrary, they are of the kind which, as the French say, *sautent aux yeux*. The language is almost everywhere as plain and easy to apprehend as, considering the nature of the matter conveyed, it could be made. The style is simple, natural, and direct; the only sort of style appropriate to the subject. The amount of information imparted is most extensive, and strictly relevant. Nowhere else will a student get nearly so much knowledge as to what has been thought and written, within the area of Christendom, on the philosophy of religion. He must be an excessively learned man in that department who has nothing to learn from this book.'—*Extract from Preface by* Professor FLINT.

A History of German Theology in the Nineteenth Century. By F. LICHTENBERGER, D.D., Dean of the Faculty of Protestant Theology of Paris. Revised and brought up to date, with important additions specially prepared for the English Edition by the Author. Translated by Professor W. HASTIE, D.D. In One large Volume, 8vo, price 14s.

'As to the importance of an accurate and comprehensive history of German theology, diversity of opinion is impossible. . . . We welcome this work as an indispensable aid to the theological student, as a valuable repertory of historical information, and a series of luminous and effective criticisms. Its learning, its calm judicial tone, its fine insight, and its lucidity and candour impart to it quite exceptional worth.'—*Baptist Magazine.*

'Such a work speaks for itself. Packed full of information, interesting in style, it will long remain a guide to the complexities of German theology.'—*Methodist Times.*

Hymns and Thoughts on Religion. By NOVALIS. With a Biographical Sketch. Translated and Edited by Prof. HASTIE, D.D., Glasgow University. In crown 8vo, with Portrait, price 4s.

'As a poet, Novalis is no less idealistic than as a philosopher. His poems are breathings of a high, devout soul.'—CARLYLE.

Christmas Eve: A Dialogue on the Celebration of Christmas. By SCHLEIERMACHER. Translated by Prof. HASTIE, D.D. Cr. 8vo, price 2s.

'A genuine Christmas book, an exquisite prose-poem.'—*Baptist Magazine.*

Kant's Principles of Politics, including His Essay on Perpetual Peace. A Contribution to Political Science. Edited and Translated by Prof. HASTIE, D.D. In crown 8vo, price 2s. 6d.

The Voice from the Cross: A Series of Sermons on our Lord's Passion by Eminent Living Preachers of Germany, including Rev. Drs. Ahlfeld, Baur, Bayer, Couard, Faber, Frommel, Gerok, Hähnelt, Hansen, Kögel, Luthardt, Mühe, Müllensiefen, Nebe, Quandt, Schrader, Schröter, Stöcker, and Teichmüller. With Biographical Sketches, and Portrait of Dr. Kögel. Edited and Translated by WILLIAM MACKINTOSH, M.A., F.S.S. Cr. 8vo, price 5s.

'Is certain to be welcomed with devout gratitude by every evangelical Christian in Great Britain.'—*Christian Leader.*

Final Causes. By PAUL JANET, Member of the Institute, Paris. Translated from the latest French Edition by WILLIAM AFFLECK, B.D. In One Volume, 8vo, Second Edition, price 12s.

CONTENTS :—*Preliminary Chapter*—The Problem. *Book I.*—The Law of Finality. *Book II.*—The First Cause of Finality. *Appendix.*

'This very learned, accurate, and, within its prescribed limits, exhaustive work . . . The book as a whole abounds in matter of the highest interest, and is a model of learning and judicious treatment.'—*Guardian.*

'A great contribution to the literature of this subject. Mons. Janet has mastered the conditions of the problem, is at home in the literature of science and philosophy, and has that faculty of felicitous expression which makes French books of the highest class such delightful reading; . . . in clearness, vigour, and depth it has been seldom equalled, and more seldom excelled, in philosophical literature.'—*Spectator.*

The Theory of Morals. By PAUL JANET, Member of the Institute, Paris. Translated from the latest French Edition. In demy 8vo, price 10s. 6d.

'As remarkable for the force and beauty of its form of expression as for its vast and varied learning, its philosophical acumen, and its uniform attitude of reverence toward religious and moral problems of the most transcendent interest to mankind.'—*Literary World.*

Commentary on St. Paul's Epistle to the Ephesians. By Rev. J. MACPHERSON, M.A., Findhorn. Demy 8vo, price 10s. 6d.

'It is an advance, and a great one, on anything we yet possess. . . . The author goes to the root, and neglects nothing that usually comes under the eye of a careful student. . . . Besides all this, the book is a living book. One is conscious of the heart of a man in it, as well as the brains.'—*Methodist Times.*

'This is a very handsome volume which Mr. Macpherson has given us, and without any doubt it will take the first place among the commentaries devoted to this Epistle. The Introduction is fuller far than we have ever had.'—*The Expository Times.*

Creation; or, The Biblical Cosmogony in the Light of Modern Science. With Illustrations. By Professor ARNOLD GUYOT, LL.D. In crown 8vo, price 5s. 6d.

'Written with much knowledge and tact, . . . suggestive and stimulating.'—*British Quarterly Review.*

'The issue of this book is a fitting conclusion to a beautiful career. . . . This, his last book, coming from the author's deathbed, will serve two causes; it will aid science by showing that it is a friend of the faith, and it will aid Christianity by showing that it need not fear the test of the latest scientific research.'—*Presbyterian Review.*

What Think Ye of the Gospels? A Handbook of Gospel Study. By the Rev. J. J. HALCOMBE, M.A., Author of 'The Historic Relation of the Gospels.' In demy 8vo, price 3s. 6d.

'The author has given the matter much earnest study, and his theory, which can only be thoroughly understood by studying his work, appears to have much in it worthy of commendation.'—*Christian Commonwealth.*

The Jewish and the Christian Messiah: A Study in the Earliest History of Christianity. By Professor VINCENT HENRY STANTON, M.A., D.D., Trinity College, Cambridge. In demy 8vo, price 10s. 6d.

'Mr. Stanton's book answers a real want, and will be indispensable to students of the origin of Christianity.'—*Guardian.*

'We welcome this book as a valuable addition to the literature of a most important subject. . . . The book is remarkable for the clearness of its style. Mr. Stanton is never obscure from beginning to end, and we think that no reader of average attainments will be able to put the book down without having learnt much from his lucid and scholarly exposition.'—*Ecclesiastical Gazette.*

An Explanatory Commentary on Esther. With Four Appendices, consisting of the Second Targum translated from the Aramaic with Notes, Mithra, the Winged Bulls of Persepolis, and Zoroaster. By Professor PAULUS CASSEL, D.D., Berlin. In demy 8vo, price 10s. 6d.

'A perfect mine of information.'—*Record.*

'No one whose fortune it is to secure this commentary will rise from its study without a new and lively realisation of the life, trials, and triumphs of Esther and Mordecai.'—*Ecclesiastical Gazette.*

Handbook of Biblical Archæology. By Professor CARL FRIEDRICH KEIL, D.D. Translated from the Third Improved and Corrected Edition. In Two Volumes, demy 8vo, price 21s.

'This work is the standard scientific treatise on Biblical Archæology. It is a very mine of learning.'—*John Bull.*

Biblical Essays; or, Exegetical Studies on the Books of Job and Jonah, Ezekiel's Prophecy of Gog and Magog, St. Peter's 'Spirits in Prison,' and the Key to the Apocalypse. By CHARLES H. H. WRIGHT, D.D. In crown 8vo, price 5s.

'Solid scholarship, careful and sober criticism, and a style which is pure and lucid.'—*Church Bells.*

Christ's Second Coming; Will it be Pre-Millennial? By Principal DAVID BROWN, D.D., LL.D. Cr. 8vo, 7th Ed., price 7s. 6d.

'This is, in our judgment, one of the most able, comprehensive, and conclusive of the numerous works which the millenarian controversy has called forth.'—*Watchman.*

The Footsteps of Christ. Translated from the German of A. CASPERS. In crown 8vo, price 7s. 6d.

'There is much deeply experimental truth and precious spiritual love in Caspers' book. . . . I own myself much profited by his devout utterances.'—Rev. C. H. SPURGEON.

Gotthold's Emblems; or, Invisible Things understood by Things that are Made. By CHRISTIAN SCRIVER. In crown 8vo, price 5s.

'A peculiarly fascinating volume. It is rich in happy and beautiful thoughts, which grow on the root of genuine piety.'—*Witness.*

WORKS BY PROFESSOR H. EWALD.

Revelation: Its Nature and Record. By Professor H. EWALD, D.D. In demy 8vo, price 10s. 6d.

'Ewald is one of the most suggestive and helpful writers of this century. This is certainly a noble book, and will be appreciated not less than his other and larger works. . . . There is a rich poetic glow in his writing which gives to it a singular charm.'—*Baptist Magazine.*

Old and New Testament Theology. 8vo, price 10s. 6d.

'Leading principles which can never be out of date enforced with the energy of genius.'—*Spectator.*

'Suggestive on every page, and therefore essential to every student of theology.'—*Record.*

Syntax of the Hebrew Language of the Old Testament. Translated from the Eighth German Edition, by JAMES KENNEDY, B.D. In demy 8vo, price 8s. 6d.

'The work stands unique as regards a patient investigation of facts, written with a profound analysis of the laws of thought, of which language is the reflection.'—*British Quarterly Review.*

BY PROFESSOR C. E. LUTHARDT, D.D., LEIPZIG.

A History of Christian Ethics before the Reformation. By Professor C. E. LUTHARDT, D.D., Leipzig. Translated by Professor W. HASTIE, D.D., Glasgow. In demy 8vo, price 10s. 6d.

'Charmingly written and adequately covers the ground. . . . The ablest and most thorough historical exposition of the subject of Christian Ethics that has been made accessible to English-speaking people.'—*Presbyterian and Reformed Review.*

The Truths of Christianity. 3 Vols. crown 8vo, price 6s. each.

1. THE FUNDAMENTAL TRUTHS OF CHRISTIANITY. Seventh Edition.
2. THE SAVING TRUTHS OF CHRISTIANITY. Fifth Edition.
3. THE MORAL TRUTHS OF CHRISTIANITY. Fourth Edition.

'We do not know any volumes so suitable in these times for young men entering on life, or, let us say, even for the library of a pastor called to deal with such, than the three volumes of this series. We commend the whole of them with the utmost cordial satisfaction. They are altogether quite a specialty in our literature.'—*Weekly Review.*

Commentary on St. John's Gospel. 3 Vols. 8vo, 31s. 6d.

'Full to overflowing with a ripe theology and a critical science worthy of their great theme.'—*Irish Ecclesiastical Gazette.*

St. John the Author of the Fourth Gospel. Translated and the Literature enlarged by Dr. C. R. GREGORY, Leipzig. 8vo, 7s. 6d.

'A work of thoroughness and value. The translator has added a lengthy Appendix, containing a very complete account of the literature bearing on the controversy respecting this Gospel. The indices which close the volume are well ordered, and add greatly to its value.'—*Guardian.*

The Church: Its Origin, Its History, and Its Present Position. By Professors LUTHARDT, KAHNIS, and BRÜCKNER. Crown 8vo, 5s.

'A comprehensive review of this sort, done by able hands, is both instructive and suggestive.'—*Record.*

Modern Doubt and Christian Belief: A Series of Apologetic Lectures addressed to Earnest Seekers after Truth. By Professor THEODORE CHRISTLIEB, D.D., Bonn. *Authorised English Translation.* In demy 8vo, Fourth Edition, price 10s. 6d.

'We recommend the volume as one of the most valuable and important among recent contributions to our apologetic literature.'—*Guardian.*

The Sinlessness of Jesus: An Evidence for Christianity. By Dr. CARL ULLMANN. In crown 8vo, Fourth Edition, price 6s.

'Ullmann has studied the sinlessness of Christ more profoundly, and written on it more beautifully, than any other theologian.'—Dean FARRAR in his *Life of Christ.*

A Chronological and Geographical Introduction to the Life of Christ. By C. E. CASPARI. In demy 8vo, price 7s. 6d.

'The work is handy and well-suited for the use of the student. It gives him, in very reasonable compass and in well-digested forms, a great deal of information respecting the dates and outward circumstances of our Lord's life, and materials for forming a judgment upon the various disputed points arising out of them.'—*Guardian.*

Sermons for the Christian Year: Advent-Trinity. By Professor ROTHE of Heidelberg. In crown 8vo, price 4s. 6d.

'The volume is rich in noble thoughts and wholesome lessons.'—*Watchman.*

Our Father's Kingdom: Lectures on the Lord's Prayer. By CHARLES B. ROSS, B.D., Lachine, Canada. Cr. 8vo, price 2s. 6d.

'This is the book to get for clear and simple presentation of the best modern expository work on this all-important section of the Gospels.'—*The Expository Times.*

History of the Passion and Resurrection of our Lord, considered in the Light of Modern Criticism. By Dr. F. L. STEINMEYER, Berlin. In demy 8vo, price 10s. 6d.

'Our readers will find this work a most valuable and suggestive help for their thoughts and teaching during Passion-tide and Easter.'—*English Churchman.*

The Miracles of our Lord, in Relation to Modern Criticism. By Professor F. L. STEINMEYER, Berlin. 8vo, price 7s. 6d.

'This work vindicates in a vigorous and scholarly style the sound view of miracles against the sceptical assaults of the time.'—*Princeton Review.*

'We commend the study of this work to thoughtful and intelligent readers, and especially to students of divinity, whose position requires a competent knowledge of modern theological controversy.'—*Wesleyan Methodist Magazine.*

BY F. W. KRUMMACHER, D.D.

The Suffering Saviour; or, Meditations on the Last Days of the Sufferings of Christ. In crown 8vo, Eighth Edition, price 6s.

David, the King of Israel. A Portrait drawn from Bible History and the Book of Psalms. In crown 8vo, Second Edition, price 6s.

WORKS BY ERNEST NAVILLE.

The Christ. By ERNEST NAVILLE, Corresponding Member of the Institute of France. In crown 8vo, price 4s. 6d.

'We look upon these Lectures as a valuable contribution to Christology; and to young ministers and others interested in the grand and exhaustive subject, they will be found to be highly stimulating and helpful.'—*Literary World.*

'M. Naville is well known as an earnest, faithful, and eloquent defender of the Christian faith, master of a rich French style, and endowed with exquisite tact in adapting his apology to the thoughts and needs of his readers. . . . The volume before us is as good English as the original is good French.'—*London Quarterly Review.*

Modern Physics: Studies Historical and Philosophical. In crown 8vo, price 5s.

'A work so remarkably able is sure to be heartily welcomed by scientific students. . . . Christian scientists should at once procure this learned and able volume.'—*Evangelical Magazine.*

'This work meets, with rare skill, some of the more subtle speculations of prominent writers in our midst.'—*Record.*

The Problem of Evil. In crown 8vo, price 4s. 6d.

'The subject is dealt with by M. Naville in a truly philosophic manner, and at the same time with a brilliancy of illustration that seizes and enchains the attention, and with a simplicity of style that places the subject within the reach of all.'—*London Quarterly Review.*

'We give this book our warmest commendation. . . . The brilliant sparkle of the French original is as nearly preserved as could be expected in any version.'—*Literary Churchman.*

The Life and Writings of Alexander Vinet. By LAURA M. LANE. With an Introduction by Dean FARRAR. In post 8vo, price 7s. 6d.

'I may say without hesitation that readers will here find a deeply interesting account of a sincere and brilliant thinker. . . . The publication of this book will be a pure gain, if it calls the attention of fresh students to the writings of a theologian so independent as Vinet was, yet so supreme in his allegiance to the majesty of truth.'—Dean FARRAR.

The Work of the Holy Spirit in Man. Discourses by Pastor G. TOPHEL, Geneva. In crown 8vo, price 2s. 6d.

'These pages are replete with clear, mellow, tender, beautiful, elevating thoughts, eminently instructive to inquiring minds, and such as the devout must delight contemplatively and prayerfully to linger upon.'—*Baptist Magazine.*

'An admirable book on a subject of the deepest importance. We do not remember a work on this theme that is more impressive, or seems more fitted for general usefulness.'—*British Messenger.*

Mediæval Missions. By Professor THOMAS SMITH, D.D., Edinburgh. In crown 8vo, price 4s. 6d.

'This is a work which will well repay careful study.'—*Watchman.*

The Way: The Nature, and Means of Revelation. By JOHN F. WEIR, M.A., Dean of the Department of Fine Arts, Yale University. In crown 8vo, price 6s. 6d.

'No one can rise from its perusal without feeling that the Scriptures are more real to him.'—*United Presbyterian Magazine.*

'Stimulative to thought on the great questions with which it deals.'—*Literary World.*

www.ingramcontent.com/pod-product-compliance
Lightning Source LLC
Chambersburg PA
CBHW021803230426
43669CB00008B/618